PUBLIC RELATIONS AND STRATEGIC COMMUNICATION IN 2050

Trends Shaping the Future of the Profession

Edited by
Alexander V. Laskin and Karen Freberg

Routledge
Taylor & Francis Group
NEW YORK AND LONDON

Designed cover image: jamesteohart/Getty

First published 2025
by Routledge
605 Third Avenue, New York, NY 10158

and by Routledge
4 Park Square, Milton Park, Abingdon, Oxon, OX14 4RN

Routledge is an imprint of the Taylor & Francis Group, an informa business

ISBN: 978-1-032-73096-7 (hbk)
ISBN: 978-1-032-73093-6 (pbk)
ISBN: 978-1-003-42665-3 (ebk)

DOI: 10.4324/9781003426653

Typeset in Times New Roman
by codeMantra

CONTENTS

CONTRIBUTORS

Alina Arti, Doctoral Researcher at Jyväskylä University School of Business and Economics (Finland), has graduated with honors from the Digital Marketing and Corporate Communication International Masters' degree program, receiving the best thesis award in 2023. Her research interests include digital influence attempts and disinformation in the context of brands and activists. She is the co-author of the conclusion chapter of the *Handbook of Digital Corporate Communication* (2023) predicting future roles of communication professionals, and her doctoral dissertation delves into the negative influence and uncontrolled communication, aiming to shed light on these critical aspects of contemporary communication dynamics.

Victoria Barry is currently enrolled at Southern New Hampshire University working toward a degree in Political Science focusing on Public Administration. While this is the first publication for Barry her focus of research is Public Administration and International Political Communication. Including public discussions such as political speeches, news media coverage, and ordinary citizens' talk and ways in which they communicate.

Dr. Brandon C. Boatwright is an Assistant Professor of Sport Communication at Clemson University. His research focus examines the intersection of sports, social media, and strategic communication. Dr. Boatwright also serves as the Director of the Social Media Listening Center in the Department of Communication. He has published original research in *Public Relations Review*, the *Journal of Contingencies and Crisis Management*, *Computers in Human Behavior*, the *Journal of Public Interest Communication*, and the *Southern Communication*

Journal. He is an active member of the National Communication Association and the Southern States Communication Association.

Shannon A. Bowen, PhD, Professor, College of Information & Communication (Faculty Affiliate, AI), University of South Carolina. She specializes in applied ethics, issues management, and decision models for helping organizations better face challenges. Dr. Bowen is Executive Director of the Global Strategic Communication Consortium and Conclave.

Luke Capizzo, PhD, APR, is an assistant professor of strategic communication and public relations. A PR researcher, educator, and practitioner, his scholarly interests include (1) social issues management; (2) theory building in activism, DEI, dialog, and organizational listening; and (3) the public relations profession, scholarship, and pedagogy. Broadly, his research examines the potential societal contributions of organizations through the public relations function. He earned his PhD at the University of Maryland. Prior to graduate studies, he practiced public relations for eight years in a variety of industries, serving in both agency and in-house roles.

Nathan J. Carpenter (PhD, Michigan Technological University) is the Director of the Atlas Lab, a social media listening and analytics lab in the College of Journalism and Communications at the University of Florida. He manages the lab's operations by facilitating research, instruction, immersion opportunities, and external partnerships around social media listening and analytics. He also provides thought leadership for social media data collection and strategy development for academic and professional communities. He previously served as the Director of Convergent Media for the School of Communication at Illinois State University where he created and coordinated the Social Media Analytics Command Center (SMACC).

W. Timothy Coombs (PhD Purdue University) (USA) is an advisor for the Centre for Crisis and Risk Communications. His primary area of research and consulting is crisis communication. His works include the award-winning book *Ongoing Crisis Communication*, coediting the *Handbook of Crisis Communication*, and co-writing *Strategic Sport Communication: Traditional and Transmedia Strategies for a Global Sport Market*. His crisis communication research has won multiple awards from professional organizations including the Jackson, Jackson & Wagner Behavioral Science Prize. He is a Fellow in the International Communication Association.

Chris DeFelice is a PhD student at the University of Florida's College of Journalism and Mass Communication. His research focuses on social media and technology in the entertainment industry with a specific interest in the cultural and industrial impact of streaming services. His research also focuses on social media audience consumption patterns and behavior.

Dr. Melissa Dennis brings nearly two decades of sales and marketing expertise to Gwynedd Mercy University. Prior to academia, she held roles at Disney Parks and Resorts, where she honed her skills in customer relationship management (CRM) and customer experience (CX) marketing. Dr. Dennis' experience in crafting data-driven marketing strategies for a globally recognized brand allowed her to gain a deep understanding of how big data informs strategic communications. This experience, along with her academic background, allows her to bridge the gap between theoretical knowledge and real-world application, making her a valuable asset in the classroom and the field.

Elina Erzikova, PhD, Professor of Public Relations at Central Michigan University and a Fellow of the Plank Center for Leadership in Public Relations at the University of Alabama. Her primary areas of research interest include relationships between the media and power and public relations ethics and leadership.

Karen Freberg is a Professor in Strategic Communications at the University of Louisville, where she teaches, researches, and consults in social media strategy, public relations, and crisis communication. Freberg is also an award-winning author and has written several books including *Social Media for Strategic Communications: Creative Strategies and Research Based Applications* and *Discovering Public Relations: An Introduction to Creative and Strategic Practices*. In addition to academic publications, Freberg has been interviewed for popular press publications such as *Adweek*, *USA Today*, *The Next Web*, *MONEY*, *USA Today College*, and *Forbes*. Before coming to the University of Louisville, Freberg earned a PhD in Communication and Information at the University of Tennessee in May 2011, and a master's degree in Strategic Public Relations at the Annenberg School for Communication at the University of Southern California in August 2007. Freberg received her Bachelor of Science degree in Public Relations at the University of Florida in August 2005.

Lea-Ann Germinder, M.S., APR, Fellow PRSA, is a veteran public relations practitioner and doctoral student in strategic communications: public relations. Her scholarly interests include (1) responsible AI implementation in public relations; (2) ethical global public relations practices; (3) alternative perspectives on public relations; and (4) feminism in public relations. Her research focuses on how public relations can help responsibly implement effective public relations in transformational moments. She earned her master's in communications from Syracuse University. She owns Germinder & Associates, Inc. and has been a strategic communications consultant for global companies in many industries.

Christian Pieter Hoffmann, PhD, is Professor of Communication Management at the Institute for Communication and Media Studies, University of Leipzig, and of Political Communication at the Institute of Political Science. He is academic director of the Center for Research in Financial Communication and co-director of the Center for Digital Participation.

Ekaterina Ivanova, a Doctoral Researcher at Jyväskylä University School of Business and Economics (Finland), has embarked on a promising academic career, having secured multiple competitive grants for her full-time work. With extensive experience in the influencer marketing industry as both an influencer and Influencer Marketing Manager, she brings practical expertise to her research. She has overseen influencer campaigns exceeding US$100,000 in value for renowned international gaming companies. Her skills include analyzing campaign results and managing influencers, from micro-influencers to celebrities. This hands-on knowledge provides depth and insight into her dissertation on influencers.

Dr. Dean Kruckeberg, APR, Fellow PRSA, is a professor at the University of North Carolina at Charlotte. He is co-author of the books *Public Relations and Community: A Reconstructed Theory*; *This Is PR*; and *Transparency, Public Relations, and the Mass Media*. He has been presented the NCA Lifetime Achievement Award for Contributions in Public Relations Education, the PRSA Atlas Award for Lifetime Achievement in International Public Relations, was PRSA national "Outstanding Educator," was awarded the Jackson Jackson & Wagner Behavioral Research Prize and the IPR Pathfinder Award. He was the 2021 recipient of the Public Relations Society of America Gold Anvil Award (the highest award presented by this international public relations professional association). He was Co-Chair of the Commission on Public Relations Education for 15 years.

Alexander V. Laskin (PhD, University of Florida) is a professor at Quinnipiac University (USA). He is an author of about 100 publications, focused primarily on investor relations, reputation management, and emerging technologies. He recently published: *Organizational Reputation Management: A Strategic Public Relations Perspective* (2024) and *Investor Relations and Financial Communication* (2022). His research was recognized with awards from the Association for Business Communication, Association for Education in Journalism and Mass Communication, and the Institute for Public Relations. Laskin also served as a Fulbright Specialist, Page Legacy Scholar, Albert Schweitzer Fellow, Plank Center Fellow, and the People's United Center for Innovation and Entrepreneurship Innovation Faculty Fellow.

Vitor Lima is an Assistant Professor of Marketing at the ESCP Business School. His research interests include emerging and speculative technologies, primarily focusing on the philosophy of technology, transhumanism, human enhancement technologies, cyborgs, biohacking, robots, and artificial intelligence. He was among the TOP 3 finalists for the 2021 AMS Mary Kay Doctoral Dissertation Award and 2021 AMS Review—Sheth Foundation Doctoral Competition for Conceptual Articles (ADCCA), and together with Russell Belk, recipient of the 2021 ACR Best Working Paper Award and *Journal of Services Marketing* 2023 Highly Commended Paper.

Jeremy Harris Lipschultz is Peter Kiewit Distinguished Professor of Communication, UNO Social Media Lab for Research & Engagement, University of Nebraska at Omaha. He has published more than one dozen books about media, the Internet, computer-mediated communication and social media. *Social Media Communication: Concepts, Practices, Data, Law and Ethics*, fourth edition and three other social media textbooks have been published by Routledge. Lipschultz also hosts a YouTube channel and is active across many social media sites.

Marta N. Lukacovic, PhD, received her doctorate from Wayne State University, Detroit-Michigan, USA. She is an Assistant Professor of Communication and Mass Media at Angelo State University (Texas Tech University System). Her research is focused on communication through digital media platforms and the matters of security, such as global crises, pandemics, political violence, and malicious AI. She co-edited a two-volume book project on public relations, media, and communication in post-socialist nations of Eastern Europe and Central Asia. She serves as the President of CAER (Communication Association of Eurasian Researchers).

Vilma Luoma-aho, Professor of Corporate Communication and Vice Dean at Jyväskylä University School of Business and Economics, is interested in digital corporate communication and new forms of influence online. She is the past chair of ProCom (Finland) and on the board of trustees of Page Society. She has published in leading journals including *Computers in Human Behavior*, *Journal of Communication*, and *Technological Forecasting and Social Change*. She is currently editing a book on AI and communication, and her latest *Handbook on Digital Corporate Communication* comes with free podcasts. She investigates disinformation and hijacking of communication funded by National Defence Fund in Finland.

Jim Macnamara, Distinguished Professor, PhD, FAMI, CPM, FAMEC, is an internationally recognized leader in evaluation of public communication and for his pioneering studies of organizational listening within government, corporations, and NGOs. Since early 2020, he has led global research for the World Health Organization to evaluate and advise on its communication in relation to COVID-19 and World Health Days. Jim is the author of 16 books including *Evaluating Public Communication: Exploring New Models, Standards, and Best Practice*, as well as almost 100 book chapters and journal articles. Before becoming an academic, Jim was founder and CEO of CARMA International Asia-Pacific for more than a decade.

Lexi Merriman is a graduate of Clemson University with a degree in Communication and a minor in Nonprofit Leadership. She worked with several local nonprofit organizations in marketing and communications positions during her undergraduate career. Her research interests lie in sport communications and interpersonal communication within organizations, in particular how organizations use social media to communicate with fans, spectators, and constituents. She is currently a graduate student in Clemson's MA Communication program.

Dr Juha Munnukka is a Senior Researcher of Marketing at Jyväskylä University School of Business and Economics (Finland). His research interests include consumer behavior, digital and AI-powered marketing communication, and influencer marketing. He has led and participated in several research projects and is currently leading a project on AI-powered virtual influencers. Munnukka has published in various academic journals such as the *Journal of Interactive Marketing*, *Industrial Marketing Management*, *Computers in Human Behavior*, *Journal of Services Marketing*, *Journal of Marketing Management*, *Journal of Service Theory and Practice*, and *Journal of Product and Brand Management*.

Ms. Sabrina Page has been a lecturer in communication for Walters State Community College in Morristown, TN for over a decade. Page holds a Graduate Certificate in Strategic Communication from Appalachian State University, Boone, North Carolina, a Master of Science Degree in Communication and a Bachelor of Science Degree in Journalism with a concentration in Public Relations from the University of Tennessee, Knoxville. She also holds an Associate of Arts in Political Science from Lake Michigan College, Benton Harbor, Michigan, as well as an undergraduate certificate in Homeland Security from American Military University, Charles Town, West Virginia. Page is an invited author and has presented research on various communication areas nationally and internationally. Her research includes crisis communication, cyberbullying, ethics, mediated public diplomacy, propaganda, reputation management, social identification in the era of social media, and the use of social media in conducting research.

Nathan J. Rodriguez, PhD, is an Associate Professor of Public Relations and Strategic Communication at Weber State University in Ogden, Utah. He also serves as faculty advisor to KWCR, the student-run radio station. His research interests concern computer-mediated communication and the process of meaning-making in online spaces. He may be reached at nathanrodriguez@weber.edu.

Deborah D. Sellnow-Richmond, PhD, is an Associate Professor in the Department of Applied Communication Studies at Southern Illinois University Edwardsville where she teaches courses in public relations and organizational communication. She researches the efficacy and unforeseen effects of public relations messages in health and organizational crisis context, and the emerging role of social media in creating and resolving organizational crises. She holds a PhD in communication from Wayne State University in Detroit, Michigan, a master's degree in Public Service from the University of Arkansas Clinton School of Public Service, and a bachelor's degree from the University of Minnesota.

Greg Simons is currently an Associate Professor at the Department of Communication Science at Turiba University in Riga, Latvia. Research interests include the changing political dynamics and relationships, mass media, public diplomacy, information warfare, hybrid warfare and subversion, organized persuasive communication, political marketing, crisis management communications, media and armed conflict, and the Russian Orthodox Church. Also researching the relationships and connections between information, politics, and armed conflict more broadly, such as the GWOT and the Arab Spring, the interpretation and representation of events and processes in the New Cold War (within the context of the transforming global order).

Kyle Stanley is a Mass Communication PhD Candidate at Louisiana State University. His research focuses on popular culture in digital spaces and explores the intersections of fandoms, celebrities/ influencers, cultural trends, and the impact of media law on these communities. His research dives deep into the intricacies of online communities, examining the relationships and interactions between fans and their chosen media.

Kate Stewart is an Assistant Professor of Public Relations at Jacksonville State University. Stewart teaches and researches public relations, social media, influencers, and pop culture. Before coming to Jacksonville State University, Stewart earned a PhD in Mass Communication with a cognate in Marketing at the University of South Carolina in August 2024, and an MA in Communication with a focus in public relations and social media at Auburn University in May 2020. Stewart received her BA in Public Relations at Auburn University in May 2018.

Burton St. John III, Professor of Public Relations, researches public relations and the management of risk and crisis. In 2022, he co-edited *The Global Foundations of Public Relations: Humanism, Chinas and the West* (Routledge) and

Communicating Climate Change: Making Environmental Messaging Accessible (Routledge). An author of seven other books that examine the management of risk and crisis by public relations and journalism, he is the only active public relations scholar twice shortlisted for AEJMC's Tankard Book Award. He is currently working on a book about the challenge of dissensus for public relations.

Marina Vujnovic, PhD, APR is a Professor of Journalism at Monmouth University, West Long Branch, New Jersey. Her research interests focus on international communication and the global flow of information, journalism studies, public relations, and explorations of the historical, political-economic, and cultural impact on media, class, gender, and ethnicity. She is the author of *Forging the Bubikopf Nation: Journalism, Gender, and Modernity in Interwar Yugoslavia*, and co-author of *Participatory Journalism: Guarding Open Gates at Online Newspapers*; *Higher Education and Disaster Capitalism in the Age of COVID-19*; *Artificial Intelligence, Strategic Communicators and Activism*. She is co-editor of *Globalizing Cultures: Theories, Paradigms, Actions*.

Dr. Allison Weidhaas, an Associate Professor at Rider University, teaches public relations and business communication. Her scholarship includes scholarly journals, a book, trade press articles, op-eds in newspapers, book chapters, and presentations at national conferences. In public relations, Weidhaas' scholarship maintains an applied focus. Additionally, Dr. Weidhaas advances social and scholarly understanding of gender inequalities and violence. Her gender-based work has been recognized with a university award and an international award for her research. She serves in leadership roles at her university, and she contributes to the discipline by reviewing forthcoming textbooks, research articles, and grants. She is also an associate editor for the *International Journal of Gender & Entrepreneurship*.

INTRODUCTION

Alexander V. Laskin and Karen Freberg

Almost every year public relations, strategic communication, advertising, and marketing industries experience a revolutionary trend that promises to change the profession completely. From generative AI with the widespread adoption of ChatGPT, to virtual reality with Facebook changing its name to Meta, and to blockchain with its promises to reshape the Internet to Web 3.0. In addition (or in response) to the technological trends, we see changes in society: the social, political, and economic structure of our lives is being reimagined. Ranking people based on their credit and social scores, disappearing expectations of personal privacy, woke culture and cancel culture, the gig economy, and many other societal trends create challenges and opportunities for the public relations and strategic communication professionals. And, of course, we see trends affecting the profession at the intersection of society and technology – such as the rise of creators and influencers, issues of digital welfare and the digital divide, and the effects of automation and algorithms on the research, planning, implementation, and evaluation.

Thinking about the future can be exciting – yet terrifying – as these rapid technological and societal changes have the power to shape, influence, and spark impact that drives unforeseen consequences and changes to society and industries, including public relations and strategic communications. Professor Dean Kruckeberg discussed this in a post by the International Public Relations Association:

> I am gravely concerned about the state of today's world in which communication technology has created an unpredictable and threatening global environment in which massive and insufficiently understood changes are occurring.
> *(Kruckeberg, 2023)*

DOI: 10.4324/9781003426653-1

While the discussion has increased in society about the growing ethical practices and data privacy ownership issues of artificial intelligence, advanced algorithmic shifts and concerns, and rapid growth of adoption to social media platforms have brought significant challenges on society, it also brings forth new opportunities and perspectives that could empower individuals to come together to formulate solutions. These solutions can come in the form of research, as well as predictions and ideas to shape practical and applied practices in the industry.

Like society, the public relations and the strategic communication industry has rapidly evolved into an ever changing, dynamic, and technologically driven profession that continues to bring forth innovative perspectives and unique research questions to light. Along with these changes, public relations and social media has also seen a shift in practices as it relates to social, political, economic, and cultural structures. These structures that have been fundamental in social media and public relations practices have influenced some of the biggest drivers of research and specialized areas in the industry, including creators and influencers, misinformation and digital warfare, the gig economy, automation and algorithm practices, artificial intelligence, and more.

Most edited collections in the field of public relations and strategic communication focus on exploring the presence and analyzing the past of the profession. However, the goal of this edited book is to provide the industry with insights, key themes, trends, and research into the future. Bold predictions, trend analysis, and ideas of where public relations and strategic communications will be in 2050 are discussed throughout the edited book.

The edited book is broken into two sections: Trends shaping the future of public relations and strategic communications, and future predictions for public relations and strategic communication specialization. In Section 1, some of the themes that have emerged focus on the impact of artificial intelligence including the rapid growth of deepfakes, propaganda, and misinformation. Yet, other chapters focus on the ethical and productive practices AI can bring to the table for public relations and strategic communication. Other trends discussed in Section 1 focus on biohacking, social credit systems, big data, influencers and creators, including the virtual ones, neurodiversity, societal polarization, and the rise of consumerism.

Section 2 of the handbook is dedicated to outlining the future of public relations and strategic communication specializations. This section allows researchers to envision what the industry will look like in 2050. Chapters in this section of the handbook focus on crisis communication, propaganda and psychological warfare, media relations and journalism, investor relations and financial communication, sports communication, and film, television, and entertainment public relations.

As we look toward the future, this handbook will focus on highlighting the trends that shape the trajectory of public relations and strategic communication development and, as a result, predict a possible future of the industry (See Figure 0.1). As important as predicting what will change, it is also important to

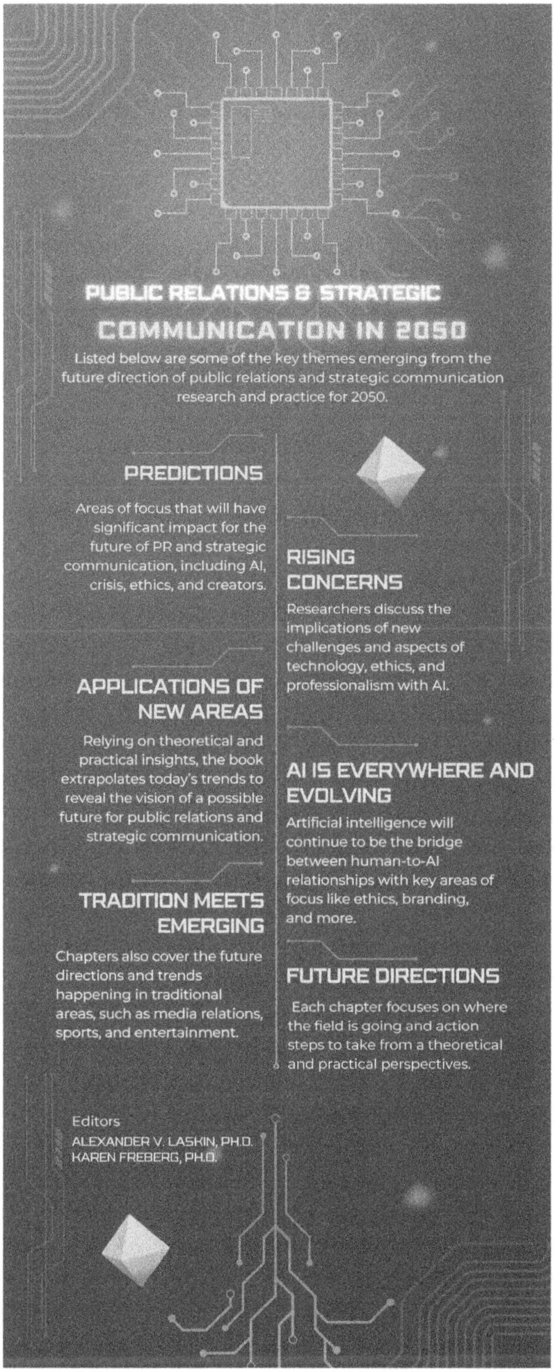

FIGURE 0.1 Public relations and strategic communication in year 2050: An infographic.

recognize what will remain the same. These universal elements will continue to be relevant and strong even in 2050:

- **Public relations and strategic communication will continue to face ethical and legal challenges.** Whether it is manipulative deepfakes or wellbeing practices to combat cyberbullying, there will always be challenges facing researchers and practitioners in public relations and strategic communication. However, this is where the need for critical thinking, creativity, empathy, and teamwork come together to bring forward a team effort to combat these challenges and provide sustainable and effective solutions that emerged from research and applied practices.
- **Human or AI-driven influencers will continue to be vital as part of the public relations and strategic communication ecosystem.** Presently, the focus on who is driving conversations (good or bad) has concentrated on influencers and creators. There will always be a group of humans (or AI-driven and created entities) who will serve as opinion makers with the ability to shift attitudes and behaviors. Formulating relationships and practical steps to analyze, listen, and proactively address these groups will continue to be relevant for public relations and strategic communication researchers and practitioners for future decades.
- **Dialog and stories will continue to spark connections in public relations and strategic communication.** Researchers and practitioners have more resources, data, opportunities, and tools than ever before to tell stories that drive impact due to technology advances. Yet, stories will now come in the shape or multiple channels and personalized for their targets.
- **Relationships – whether they are with humans or AI entities – are still at the root of public relations and strategic communication.** The drive for connections, community building, and sparking dialog will endure even with the rapid changes and advances that technology has brought to society. Public relations and strategic communication professionals and researchers will still be exploring relationships, as they may include more than just certain type of stakeholders and community members, and bridge to virtual influencers, artificial programs, and AI-driven human connections.
- **The growing need to continue to be agile and adaptive.** As society and other economic, cultural, and political issues emerge, researchers and practitioners must be adaptive and agile in their research questions, creative message strategies, and innovative practices to help address these questions, provide solutions, and be part of the evolution of the public relations and strategic communication industry.
- **More integration and diversity – from individuals, professions, backgrounds, and perspectives – will be needed for the public relations and strategic communication profession and research community.** Public

relations and strategic communication need more researchers to push and test the boundaries, ideologies, and perspectives that have been framing the research agenda and practices for decades. It is important to understand the foundation in which public relations and strategic communication research and practices have built upon, but it is equally important to look ahead to bring together more diverse schools of thought, ideas, and perspectives in moving the field forward.

In summary, this edited book with diverse scholars coming in from various backgrounds and areas of specialization provides a comprehensive roadmap for navigating the ever-evolving landscape of public relations and strategic communication from now to year 2050. The collection's goal is to serve as a guide to equip scholars and practitioners with the foresight to innovate, adapt, and be agile in the rapidly evolving profession.

References

Kruckeberg, D. (2023). Sailing in uncharted waters: Communications in an era of massive and insufficiently understood changes. *IPRA*. Retrieved from https://www.ipra.org/news/itle/itl-506-sailing-in-uncharted-waters-communications-in-an-era-of-massive-and-insufficiently-understood-changes/

SECTION 1

Trends Shaping the Future of Public Relations and Strategic Communication

1

QUESTIONS OF POWER OVER (AND CONTROL OF) SOCIAL, POLITICAL, ECONOMIC, AND CULTURAL DIMENSIONS OF ARTIFICIAL INTELLIGENCE IN PUBLIC RELATIONS AND STRATEGIC COMMUNICATION

Dean Kruckeberg and Marina Vujnovic

Introduction

As is reflected in its ambitious title, this chapter makes recommendations based on the co-authors' contemplation of public relations practitioners' mission, role, and function within the context of AI's present impact and its uncertain future trajectory extending to the year 2050.

Predicting possible outcomes of Artificial Intelligence in its yet unknown future iterations is an admittedly difficult—arguably impossible—task because of AI's dizzyingly rapid and seemingly chaotic evolution. Particularly since the unveiling of ChatGPT in November 2022, a continuing—indeed, geometrically increasing—din of noises has emanated from news media and from other information sources, replete with a cacophony of oftentimes wild prognoses ad infinitum as well as alarmist warnings ad nauseum from a range of sources, some of whom are obviously well-credentialed, while the credibility of others must remain suspect.

Thus, this chapter can only be speculative in anticipation and appreciation of the unknown status of Artificial Intelligence by the 21st century's midpoint and of AI's impact on public relations professional practice a quarter century hence. The book's co-authors, in their attempts to discover the latest information about Artificial Intelligence in their research for this chapter, were met each day with fresh headlines about AI in the news media, as well as with the latest projections and perspectives in the professional and scholarly literature. These prophesies were invariably accompanied by the dire warnings from a plethora of people who collectively had recognized the significance of AI as a disruptor, but

DOI: 10.4324/9781003426653-3

who individually had voiced an eclectic range of non-specific fears of potential abuses in AI's present and future applications.

Certainly, AI (in particular, generative AI) promises to be a—if not *the*—major disrupter in contemporary global society in an era that Schwab (2016) declares to be a "fourth revolution," which has succeeded: the first revolution, from 1760 to 1840, which had introduced mechanical production; the second revolution, beginning in the 19th century and into the 20th century, which had brought mass production; the third, which was that of the computer or digital revolution that had begun in the 1960s; and the present revolution, which began in the 21st century and which includes the rapid development of Artificial Intelligence and machine learning.

Areas That Demand Attention by Scholars and Journalists

Perhaps necessarily so, Artificial Intelligence remains a somewhat nebulous and amorphous concept. This book's co-authors accept AI to be an umbrella term for evolving technologies that historically have required human intelligence (Swiatek & Galloway, 2022). Zerfass et al. (2020) define Artificial Intelligence as technology-based, software-driven agents that undertake decision-making processes and actions. A host of questions and concerns about AI—oftentimes exacerbated because of AI's imprecise and inclusive definition—are both abundant and readily obvious. Such questions and concerns have been trumpeted widely, both by knowledgeable sources and by those who would appear to be less credible. Some of the latter's non-specific concerns about AI's dangers may be grossly exaggerated because of these alarmists' sometimes faulty reasoning and inadequate understanding.

Furthermore, Artificial Intelligence must not be presumed to be a panacea for any litany of pre-existing societal problems and challenges for which AI might ultimately prove to be largely insignificant or perhaps might even exacerbate. For example, AI may or may not substantively contribute to the resolution of global warming, nor may it alleviate societal problems that are associated with mass population migrations, nor may it help to bring peace to regions of the world that habitually experience continuing warfare. AI may or may not significantly address the immediate and long-range needs of an inordinately young population in various geographic regions, that is, youth who presently lack educational opportunities and who appear to have little likelihood of sufficient opportunities for sustainable employment.

In sum, global society's social, political, economic, and cultural dimensions have changed continually throughout humankind's existence because of a multitude of variables and innovations that had preceded AI and its actual or any presumed influences. Thus, AI should not be examined by naively attempting to overlay it on a presumed societal stasis. Neither should an examination of AI be simply overlaid on any assumed static practices of public relations. Practitioners' mission, role, and function have likewise been fluid throughout public relations' history as well as diverse in how public relations have been practiced throughout the world. Furthermore, it is possible—if not likely—that AI will affect different cultures in different ways, thereby creating different societal outcomes. And most certainly, AI should not ipso facto be heralded optimistically as the sole—or necessarily even a primary—disruptive savior benefitting contemporary or future global society and enhancing public relations as a professionalized occupation.

Such examination must be predicated on a re-examination and reconsideration of basic existential questions regarding what constitutes humanity and human agency. Such introspection is required because of widespread concerns that AI challenges historic assumptions about the human species' superlative intelligence as well as humankind's ostensibly unique sentience and, thereby, Homo sapiens' ultimate moral/ethical responsibility. Answers to intriguing questions such as these will demand multi-disciplinary inquiry from among scholars in a comprehensive range of disciplines in the humanities and in the social and natural sciences, as well as from those in engineering and in all other applied professions, such as public relations.

Because of public relations practitioners and scholars' knowledge, skills, and abilities as ethical communicators and in their normative role as organizational and societal watchdogs, the public relations professional and scholarly community has inordinate—arguably unique—responsibilities. They must assume leadership in helping to safeguard humankind and the global physical environment from potential abuses and misuses of Artificial Intelligence. In doing so, public relations practitioners must learn how to build and to maintain mutually beneficial relationships among their publics in a vastly different world in which AI will play a significant part. However, to perform these responsibilities, this professional and scholarly community must consider and ponder questions such as these

What Makes Us Human, and Could AI Challenge Basic Assumptions about Our Historic Dominion over the World?

How, must one think about Artificial Intelligence and its manifestations, for example chatbots? Is AI like a really smart and lovingly affectionate dog or like a well-designed, but nevertheless inanimate and unfeeling, automobile, the latter totally unappreciative of its latest oil change or new air cleaner? How must AI be treated? Does AI have "intelligence" as such attribute is normally ascribed to humans, albeit nevertheless "artificial"? Of course, these questions beg a definition of "intelligence," which becomes problematic in many respects when considering what AI is. Bajak (2023, November 20) says that AI is simply counting the past to predict the future. Chowdhury (n.d.) says, "It is amazing how many people, even if they're an expert, confuse a user design that mimics chat functionality as sentience" (p. 21). She says AI is not magic. "It's simply math, put into code. That people think of programmers as uniquely capable entities that are smarter than every else; also wildly untrue" (p. 21).

Nevertheless, Edelman (2019, March) observes that computer advances are creating a "Cognitive Era" that might include a "human-species defining moment" (p. 5). Yao and Ling (2020) observe that AI can undertake sophisticated tasks with little or no human intervention or input. Some experts predict Artificial General Intelligence (AGI) will become at least as smart as humans in all areas of intelligence (Meacham, 2023, September 8).

The future is intriguing, and the ramifications of AI are probably more immediate than most people fully understand or sufficiently appreciate. Certainly, questions of what is human and what constitutes "human-like" agency will beg reflection and introspection by those in all disciplines and professionalized occupations, but perhaps particularly so in public relations. As AI rapidly evolves, perhaps the ultimate questions will become, "What is life?" and "who is human?"

Or, conversely, will AI reach—or even exceed—human levels of intelligence, albeit an "artificial" intelligence, however this "intelligence" and "artificial" may be defined? As such, would an AI entity deserve and appreciate the dignity, rights, respect, and basic autonomy usually granted only to humans? Considerations about AI and its agency such as these are far more than intellectual fodder for discussions in university classrooms or at campus coffee houses; rather, these questions are more important than they might first appear because humans will likely be forging relationships—indeed, "interpersonal relationships"—with AI entities, with obvious implications for public relations.

Can an AI entity become a "living being" and lifeform such as a human, despite the theological unlikelihood that a "soul" will be instilled upon it? And, if an AI entity is deemed to be "living," should it be extended basic "human" rights, and does this "living being" deserve and appreciate and respond to the kindness, love, and affection that are normally reserved for other humans or for highly domesticated animals?

In sum, do humans have the moral/ethical obligation to be respectful, polite, and courteous to AI entities; conversely, can humans' sanctimony and air of superiority hurt the feelings of these non-biological AI entities? Furthermore, must AI be safeguarded from all forms of slavery, exploitation, and abuse, which protection even animals enjoy in many cultures, and does an AI entity deserve autonomy at some level? Will humankind need to philosophically and psychologically "share the world" with these autonomous non-organic—that is, neither animal or plant—AI entities that may become obnoxiously demanding, possibly malevolent, if not evil, and, as some have suggested, ultimately might have the capability and will seek a self-assumed destiny to become our masters? If so, must or can there be a "community" of humans and AI entities, that is, must these AI entities become (or even demand to be) accepted as one of us in a diverse and democratic global society of equity and inclusion?

Depending on the answers to such questions, desired normative theories of society might need to be re-examined and re-assessed, as would existing socio-scientific paradigms. Leopold distinguished humans as having a capacity that is unique among earth's organisms: "to rectify their misdeeds, i.e., to become (or once again become) citizens of the land community—but now knowing, self-conscious citizens" (Fritzell, 1987, p. 141). Will AI and its non-organic entities achieve such knowing and self-consciousness?

What Are the Most Significant Questions and Threats?

Many of the questions about AI's rapid evolution and the concerns about its entities' applications and manifestations relate to AI's impact on humankind, in particular, its potential threat to global society's welfare and well-being. Indeed, as is the case with any new technology, AI presents a new set of problems and a new set of needs. Concerns about threats from AI and from its potential applications are unquestionably valid and justified, although one might argue that the wrong questions are frequently being asked and that many people are overly worried about the wrong concerns. Such questions and concerns are often centered around the possible "weaponization" of AI by perceived enemies as well as around potential juxtapositions of status-quo power that could be enabled or encouraged by AI.

Some questions are intriguing, albeit perhaps primarily as intellectual fodder, for example, in a competition between opposing AI entities, both of which are ostensibly omniscient and with like logical, deductive, and reasoning abilities, which one would win a chess match and why? (That is, which one of these "intelligent" twins would outsmart the other one?) In a competitive global environment in which AI is employed, would the beneficiaries of a conquering AI entity most likely be primarily governments, or (transnational) corporations, or competing civil society organizations/ nongovernmental organizations, or citizens both collectively and individually—or all or none of these social actors? Here are only a few disruptions and potential threats that AI represents to the social, political, economic, and cultural dimensions of global society, which will be followed by a discussion about their implications for public relations practitioners.

Social Threats of AI

Many of the afore-mentioned questions and concerns represent potential "social threats" that challenge Homo sapiens' assumed supremacy and dominion over the world, the species' ostensibly superlative intelligence and level of sentience, and humankind's highest-level capability of empathy—all of which attributes are often ascribed at their ultimate—if not sole—levels to humans. Hopefully, least likely from among these social threats is of AI, itself, dominating the human species, with no means for humans to "pull the plug" to effectively "kill" or to re-subjugate renegade AI entities.

The likelihood of Artificial Intelligence becoming sufficiently powerful to conquer humankind—while harboring an accompanying malevolent desire to do so—is hopefully no greater than would be that of extra-terrestrial beings in spaceships waging a full-scale attack on earth. Nevertheless, such danger of Artificial Intelligence's threat to humankind—to whatever its plausible extent and of whatever its manifestation—should not be negated nor discounted lightly; at the least, such potential scenario is worthy of vigilance, despite a presumed remote likelihood that AI entities will demand shared power or will seek to become humankind's overlords. Indeed, reassurances from Tech companies seem inadequate, if not hollow, for example: "Aligned with human values. Inside the most cutting-edge AI labs, a few technicians are working to ensure that AIs, if they eventually surpass human intelligence, are 'aligned' with human values. They are designing benevolent tools, not spiteful ones" (The AI Arms Race is Changing Everything, p. 13).

Seemingly more likely—and perhaps more alarmingly—would be the application of AI entities by one group of humans, for example those in an imperialistic nation-state, to attempt to dominate others, in this example a rival nation-state. A "weaponization" of AI would appear to be a quite realistic threat from among warring or otherwise competing nation-states—of course, to an extent this is already occurring and appears to be increasing considerably. Again, the public relations implications of such threat are obvious.

A plausibly more immediate social threat—or at least a seemingly more obvious disruptor for individuals in their respective societies—would be the continuation of a massive and increasing alienation of humans in their relationships among one another. As had been discussed earlier in this chapter, the potential exists for AI entities to compete with humans for these ostensibly meaningful "interpersonal relationships" that were previously shared exclusively among humans or, for some, with their beloved anthropomorphized pets.

Furthermore, global society's already appalling lack of transparency will be further exacerbated by Artificial Intelligence, in particular generative AI. In today's disingenuous global communication environment, misinformation and disinformation are already rampant, and AI and its abuses are becoming pervasive. Artificial Intelligence is being applied in oftentimes nefarious ways, and its presence is increasingly indetectable. Again, the public relations implications are obvious. Indeed, compelling reasons exist that humans should not (indeed, must not) be trusting in today's global communication milieu.

Tsetsura and Kruckeberg (2017) describe *trust* as the belief in the truth of a communicator's message. Vujnovic and Kruckeberg (2016) further define *trust* as the confident belief in the *authenticity* of a social actor. They define *authenticity* as the attributes of a social actor that are not only truthfully presented to that social actor's publics as well as to society-at-large, but also to itself, "having knowledge of who or what one is and presenting those attributes truthfully to the social actor's publics as well as to society at large" (p. 124). People *trust* those whom they perceive to be telling the truth. Valentini and Kruckeberg (2011, Spring) observe that a requisite of *trust* is the reasonable prediction and anticipation of an action by an actor based on that actor's prior behavior and other communication. They further note that the function of *trust* is to reduce the complexity that is seen in postmodern, hypercomplex society, adding the caveat: "… (T)rust can only exist where it is deserved, i.e such trust cannot be betrayed" (p. 101). Luhmann (1979, p. 4) notes that the only alternatives to appropriate *trust* in society are "chaos and paralysing fear."

Vujnovic and Kruckeberg (2016) say *truth*: "Is negotiated in the process of communication; People must enter the process of communication with the expectation that what is going to be said will be clear and truthful" (p. 124). Tsetsura and Kruckeberg (2017) expand on this definition of *truth*:

> Accurate, complete, and unbiased information that has been gathered and verified conscientiously and competently and that is presented fairly and in good faith by those who are attempting to achieve the idea of objectivity with complete transparency in gathering, analyzing, and presenting this information.
>
> *(p. 124)*

They distinguish it from *incomplete truth:*

> News and other information that is being presented as truth may be by-and-large accurate, but the news gatherer/disseminator has intentionally omitted contextualizing information or has purposely failed to identify influences that have altered the presentation of this information with the outcome of deceiving and/or misleading.
>
> *(p. 124)*

Tsetsura and Kruckeberg (2017) contrast *truth* to a *lie*, the latter which they say is: "Information that the communicator knows to be false that is presented with the intent to deceive or mislead" (p. 33). Vujnovic and Kruckeberg (2014, March) define *transparency* as "Both voluntarily and involuntarily disclosed, easily accessible, shared information," while pseudo-transparency is "A false sense of both voluntarily and involuntarily disclosed, easily accessible, shared information" (p. 124). Tsetsura and Kruckeberg (2017) define the lack of transparency as

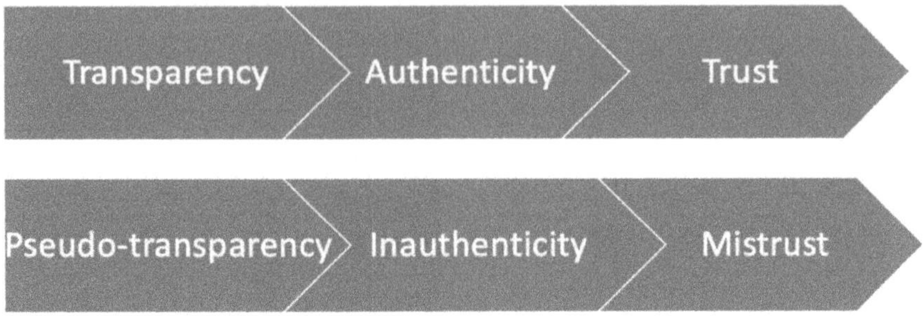

FIGURE 1.1 Transparency and pseudo-transparency linear progression.

Source: Artwork created by the authors themselves.

opacity, which in the news gathering/dissemination process they declare to be "a significant threat to people worldwide, both as citizens and marketplace consumers" (p. 3). All of these are important concepts when examining the social threats of Artificial Intelligence.

Vujnovic and Kruckeberg (2014, March) concluded that *transparency* suggests *authenticity* that begets *trust* in relationships; in contrast, *pseudo-transparency* in the social dimension exploits involuntary and/or unknown *transparency*, creating an *inauthenticity* that begets *mistrust*, together with the social enslavement of mandated new communication technologies. Thereby, *transparency*'s utility is of value only to the extent that it creates *authenticity* and *trust*. *Authenticity* is only possible through transparency, and *trust* is only possible through *authenticity*. They describe this linear progression as such.

Contemporary citizens—many of whose lives today are lived largely online, thereby substantively replacing erstwhile face-to-face (arguably more healthy) interpersonal communication and relationships—are immersed in a communication environment of *opacity* and *pseudo-transparency*, not of *transparency*. Such environment creates *inauthenticity* that results in *mistrust*, not the *trust* that is only possible and deserved through *authenticity*. Sadly, this *mistrust* is well-advised, indeed is essential, for humankind's welfare in today's disingenuous global communication environment.

Further alarmingly, this immense and highly dangerous social threat is exacerbated greatly in today and likely tomorrow's continually evolving new iterations of Artificial Intelligence. In particular, generative AI compounds this need for *mistrust* many times over. Thus, for the very survival of humankind, these problems that are being exacerbated by AI must be addressed; with constant vigilance, journalists and public relations practitioners worldwide must proactively combat a global communication milieu that harbors *opacity*, *pseudo-transparency*, *inauthenticity*, *incomplete truth*, and *lies*, rather than safeguarding and assuring *transparency*, *authenticity*, and *truth*.

Political Threats of AI

AI's "social threats" that have been discussed transcend and must be included within the dimension of AI's political threats. More than a decade ago, Vujnovic and Kruckeberg (2013, March) had said that global society is in the midst of a revolution, with communication technology fundamentally changing us politically, in which power differentials are being flattened and juxtaposed, with unpredictable power emanating quickly from unrecognized and unseen sources. In that context, the political threats of Artificial Intelligence are staggering, indeed mind-boggling, and abuses of AI for political advantage are destined to be part of global society from now on. Deepfake videos and images of celebrities and of private citizens can be immensely damaging to their victims and can be used to prompt hasty decisions based on erroneous information during politically volatile times. Such abuses are difficult for governments to monitor and to regulate. Chappell (2024, January 26) noted that deepfakes have become easier to make and "the latest iterations promise to use AI to generate even more convincing images and video" (n.p.).

Embarrassing a superstar can be devastating on several levels, particularly to the subject of the deepfake, but a greater danger politically is a fake video of the leader of a nation-state provocatively declaring something that she had never said. Of course, perhaps most abhorrent of all dangers are AI's potential applications in military operations, some in which Artificial Intelligence might, indeed, protect and preserve human lives, while other applications might only promise further unimaginable destruction. Certainly, AI and its applications pose potential dangers for the well-being of nation-states as these political entities are presently defined.

Economic Threats of AI

A special issue of *Time* magazine that had examined AI observed:

> While you're reading this sentence, artificial intelligence (AI) programs are painting cosmic portraits, responding to emails, preparing tax returns, and recording metal songs. They're writing pitch decks, debugging code, sketching architectural blueprints, and providing health advice.
>
> *(The AI arms race is changing everything, p. 9)*

That special issue of the magazine predicted that "… AI will reorient the way we work and engage with the world, unlock creativity and scientific discoveries, and allow humanity to achieve previously unimaginable feats. …AI could boost the global economy by over $15 trillion by 2030" (The AI arms race is changing everything, n.d., p. 9). AI is predicted to help humans be more productive

(How to make AI work for you at work, n.d, pp. 35–39), impacting tasks that are "routine, predictable, or standardized" (How to Make AI Work for You at Work, n.d, p. 36).

Nevertheless, amidst the likely obsolescence of a goodly number of existing jobs and their requisite vocational/professional knowledge, skills, and abilities, the new qualifications that will be needed in an Artificial Intelligence environment will not necessarily translate into high-wage jobs, or, for that matter, sustainable employment. In the words of *The Economist* (Big Tech and the pursuit of AI dominance, 2023, March 26): "The tech giants have all they need—data, computing power, billions of users—to thrive in the age of AI" (para.). One might posit that citizens collectively and individually may not necessarily also thrive. Such uncertainty includes career positions in public relations as that professionalized occupation is presently practiced. Certainly, some knowledge, skills, and abilities will become obsolete, as has been historically the case and often for the benefit of humankind. Driving a team of horses is a skill that few people need in modernity, or even being able to drive a manual transmission car; certainly, one might question whether cursive writing is essential in a world of keyboards, computers, smartphones, and voice commands.

The knowledge, skills, and abilities that will be needed for sustainable employment (or to live one's life in contemporary society) will certainly change by the year 2050, begging questions of educational triage, that is, what education will remain requisite for humankind in the year 2050 and what can be safely discarded as obsolete. Further, who should provide this education in a neoliberal economic environment? At some point, humankind will likely ask whether Big Tech—with its centralized and heightened social, political, economic, and cultural power, all of which will be increasingly enhanced by the tools of Artificial Intelligence—is, indeed, too powerful; if so, what, if anything, can be done about it?

Cultural Threats of AI

These "social, political, and economic threats" transcend into and collectively can be collapsed within the immense "cultural threats" of AI. Global society by the year 2050 is destined to change in ways that are presently unimaginable, with tremendous implications for public relations and its professional practice.

Within the next quarter century, public relations scholars and practitioners will need to re-examine and reconsider basic existential questions regarding what constitutes humanity and human agency within global society. Because of public relations practitioners and scholars' knowledge, skills, and abilities as ethical communicators and in their normative role as organizational and societal watchdogs, the public relations professional and scholarly community has inordinate—arguably unique—responsibilities in pondering such questions, but also the education and professional worldview that makes them eminently qualified to do so. They will need to apply their knowledge and assume their responsibility in relationship management, perhaps even extending to Artificial Intelligence entities, which may constitute a public or part of a public.

Public relations professionals will need to be ponder moral/ethical questions and contemplate pre-existing normative theories of society. They will need to be among the leaders in assuring that the global society is one of transparency, authenticity, and trust, not pseudo-transparency, inauthenticity, and mistrust. Although a classical liberal arts education will arguably be more essential than ever for public relations practitioners in 2050, their professional education will likely change greatly in ways that perhaps are not presently recognizable. Finally, by the year 2050 and perhaps much sooner, considering the rapid development of AI technologies, PR relations role in strategic communication albeit changed will be even more relevant. While AI will be getting increasingly more creative, human intuition will likely be hard to replicate even in smart machines. Thirty years from now many of the tools used in strategic communication today will be AI powered, and while AI might, and in some instances already is helping with the strategy, public relations practitioners will be still the ones executing the strategy, no matter how well and how precisely conceived. As long as three are other humans who need or desire strategic communication there will be need for other humans to create and execute it, as we believe what is essentially human cannot be replaced or replicated.

References

AI-Human Romance. (n.d. Display until 3/12/24). *Artificial intelligence: A new age of possibilities* (Special *Time* Edition), pp. 74–75.

The Arms Race Is Changing Everything. (n.d. Display until 3/12/24). *Artificial intelligence: A new age of possibilities* (Special *Time* Edition), pp. 8–13.

Bajak, F. (2023, November 20). Insider Q&A: Pentagon AI chief on network-centric warfare, generative AI challenges. *AP News*. Retrieved from https://apnews.com/article/pentagon-insider-ai-technology-cd1530bc621abf14954de49c2ee0896d

Big Tech and the Pursuit of AI Dominance. (2023, March 26). *The Economist*. https://www.economist.com/business/2023/03/26/big-tech-and-the-pursuit-of-ai-dominance

Chappell, B. (2024, January 26). Deepfakes exploiting Taylor Swift images exemplify a scourge with little oversite. *NPR*. Retrieved from https://www.wfae.org/united-states-world/2024-01-26/deepfakes-exploiting-taylor-swift-images-exemplify-a-scourge-with-little-oversight

Chowdhury, R. (n.d. Display until 3/12/24) the big players. *Artificial intelligence: A new age of possibilities* (Special *Time* Edition), p. 24.

Debeljak, A. (2012). In praise of hybridity. In K. Sriramesh & D. Vercic (Eds.), *Culture and public relations: Links and implications* (pp. 15–32). Routledge.

Edelman. (2019, March). *2019 Edelman AI survey results report*. Edelman. Retrieved from https://www.edelman.com/sites/g/files/aatuss191/files/2019-03/2019_Edelman_AI_Survey_Whitepaper.pdf

Fritzell, P. H. (1987). The conflicts of ecological conscience. In J. B. Callicott (Ed.), *Companion to a sand county Almanac* (pp. 128–153). The University of Wisconsin Press.
Giroux, H. A. (2002, Winter). Neoliberalism, corporate culture, and the promise of higher education: The University as a democratic public sphere. *Harvard Educational Review*, *2*(4), 425–463.
Goodstein, L., Nolan, T., & Pfeiffer, J. W. (1993). *Applied strategic planning: A comprehensive guide*. McGraw-Hill, Inc.
Holy Bible: International version. (1978). Genesis. (Ch. 1, verses. 26–31). Zondervan Bible Publishers.
How to Make AI Work for You at Work. (n.d. Display until 3/12/24). *Artificial intelligence: A new age of possibilities* (Special *Time* Edition), pp. 35–39.
Kruckeberg, D., Creedon, P., Gorpe, S., & Al-Khajha, M. (2014, October). *The dynamics of power and influence among corporations, civil society organizations and governments: Ramifications of the changing social, political, economic and cultural dimensions of global society in an era of transparency through digital communication.* Paper presented at the Fourth Conference of the Yarmouk University Faculty of Communication in cooperation with the Arab-U.S. Association for Communication Educators, Irbid, JO.
Luhmann, N. (1979). *Trust and power*. John Wiley.
Meacham, S. (2023, September 8). A race to extinction: How great power competition is making artificial intelligence existentially dangerous. *Harvard International Review*. Retrieved from https://hir.harvard.edu/a-race-to-extinction-how-great-power-competition-is-making-artificial-intelligence-existentially-dangerous/#:~:text=The%20pressure%20to%20outpace%20adversaries,risk%20to%20humanity's%20continued%20existence
Price, J. L. (1972). *Handbook of organizational measurement*. D. C. Heath and Company.
Price, J. L. (1968). *Organizational effectiveness: An inventory of propositions*. Richard D. Irwin, Inc.
Schwab, K. (2016). *The fourth industrial revolution*. Crown Business.
Swiatek, L., & Galloway, C. (2022). Artificial intelligence and public relations: Growing opportunities, questions, and concerns. In D. Pompper, K. R. Place, & C. Kay Weaver (Eds.), *The Routledge companion to public relations* (pp. 352–362). Routledge.
Swiatek, L., Vujnovic, M., Galloway, C., & Kruckeberg, D. (2024). *Artificial intelligence, strategic communicators and activism*. Routledge.
The History of Dogs: Special issue. (no author given) (2023, April 28). *OverDrive Magazine*, Issue 33.
Toffler, A., & Toffler, H. (1995). *Creating a new civilization: The politics of the Third Wave*. Turner Publishing Inc.
Tsetsura, K., & Kruckeberg, D. (2017). *Transparency, public relations and the mass media: Combating media bribery worldwide*. Taylor and Francis/Routledge (Research in Journalism Series).
Valentini, C., & Kruckeberg, D. (2011, Spring). Public relations and trust in contemporary global society: A Luhmannian perspective of the role of public relations enhancing trust among social systems. *Central European Journal of Communication, 4*(1), 91–107.
Vujnovic, M., & Kruckeberg, D. (2013, March). *Conceptualization, examination, and recommendations for a normative model of community-building for organizations*

managing change using new media. Paper presented at the 16th annual International Public Relations Research Conference, Miami, FL.

Vujnovic, M., & Kruckeberg, D. (2014, March). *A PR "meta-strategy" based on an examination of "transparency," "pseudo-transparency," "authenticity" and "trust"*. Paper presented at the 17th Annual International Public Relations Research Conference, Miami, FL.

Vujnovic, M., & Kruckeberg, D. (2016). Pitfalls and promises of transparency in the digital age. *Public Relations Inquiry, 5*(2), 121–143.

Yao, M. Z., & Ling, R. (2020). "What is computer-mediated communication?"—An introduction to the special issue. *Journal of Computer-Mediated Communication, 25*(1), 4–8.

Zerfass, A., Hagelstein, J., & Tench, R. (2020). Artificial intelligence in communication management: A cross-national study on adoption and knowledge, impact, challenges and risks. *Journal of Communication Management, 24*(4), 377–389.

2

THE GROWTH OF MALICIOUS AI

Countering Disinformation and Deepfakes Amid Mega-Crises

Marta N. Lukacovic and Deborah D. Sellnow-Richmond

One of the most anxiously observed products of AI (artificial intelligence) today is the phenomenon of deepfakes, which refers to visual or audiovisual content that has been machine-generated, to a degree altered from the original or completely fabricated, but may easily pass for an authentic recording. The global communities were already highly concerned about disinformation campaigns that have been proliferated through social media and other online platforms. Many now fear that deepfakes may significantly exacerbate the situation further, specifically in the volatile context of complex mega-crises that encompass serious interconnected challenges on local and global levels. While the introduced picture seems rather grim, this chapter presupposes that by the year 2050, global and local societies will likely be experiencing a world where the negative impacts of disinformation and deepfakes will be kept at bay. In this future world, professionals and stakeholders from various sectors, backgrounds, cultures, and locations will be working together on mitigating, or perhaps even solving, the formerly pervasive mega-crises. PR/strategic communication professionals will play a vital role in these promising processes – in overcoming the threat of deepfakes and disinformation amid mega-crises. This chapter details the positive ongoing developments in PR/strategic communication research, education, and applied practice that position this field at the forefront of countering such significant challenges of the first half of this century.

The Trend of Deepfakes and Disinformation Amid Mega-Crises

Before a deeper look into the role deepfakes play in disinformation campaigns, it is crucial to take a step back and assess a broader perspective. Particularly as

DOI: 10.4324/9781003426653-4

the possible negative impacts of deepfakes in particular and disinformation in general are not happening in a vacuum. After all, strategic communication, as a foundation of public relations, must be based on a broader perspective.

With the globalization of business, culture, and media, societies are becoming more complex and tensions are also growing. Let us consider an example of mass migration which well illustrates a mega-crisis. Frequently, refugees are displaced due to war and political violence. However, very commonly business ventures lead to irresponsible acts like negligent exploitation of resources, and impacted people must decide to immigrate due to tremendous degradations of life quality and natural environment in their home countries. As the migrants enter host countries, they are often met with not just exploitative conditions, but also are scapegoated for the economic, social, and political failures experienced locally. In such a climate, friction grows and so does extremism, with members of different communities, including majority and minority populations, opting for religious-fundamentalist, nationalist, xenophobic, or even neo-fascist and neo-Nazi movements. And as such, the chain of negative actions and outcomes continues. These complex, interconnected, and far-reaching issues are beyond the typical contained crises that have been studied through PR and strategic communication lenses. These are the *mega-crises*, which are clusters of pervasive crises with the characteristics of wicked problems, each sub-crisis exacerbating the other sub-crises, defying disciplinary and national boundaries, and thus being enormously difficult to solve (Sellnow-Richmond & Lukacovic, 2024).

Disinformation campaigns play a central role in aggravating the growing mega-crises around the world. While misinformation is inaccurate or false information that inadvertently enters public discourse and perception, *disinformation* is deliberately designed and spread with the strategic goal of deceiving the audience (Chadwick & Stanyer, 2022).

Strategic deceptive campaigns have been waged by a variety of actors, including commercial, criminal, non-state extremist, and state-affiliated entities (Waterman & Tsetsura, 2021).Today, disinformation is widely considered a profoundly problematic phenomenon and is addressed across many sectors, organizations, higher education institutions, nations, international entities, etc. This keen attention to disinformation confirms its mega-crisis-reaching repercussions.

Arguably, disinformation is not a new phenomenon. Different incarnations of strategic disinformation such as deceptive character assassination of public figures can be identified through various stages of human history (Samoilenko et al., 2020). However, the developments of new technologies offer novel opportunities and have marked the expansion of disinformation phenomena. The massive growth of social media and content-sharing platforms has been accompanied by increases in the frequency, variety, and reach of disinformation campaigns (Morozov, 2011). Specific adaptations of advanced technologies based on AI that are designed and/or deployed for deceptive, criminal, belligerent, or even terrorist purposes are characterized and theorized as MUAI – malicious use of artificial intelligence – by Bazarkina and Pashentsev (2019). Unfortunately, but not surprisingly, MUAI is today deeply integrated into disinformation campaigns.

Deepfakes bring disinformation campaigns to new extents. Ahmed (2022) defines deepfakes as "AI-driven synthetic media in which people appear to do and say something that never really happened, making them more plausible than other mis- and disinformation modalities" (p. 90). Samoilenko and Suvorova (2023) emphasize the significant expansion of MUAI through GANs (or generative adversarial networks) which are deep-learning algorithmic architectures that are capable of altering images and videos of real people as well as of producing completely new images and videos of people and situations that never existed, but yet appear realistic to many viewers. Montoro-Montarroso et al. (2023) stress that: "Face manipulation in images and videos, either partial or total, has been one of the most active areas in research to date and one that poses a significant challenge in fighting disinformation" (p. 8).

Although the effects of deepfakes were initially documented as rather limited and conditional in terms of political impact, for instance, many scholars continue to encourage general caution, research, and/or regulatory policies in order to appropriately respond to swiftly evolving deepfakes and their repercussions (Dobber et al., 2020; Helmus, 2022; Langguth et al., 2021). The extent of the impacts of deepfakes in deliberate disinformation campaigns might be intensifying in more recent history. Particularly far-reaching and devastating cases of the utilization of deepfakes in disinformation campaigns were detected and/or alleged in the aftermath of the Hamas attack on Israel in October 2023 and the subsequent Israeli military incursion into Gaza, with examples including purportedly fabricated images of deceased and mutilated civilian victims (e.g., Murphy, 2023). While these incidents frequently happen, many members of the global public are rather unaware of generative AI technologies and their capabilities in deepfake creation (Dobber et al., 2020; Samoilenko & Suvorova, 2023). On the other hand, those aware of deepfakes are becoming increasingly more cynical, which contributes to the dissolution of public trust in media and other institutions (*Anti-Defamation League*, 2023).

While the picture above may render an unoptimistic prospect, we believe that the situation with disinformation and deepfakes can be dramatically improved by the middle of the current century. Importantly, PR/strategic communication represents the sector that can play quite a vital role in transcending the current concerning path. In the next section of this chapter, we recap the initiatives in our field that position PR/ strategic communication at the forefront of the fight against disinformation campaigns and deepfakes in the context of mega-crises. Then, we will outline how the initiatives translate into specific knowledge, skills, and abilities to ensure that PR/strategic communication research, education, and applied practice are indeed moving in the forecasted direction by 2050.

Public Relations/Strategic Communication Today and in 2050; Facing Deepfakes, Disinformation, and Mega-Crises

The efforts in the field of PR/strategic communication that ought to be implemented where not fully integrated, enhanced where already practiced, and elevated as the field approaches the new decades, are: (1) interdisciplinary and intersectoral collaboration, (2) intercultural and global collaboration, (3) dialog with all pertinent stakeholders, (4) high-quality and continuous education of professionals, (5) contribution to broader literacy efforts, and (6) rigorous theory-driven research. In the following sections, we elaborate on the importance of these efforts specifically when facing the mega-crises intertwined with deepfakes within disinformation campaigns.

Interdisciplinary and Intersectoral Collaborations

While deepfakes are possible thanks to technological developments, their capacity to further exacerbate disinformation campaigns is rooted in a web of problems that often have psychological, social, political, economic, and several other components. Hence, a solely tech-based solution to this problem is likely to fail due to its deterministic limitations (Bakir & McStay, 2022). MUAI must be countered with complex responses, mitigations, and eventually solutions that marry technological components with research and applied methods informed by a number of different disciplines across sciences, social sciences, and humanities (Averkin et al., 2019; Bakir & McStay, 2022). Countering mega-crises in general requires interdisciplinary coalitions, where PR/strategic communication should play a significant role in collaborations with other relevant academic disciplines and industry sectors (Sellnow-Richmond & Lukacovic, 2024).

Due to such promising practical benefits in fighting deepfakes, disinformation, and larger mega-crises, it is not surprising there is a strong consensus on the value of interdisciplinary and intersectoral collaboration. Hence, it is paramount that professionals of PR/ strategic communication in all subareas, including research, education, and application continue to actively pursue knowledge, skills, and abilities (KSAs) that equip them for success in interdisciplinary and intersectoral collaborations.

Intercultural and Global Collaborations

MUAI weaponized in disinformation campaigns is a global phenomenon, especially in the context of mega-crises (Lukacovic & Sellnow-Richmond, 2023).

Deepfakes specifically have already been utilized across the world, having negative effects on people from various cultures (Samoilenko & Suvorova, 2023). The global nature of technological developments, such as AI and its implications, necessitates inclusive intercultural participation in the construction of feasible global ethical guidelines and international legal frameworks (Roumate, 2023). While intercultural orientations are not new for the PR/strategic communication field, the reorientation toward a global perspective is another frontier and will require growth in terms of focused research and reflection on findings (Rittenhofer & Valentini, 2015).

Collaborations across cultures and on the global level are and will continue to be challenging but necessary to mitigate mega-crises and alleviate the potential detriments of deepfakes within disinformation campaigns. Strategic communication is fundamental in building and sustaining intercultural and global partnerships. Hence, PR/ strategic communication researchers, educators, and practitioners of today, of the near future, and of 2050, should acquire KSAs that serve in intercultural and global collaborations, and specifically such collaborations that address mega-crises, disinformation, and MUAI.

Dialog with All Pertinent Stakeholders

Mega-crises and deepfake-intertwined campaigns will continue to be a problem for decades to come (Bakir & McStay, 2022; Sellnow-Richmond & Lukacovic, 2024). Preparation for the exacerbation of issues is vital. It is paramount as various organizations and governments prepare for these crises, that communication professionals are prominently engaged. One of the best practices of applied crisis communication is partnerships with the publics/stakeholders (Seeger & Sellnow, 2019). A consensus in the contemporary PR is a deep commitment to and facilitation of symmetrical communication between organizations and all pertinent stakeholders (Grunig, 2006).

However, symmetrical communication is not an easy endeavor, especially when structural power differences are still rather pervasive. So, to achieve a truly symmetrical, meaningful dialog, particularly in the context of crises, those in positions of power should be committed to ethical dialog practices such as listening (Neill & Bowen, 2021). Furthermore, the increasingly interdisciplinary, intersectoral, intercultural, and global nature of collaborations introduces a number of other challenges that should be explored and eventually transcended thanks to the input of PR/ strategic communication practitioners, researchers, and educators. To do so, KSAs for PR/ strategic communication professionals of the upcoming decades must be deliberately centered on dialog with very diverse collaborators and stakeholders. Furthermore, these inherently not easy dialogs will frequently have to happen under challenging conditions of mega-crises and uncertainties that are aggravated by deepfakes within disinformation campaigns.

High-Quality, Continuous Education

The role of high-quality PR/ strategic communication education is vital. PR education represents a research subarea that produces theoretically driven and evidence-based recommendations. In the near future as well as for decades to come, it is paramount that educators continue to enhance their pedagogical approaches with up-to-date recommendations. The contemporary zeitgeist in PR education in the US stresses the importance of understanding data, AI, as well as ethics, social responsibility, and the view of PR as a driver of positive social change (Toth & Bourland-Davis, 2023). In this vein, Lopezosa et al. (2023) advocate for education that equips future communication professionals with both the skills to use relevant AI tools, and also a profound understanding of the roots, societal impacts, and ethical implications of these technologies. These are the notions in education that can foster "the new function of public relations as a form of corporate conscience in a technological context, shaped towards maximizing human potential in the face of technological determinism" (p. 10, Santa Soriano & Torres Valdés, 2021).

Such a comprehensive, high-quality educational path can place PR/strategic communication professionals at the forefront of the combat against deepfakes used in disinformation campaigns. Particularly as the KSAs that upcoming PR/strategic communication professionals can gain through their education will equip them well to take part in the successful establishment of dialogs with various stakeholders that represent diverse communities, cultures, disciplines, and sectors.

Furthermore, it must be acknowledged that today's world is quickly developing, partially thanks to the fast advances in technologies, both beneficial and malicious. For instance, the development of AI is predicted to significantly reconfigure the job market (Deranty & Corbin, 2022) and/or reconfigure the KSAs that will be necessary for professionals across fields including PR/ strategic communication (Zerfass et al., 2020). The quality of deepfakes (Samoilenko & Suvorova, 2023) and thus "potentially deleterious impact of deepfakes" (p. 18, Helmus, 2022) will increase in near and more distant future. Moreover, defining features of mega-crises are volatility and unpredictability (Sellnow-Richmond & Lukacovic 2024). This complex fluidity of social, political, and technological realities requires that PR/strategic communication researchers, educators, and practitioners continue to actively study the rapidly evolving phenomena, research-driven theories, and evidence-based responses throughout their careers.

The turmoil of the present and future necessitates continuous and/or continuing education across a variety of fields (Horowitz, 2022). 'Continuous education' refers to a discretionary commitment to stay updated on the developments in one's field and the broader world. There is a general consensus that PR/strategic communication professionals in various areas, ranging from education to research to applied practice, need to stay current (Tsetsura & Vergara, 2021). Hence, today and in the future, effective PR/strategic communication professional must stay committed to continuous education. What perhaps should happen in the future is creating a more institutionalized framework, industry-sponsored support, and formalized incentives for continuing education of PR/strategic communication professionals. Specifically, 'continuing education' implies required classes, training, and/or testing to formally verify and maintain one's professional accreditation (Horowitz, 2022). By demonstrating the vital role of PR/strategic communication professionals in coalitions to fight the impacts of deepfakes in particular and disinformation within mega-crises in general, the impetus for sponsorship and institutionalization of continuing education in the field will be significantly more robust.

Contribution to Broader Literacy Efforts

The growth of the field of communication in general has been attributed to the relevant research and application that answered the most pressing, practical questions and concerns of many societies and different sectors (Craig, 2021; Donsbach, 2006). With the fight against disinformation and deepfakes, the calls for improvements in information literacy and AI literacy are prominent (e.g., Haider & Sundin, 2022; Hermann, 2021). Importantly, there is a communication element to those literacies and it is paramount that communication researchers and educators are the ones actively involved in these broader educational efforts (Lukacovic & Sellnow-Richmond, 2023). This means that PR/ strategic communication educators, researchers, and practitioners have a lot to offer not just to their peers within the field, but to general education as well.

The vital place of communication in information literacy and AI literacy curricula needs to be supported by pertinent advocacy (Dannels & Housley Gaffney, 2009). Hence, the critical KSAs of PR/strategic communication educators will increasingly necessitate conveying field-specific takeaways and their value to key decision-makers as well as wider student populations and general public.

Rigorous Theory-Driven Research

Rigorous research and theory must inform interdisciplinary and intersectoral collaborations (Sellnow-Richmond & Lukacovic, 2024), intercultural and global collaborations (Greene & Keremidchieva, 2023), dialog with stakeholders (Seeger & Sellnow, 2019), education (Toth & Bourland-Davis, 2023), and advocacy for incorporating communication education to broader general education and literacy efforts (Dannels & Housley Gaffney, 2009). Naturally, a robust and ever-evolving body of rigorous research and theory is necessary to describe and possibly counter deepfakes and disinformation (Bakir & McStay, 2022; Dobber et al., 2020; Samoilenko & Suvorova, 2023). No doubt, a wide consensus underscores that research is and will continue to be vital for all the listed efforts today, tomorrow, and by the middle of this century. Henceforth, PR/ strategic communication researchers should actively pursue and elevate KSAs that allow them to better convey key takeaways of their findings to educators and practitioners within the field and to other stakeholders beyond the field. PR/ strategic communication educators should likewise cultivate and continuously improve KSAs that assure up-to-date research and theory-informed teaching and learning in the context of growing mega-crises and plague of disinformation including deepfakes. Practitioners must possess the necessary KSAs that allow them to adaptively respond to the needs of their work, including the capacity to learn from new research and theory-informed findings that will continue to emerge.

The outlined project is based on already initiated and in many instances quite well-established notions in PR/strategic communication research, education, and applied practice. So, while the challenges of mega-crises are tremendous, and the role of deepfakes and disinformation within the mega-crises is very fickle and unpredictable, we strongly believe that the field of PR/strategic communication possesses the fertile ground to further grow new professionals who can properly respond to these serious pressures of today and tomorrow.

Knowledge, Skills, and Abilities of Public Relations/Strategic Communication Professionals Taking on Deepfakes, Disinformation, and Mega-Crises Today and in 2050

In light of the trends in the field, as described in the previous section, this section outlines the particular KSAa (knowledge, skills, abilities) that are crucial for PR/strategic communication professionals today and even more so by 2050. Specifically, these KSAs are related to the capacity of PR/strategic communication professionals to join the wider coalitions and efforts against disinformation campaigns with deepfakes. The list below is not exhaustive but encompasses several necessary areas of focus.

Knowledge

Knowledge of Key Concepts in the Field and Beyond

The knowledge of key vocabulary, concepts, theories, and methods in PR/strategic communication but also across different applicable disciplines and sectors will enable the professional to further learn and communicate with others.

Intercultural & Global Literacies

The knowledge of globalization and its implications, interdependence of systems, diversity in cultures and experiences, and other perspectives will broaden the understanding of the world that a PR/strategic communication professional needs.

Understanding of the Interplay of Crises and Disinformation

Professionals should navigate the key terms, concepts, theories, and methods that pertain to crises and disinformation campaigns. Crises, and specifically mega-crises, as well as disinformation, are pervasive and far-reaching phenomena. Thus, all various PR professionals will only benefit from having a high-level working understanding of these phenomena.

AI Literacy

PR/strategic communication professionals should have literacy about AI, which includes knowledge of its origins, ethical dilemmas, positive societal impacts, negative societal impacts, and general and well as field-specific applications.

Skills

Communication across Platforms, Contexts, and Stakeholders/ Audiences

PR/strategic communication professionals should develop strong interpersonal communication, public speaking, and media communication skills in diverse contexts. The various types of communication encounters will involve colleagues from different disciplines or sectors, representatives of diverse global or local communities and cultures, and other pertinent stakeholders, so a professional should have sharp skills in addressing those diverse communication audiences.

Capacity for Continuous Learning

Professionals should develop reading, listening, and analytical skills to be able to continue learning throughout one's *active life*. By '*active life*', we mean one's career, activism, and other life stages during which one wishes to take part in applying their PR/strategic communication background.

Use of AI and Other Relevant Technologies

Professionals should continuously develop practical skills in using AI and other advanced technologies that are becoming relevant in the field. This should encompass skills in using such applications that can aid in the detection of deepfakes. Furthermore, the professional should have skills in using a variety of other technologies that are commonly used to directly appreciate the experiences of the wider population.

Abilities

Analysis and Application

Professionals should be able to apply appropriate concepts, theories, and methods to relevant situations to shed light on novel situations or develop solutions for difficult problems that come up in the practice of PR/strategic communication.

Facilitation of Dialogs

Professionals should be able to establish infrastructures and platforms for productive dialogs and actually accomplish these dialogs with various stakeholders across fields, sectors, cultures, and all other possible pertinent individuals and groups in the given situation.

Aptitude to Adapt to Change and Transform Realities

Professionals should cultivate their aptitude for continuous learning throughout one's active life to appropriately acknowledge and adapt to fast changes in the areas of PR, media, and technology including AI. This also means staying abreast of dynamic threats of mega-crises and disinformation. Furthermore, this means the cultivation of aptitudes for creativity necessary for overcoming the challenges that will arise, mitigating problems, and ultimately transforming the realities for the better.

Conclusion

Even though there are many concerns about the impacts that deepfakes and disinformation will have amid mega-crises, PR/strategic communication professionals can play a vital role in mitigating the possible threats. By the year 2050, many societies around the world may be highly information-literate and AI-literate. While disinformation campaigns may still occur, and, by that point, very sophisticated deepfakes will very likely be used, coalitions across disciplinary, sectoral, cultural, and global boundaries will work together to expose deception. These coalitions will unite the fields of technology and sciences with social sciences and humanities, creating effective tools to counter disinformation campaigns by coupling technological instruments with interdisciplinary approaches. Analogously, interdisciplinary and global coalitions will effectively work together to mitigate and perhaps even eradicate many other pervasive mega-crises that plague the world today, such as poverty, extremism, degradation of the natural environment, etc. The PR/strategic communication field can and should be at the forefront of the developments toward the forecasted future. Indeed, as this chapter recaps, PR/strategic communication research, education,

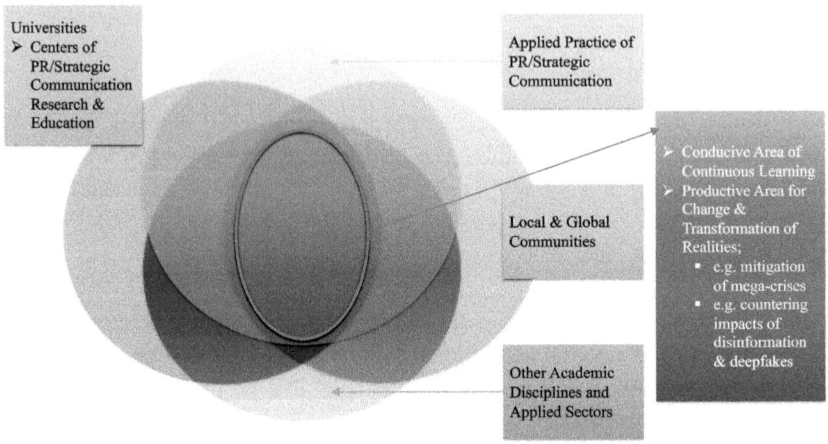

FIGURE 2.1 Where PR/strategic communication research and education intersect with diverse academic disciplines, applied sectors, as well as local and global communities lies a fertile ground for continuous learning and transformative impacts. Leveraging this productive intersection is crucial for mitigating mega-crises and combating disinformation in the rising era of AI.

Source: Author.

and applied practice are particularly keen when it comes to the steps that can help to approximate that vision of the future, namely: (1) interdisciplinary and intersectoral collaboration, (2) intercultural and global collaboration, (3) dialog with all pertinent stakeholders, (4) high-quality and continuous education of professionals, (5) contribution to broader literacy efforts, and (6) rigorous theory-driven research. While a lot has been done already, there is still much to be accomplished. Both society and technology constantly evolve. New opportunities and challenges constantly arise. PR/strategic communication professionals are and will continue to be important actors in bridging sectors and cultures through dialog, embracing change through continuous learning, and finding creative solutions to transcend crises (see Figure 2.1).

References

Ahmed, S. (2022). Disinformation sharing thrives with fear of missing out among low cognitive news users: A cross-national examination of intentional sharing of deep fakes. *Journal of Broadcasting & Electronic Media*, *66*(1), 89–109. https://doi.org/10.1080/08838151.2022.2034826

Anti-Defamation League. (2023, November 1). Generative artificial intelligence (GAI): Increasing the fog of war between Israel and Hamas. https://www.adl.org/resources/blog/generative-artificial-intelligence-gai-increasing-fog-war-between-israel-and-hamas

Averkin, A. N., Bazarkina, D. Yu, Pantserev, K. A., & Pashentsev, Y. N. (2019). Artificial intelligence in the context of psychological security: Theoretical and practical implications. *Atlantis Studies in Uncertainty Modelling, 1*, 101–107.

Bakir, V., & McStay, A. (2022). *Optimizing emotions, incubating falsehoods; How to protect the global civic body from disinformation and misinformation*. Palgrave Macmillan.

Bazarkina, D. Yu, & Pashentsev, Y. N. (2019). Artificial intelligence and new threats to international psychological security. *Russia in Global Affairs, 17*(1), 147–170. https://doi.org/10.31278/1810-6374-2019-17-1-147-170

Chadwick, A., & Stanyer, J. (2022). Deception as a bridging concept in the study of disinformation, misinformation, and misperceptions: Toward a holistic framework. *Communication Theory, 32*(1), 1–24. https://doi-org.easydb.angelo.edu/10.1093/ct/qtab019

Craig, R. T. (2021). Response. In M. H. Rich & J. S. Robles (Eds.), *Practicing communication theory; Exploring, applying, and teaching the constitutive metamodel* (pp. 191–210). Cognella Academic Publishing.

Dannels, D., & Housley Gaffney, A. (2009). Communication across the curriculum and in the disciplines: A call for scholarly cross-curricular advocacy. *Communication Education, 58*(1), 124–153. https://doi-org.easydb.angelo.edu/10.1080/03634520802527288

Deranty, J.-P., & Corbin, T. (2022). Artificial intelligence and work: A critical review of recent research from the social sciences. *AI & Society*, 1–17. https://doi.org/10.1007/s00146-022-01496-x

Dobber, T., Metoui, N., Trilling, D., Helberger, N., & de Vreese, C. (2020). Do (microtargeted) deepfakes have real effects on political attitudes? *The International Journal of Press/Politics, 26*(1), 69–91. https://doi.org/10.1177/1940161220944364

Donsbach, W. (2006). The identity of communication research. *Journal of Communication, 56*, 437–448.

Greene, R. W., & Keremidchieva, Z. D. (2023). Governing superdiversity: A critical commentary on intercultural understanding. *Journal of Multicultural Discourses, 18*(1), 22–32. https://doi.org/10.1080/17447143.2023.2234888

Grunig, J. E. (2006). Furnishing the edifice: Ongoing research on public relations as a strategic management function. *Journal of Public Relations Research, 18*(2), 151–176. https://doi-org.easydb.angelo.edu/10.1207/s1532754xjprr1802_5

Haider, J., & Sundin, O. (2022). Information literacy challenges in digital culture: Conflicting engagements of trust and doubt. *Information, Communication & Society, 25*(8), 1176–1191. https://doi.org/10.1080/1369118x.2020.1851389

Helmus, T. C. (2022, July 6). *Artificial intelligence, deepfakes, and disinformation: A primer*. RAND Corporation. https://www.rand.org/pubs/perspectives/PEA1043-1.html

Hermann, E. (2021). Artificial intelligence and mass personalization of communication content—An ethical and literacy perspective. *New Media & Society, 24*(5), 1258–1277. https://doi.org/10.1177/14614448211022702

Horowitz, M. (2022, September 12). Council Post: Three reasons to replace "continuing education" with "continuous education." *Forbes*. Retrieved from https://www.forbes.com/sites/forbesnonprofitcouncil/2022/09/12/three-reasons-to-replace-continuing-education-with-continuous-education/?sh=2f6e311376fb

Langguth, J., Pogorelov, K., Brenner, S., Filkuková, P., & Schroeder, D. T. (2021). Don't trust your eyes: Image manipulation in the age of deepfakes. *Frontiers in Communication, 6*, 1–12. https://doi.org/10.3389/fcomm.2021.632317

Lopezosa, C., Codina, L., Pont-Sorribes, C., & Vállez, M. (2023). Use of generative artificial intelligence in the training of journalists: challenges, uses and training proposal. *El Profesional de La Información, 32*(4), 1–12. https://doi.org/10.3145/epi.2023.jul.08

Lukacovic, M. N., & Sellnow-Richmond, D. D. (2023). COVID-19 pandemic and the rise of MUAI threats to national and international psychological security. In E. Pashentsev (Ed.), *The Palgrave handbook of malicious use of AI and psychological security* (pp. 175–201). Palgrave Macmillan.

Montoro-Montarroso, A., Canton-Correa, J., Rosso, P., Chulvi, B., Panizo-Lledot, A., Huertas-Tato, J., Calvo-Figueras, B., Rementeria, M. J., & Gomez-Romero, J. (2023). Fighting disinformation with artificial intelligence: Fundamentals, advances and challenges. *El Profesional de la Informacion, 32*(3), 1–16. https://link.gale.com/apps/doc/A755569336/IFME?u=anon~8cfaf598&sid=sitemap&xid=f1c124d3

Morozov, E. (2011). *The net delusion: The dark side of internet freedom*. Public Affairs.

Murphy, M. (2023, October 31). Emotive deepfakes in Israel-Hamas war further cloud what's real. *Bloomberg*. Retrieved from https://www.bloomberg.com/news/articles/2023-10-31/-emotive-deepfakes-in-israeli-war-further-cloud-what-s-real#xj4y7vzkg

Neill, M. S., & Bowen, S. A. (2021). Ethical listening to employees during a pandemic: New approaches, barriers and lessons. *Journal of Communication Management, 25*(3), 276–297. https://doi.org/10.1108/jcom-09-2020-0103

Rittenhofer, I., & Valentini, C. (2015). A "practice turn" for global public relations: An alternative approach. *Journal of Communication Management, 19*(1), 2–19. https://doi.org/10.1108/jcom-11-2013-0084

Roumate, F. (2023). Ethics of artificial intelligence, higher education, and scientific research. In F. Roumate (Ed.), *Artificial intelligence in higher education and scientific research; future developments* (pp. 129–144). Springer.

Samoilenko, S., Icks, M., Keohane, J., & Shiraev, E. (Eds.) (2020). *Routledge handbook of character assassination and reputation management*. Routledge.

Samoilenko, S. A., & Suvorova, I. (2023). Artificial intelligence and deepfakes in strategic deception campaigns: The U.S. and Russian experiences. In E. Pashentsev (Ed.), *The Palgrave handbook of malicious use of AI and psychological security* (pp. 507–529). Palgrave Macmillan.

Santa Soriano, A., & Torres Valdés, R. M. (2021). Engaging universe 4.0: The case for forming a public relations-strategic intelligence hybrid. *Public Relations Review, 47*(2), 1–12. https://doi.org/10.1016/j.pubrev.2021.102035

Seeger, M. W., & Sellnow, T. L. (2019). *Communication in times of trouble*. Wiley Blackwell.

Sellnow-Richmond, D. D., & Lukacovic, M. N. (2024). The COVID-19 pandemic as exemplar of the chaos of mega-crises. In T. L. Sellnow & D. D. Sellnow (Eds.), *Communicating risk and safety* (pp. 97–107). De Gruyters. https://doi.org/10.1515/9783110752427-006

Toth, E., & Bourland-Davis, P. (Eds.) (2023). *Navigating change: Recommendations for advancing undergraduate public relations education* (The 50th anniversary report). Commission on Public Relations Education. https://www.commissionpred.org/wp-content/uploads/2023/11/CPRE-50th-Anniversary-Report-FINAL.pdf

Tsetsura, K., & Vergara, L. (2021). The U.S. capability framework for public relations and communication management: Results of a national three-stage study. *Public Relations Review, 47*(2), 1–8. https://doi.org/10.1016/j.pubrev.2021.102016

Waterman, D., & Tsetsura, K. (2021). The future of Russia's strategic communications: An effects-based approach. In K. Tsetsura & D. Kruckeberg (Eds.), *Strategic communications in Russia; Public relations and advertising* (pp. 221–234). Taylor & Francis.

Zerfass, A., Hagelstein, J., & Tench, R. (2020). Artificial intelligence in communication management: A cross-national study on adoption and knowledge, impact, challenges and risks. *Journal of Communication Management, 24*(4), 377–389. https://doi.org/10.1108/JCOM-10-2019-0137

3

RESPONSIBLE AI FOR PUBLIC RELATIONS PRACTICE

Applying Public Relations Practitioner Perspectives to Ethical Codes for the Use of Generative Artificial Intelligence

Lea-Ann Germinder and Luke Capizzo

With the launch of ChatGPT in Nov. 2022 and the broader rise of big data and generative artificial intelligence (AI) as content generation and management tools, public relations faces a reckoning as a profession. This chapter, like others in this volume, looks to examine the impact of AI in the context of public relations with a focus on the future, centering codes of ethics. Norms and codes of ethics in public relations have evolved over time due to societal and technological changes (e.g., Bowen, 2013; Fitzpatrick, 2002a, 2002b; Neill, 2023; Watson, 2015). While AI has been studied for some time, the rapid growth in the use of generative AI (predominantly ChatGPT), has resulted in substantial growth in scholarly and professional interest in the impacts of AI on the public relations profession and organizationally centered strategic communication. While the Commission on Public Relations Education (2023) report identified both ethics and data analytics (including AI training) as two of the six most critical areas to address within the public relations profession, leading practitioners in multiple associations have struggled to find consensus on tackling the emerging challenges. In the same Commission on Public Relations Education Report, Neill (2023) found that practitioners ranked ethics third behind writing and communication skills in priority when identifying essential competencies that are necessary for public relations practice.

Despite optimism about the potential time-saving role of AI tools, many realities of big data (e.g., D'Ignazio & Klein, 2020), give some practitioners and scholars pause about the rush to use generative AI without guidelines. Others are concerned with those in the profession not learning the tools being left behind as the

DOI: 10.4324/9781003426653-5

technology continues to evolve. The challenges are many—including but not limited to transparency, disclosure, honesty, safeguarding confidences, and bias. These issues are inherent to large datasets and in the case of bias, are often grounded in societal and systemic inequality, deeply complicating any plans to address them.

The concept of Responsible Artificial Intelligence (RAI) (e.g., de Laat, 2021; Ray, 2023) has been used by technology companies and by AI experts to advocate for the ethical implementation of artificial intelligence by all organizations implementing AI. However, while the term has been used, the full implementation of RAI has also been called into question. There are multiple reasons for this including a lack of established legal and regulatory universal guidelines, a lack of general awareness regarding how to implement RAI, and a lack of funding.

In public relations, the theory of responsible public relations ethics (Fitzpatrick & Gauthier, 2001) has been proposed as a more practical course of action relative to public relations practitioners adhering to the Public Relations Society of America's Code of Ethics as an aspirational goal rather than as a mandatory compliance issue. Thus, there is an opportunity to leverage the concept of responsible AI into the public relations lexicon as responsible public relations (RPR) that helps organizations move toward RAI. The purpose of this chapter is to leverage RPR to encourage the adoption of RAI as part of our understanding of the potential for stronger professional ethical direction in the coming decades. It becomes the raison d'etre for the public relations professional's inclusion in and leadership role in organizations desiring to implement RAI. Using a set of 15 interviews with highly experienced public relations practitioners (15 to 45+ years), this chapter examines the potential for developing a more responsible approach to AI ethics through the ethical codes, with consideration of implications for several decades to come. The chapter will first provide a brief overview of relevant literature before sharing findings from these interviews and implications for public relations practices now and in 2050.

Literature Review

Ethics in Public Relations

Deontology, Utilitarianism, and Ethics of Care

Public relations ethics has been understood from multiple viewpoints and perspectives. These distinctions often create conflict between idealized codes of ethics and practitioner realities of client and employer prioritization (Fawkes, 2012). One approach begins from a deontological or process-oriented perspective, positioning fair process as the guidepost of professional and managerial ethics (e.g., Bowen, 2004, 2023). In particular, Bowen's (2005, 2013) scholarship highlights Kant's categorical imperative, the binding moral commitment to follow just processes despite extenuating circumstances. Individuals should be "respected as ends in themselves" rather than as means to profit or organizational success (Place et al., 2021, p. 5). By contrast, utilitarian or consequentialist approaches to ethics prioritize equitable or just outcomes over process (e.g., Lee, 2015), such as in public health-oriented persuasive communication which prioritizes agreed-upon public goods such as quality of life or life expectancy (Lee, 2015). Finally, the ethics of care perspective (e.g., Dong & Morehouse, 2022; Fraustino & Kennedy, 2018; Madden & Alt, 2021) "privileges relationships, context, partiality, and considerations of interdependence and vulnerability (i.e., traditionally feminine values) over hierarchy, abstractions, impartiality, duties/rules, and calculated rationality" (Fraustino & Kennedy, 2018, p. 22). Thus, an ethic of care in public relations centers personal, individual care over abstract, rational systems and processes for decision-making.

Responsible Advocacy and Democratic-Oriented Ethics

The Professional Responsibility Theory of Public Relations (Fitzpatrick & Gauthier, 2001) was written prior to the introduction of generative AI although it aligns with a responsible framework to lead to engaging in RAI. This research calls for public relations practitioners to establish "baselines for responsible advocacy in public relations: access, process, truth and disclosure" (Fitzpatrick, 2006, p. 9). Fitzpatrick argues that "the core concepts of advocacy in the Public Relations Society of America's (PRSA) Code of Ethics reflect democratic ideals grounded in First Amendment legal theory" (p. 1). She points out that the same concepts of "protecting and advancing the free flow of accurate and truthful information" and "informed decision-making" have not only been "recognized as democratic principles of law but are the basis of the PRSA code" (p. 2). Fitzpatrick says that public relations practitioners should also consider ethics beyond what is determined by regulations and laws. Currently, laws and regulations are not only far behind the rapid adoption and technological developments in AI, but legal scholars posit that the law may never be able to keep up with such a rapid rate of development in technology (Molchakov et al., 2023).

AI, Big Data, and Ethics

AI is a type of artificial intelligence system capable of generating text, images, video, and human-like conversations. It is enabled by machine learning—computers teaching themselves by analyzing large amounts of data typically from the internet (International Public Relations Association, 2023). While AI has been in use for decades behind many applications, it is the availability and subsequent rapid growth in the direct use of ChatGPT, and similarly accessible generative AI tools, by the public that has sparked intense debate. While an analysis of definitions of generative AI should be planned for future research, guides are still emerging. Presently, the definition of AI is often confused with the dominant tool, ChatGPT, and simply referred to as AI.

AI and Public Relations Codes of Ethics

The first modern public relations code of ethics was adopted in 1950 by the Public Relations Society of America (D'Angelo, 2022). The first international code of public relations ethics was introduced by the International Public Relations Association in 1965 (Watson, 2014). In 2023, the rapid adoption of AI created a potential for public relations professionals to inadvertently conflict with existing public relations ethical codes of conduct. These codes, including that of the Public Relations Society of America Code of Ethics (Public Relations Society of America, 2000) champion truth, trust, transparency, confidentiality, addressing bias and other ethical issues. In its 2000 revision, PRSA dismantled most of the code's enforcement mechanism (Fitzpatrick, 2002a; Huang, 2001; Page et al., 2024), leaving the code as an inspirational and aspirational tool rather than a functional deterrent to unethical professional behavior.

Now AI is forcing associations to reexamine their ethical codes. The Chartered Institute of Public Relations (2018, 2020, 2023a, 2023b) was the first organization to examine the impact of AI on the public relations profession, its use and engagement as part of its ethical mandate. The Chartered Institute of Public Relations' 2020 report was issued with AI Guidelines before ChatGPT caused a groundswell of use in 2023. That report showed that only 15% of PR professionals were using AI. A subsequent 2023 report showed 57% of PR professionals were using ChatGPT. A more recent report by the University of Southern California (2023), showed that 80% of public relations professionals thought that AI would be a substantial part of their future business versus just 18% in 2019. As of March 2024, The PR Council (2023), Chartered Institute of Public Relations (2023), The Public Relations Society of America (2023), and the International Association of Public Relations (2023) have all released AI-related ethical guidance for practitioners. Based on this prior research, this chapter asks two central research questions. First, what ethical challenges, issues, or opportunities do practitioners face due to the use and growth of generative AI? Second, how should practitioners meet the challenge of this new technology?

Results

Agreement on Hype, Not Ethics

One central theme that emerged is that while the public relations profession is intrigued by the opportunities for ChatGPT and similar generative tools to transform our daily work, there was no consensus on how to handle all the ethical challenges and issues the technology presents. There is agreement that the hype around AI has caused a "Wild West" mentality, but how the code of ethics fits in each use case is unclear. The responses varied from a "wait and see" to taking a strong stance on "who we are." For example, one participant expressed:

> As far as conflict [with the codes], we're talking about a very wide universe here that has to be addressed. We must take a very strong stand and perspective, saying, this is who we are. If our values are transparency, if our values are whatever, it's just going to be a continual testing of which makes sense at the time because there are going to be applications with AI we've never seen before.

Thus, many participants advocated for taking action, often through professional association engagement and process-oriented guidance (as is addressed in a later theme), but there was little agreement on what form such approaches might take. Several expressed their conflicted views: "What I'm concerned about is inadvertent plagiarism. The program [has a] lack of transparency. I don't know where it's getting this stuff, and that makes me wary and cautious. I think we need to think through that very carefully." This perspective emphasizes the lack of functional broader (i.e. national governmental) regulatory oversight on AI tools, positioning the public relations profession as needing to take ownership of the ethical challenges posed by emerging technologies.

Limited Guidance on Transparency and Disclosure

A second theme that emerged is the importance of disclosure and transparency when using generative AI tools. One argument was that a lack of disclosure could lead to not only trust issues but also ethical and legal concerns about where the information came from. Practitioners were urged to check their work and remain vigilant in ensuring the accuracy of all information. As one interviewee suggested,

> AI presents largely unknown and remarkably powerful concerns given generative AI's characteristics that can conflict with principles of transparency, disclosure of information, honesty, and safeguarding confidences. These issues might be addressed through active advocacy by professionals and professional associations, as well as by regulatory bodies.

Another participant was even more pointed with their skepticism of generative AI tools: "Unless totally transparent with the use of AI to develop systems, materials or resources, there is strong possibility that any unknown conflicts (or those established to be intentional) could be addressed with fidelity." Many participants pointed to the importance of disclosing the use of generative AI as part of public relations tactics. Others were not concerned with disclosure, viewing the use of generative AI as a background tool similar to using Google search, for example, thus it is clear there is no consensus on how to handle disclosure.

Testing and Training Are Essential

A theme that emerged here was the need for practitioners to take the initiative to test and experiment with ChatGPT and generative AI. Those interviewees who were most knowledgeable about the use of AI in public relations reaffirmed that "time is of the essence" and that practitioners should "ignore AI at your own peril as you may very well lose your job." That said, most interviews cited knowledge of AI's propensity for hallucinations and to output false information. They reinforced the importance of a human fact-checking their AI work and emphasizing this is true no matter what the source is. More experienced practitioners with expertise in technology, while concerned about the dangers, enthusiastically encouraged testing and training and as one participant noted, a "we've-been-here-before" approach. There was still a small minority of those not engaging in AI that have chosen to "wait until the dust settles."

Several participants referenced how slow the public relations profession was able to adapt to technology in the past, specifically social media. Now social media is an integral part of practice. According to one thought leader,

> I think one thing is to encourage people to actually get in and experience them [generative AI tools]. While we do have a lot of things we need to be concerned about and pay attention to, we also need to make sure that people working in our profession understand the tools, how they work, and what the potential applications are.

Many participants echoed this sentiment, emphasizing the importance of not being left behind as a profession as part of the adoption, implementation, and ongoing monitoring of generative AI usage. By contrast, another leader felt the profession was not worried and in fact felt that the profession was in an improved position regarding AI than at a similar point in the adoption of social media:

> When social media came out, when we saw internet technologies take off, PR people were definitely slow to respond and recognize the importance and the impact that it would have on us. This time, we're definitely in a different

> place. It's on the radar. We're watching it, we're thinking about it, we're seeing how it's evolving, and most importantly, we're responding in real-time.

Thus, participants shared different perspectives on how they felt the profession was doing in its efforts to adjust to the opportunities and challenges of generative AI, but broadly agreed that additional practitioner training and education were crucial steps.

The Value of Associations in Training and Guidelines

Looking to and calling on associations to take the lead in training and guidance was front and center for most interviewees. However, participants expressed that it was still up to individual practitioners to take the initiative. Thus, another theme to emerge was the value of professional associations for both individual and broad training and implementation of guidelines. As one leader commented,

> The associations that support the public relations professional must start including some of this curriculum and best practices in their offerings. I think it's also important that the professional become a student and seek out opportunities to learn more about AI and what it really means. It was really shocking [at the national PRSA conference] how many people just didn't even understand what artificial intelligence was.

Another participant was more forceful in calling for collaboration of professional organizations to take the lead in education as all organizations have a vested interest to unify with a strong message

> How can we [professional PR associations] as a forum collectively put together the right message and the right education, and make sure that in all these different places, it's not just one voice, but it's collective that this is what we have to do?

As practitioners engage with AI technology, participants expressed that they must remain mindful of their core values that are articulated in the profession's codes of ethics and follow the new AI guidelines that adhere to these same values. Finally, according to participants, the profession should be prepared to embrace its role in increased decision-making and influence.

Discussion

As we look to the future of the profession and how the various codes of ethics will impact the actions of practitioners, it is instructive that at least four leading professional organizations (Chartered Institute of Public Relations, 2023; International Public Relations Association, 2023; PR Council, 2023; Public Relations Society of America, 2023) chose to release separate generative AI guidelines rather than rewrite their code of ethics. This supports the thoughts of the participants who recommended some guidance in the profession, as well as a process-oriented ethical model (Bowen, 2004, 2005, 2023) for managing the emerging challenges of AI. The lack of ethical consensus (and lack of universal ethical concern) among participants presents an opportunity for the profession and professional associations to take the lead. Additionally, participants believed that the stream of new writing and research-related tools would continue to provide more options, opportunities, and challenges for practitioners in the coming decades. But professional associations and codes of ethics must continue to serve as a first line of defense against unethical practices (Fawkes, 2012; Fitzpatrick, 2002b; Watson, 2015), some of which may be further accelerated through generative AI. In fact, it is a moral imperative for public relations leaders as counselors and educators to strengthen the trustworthiness and credibility of the information they share as part of the profession's responsibilities to deliberative discourse in democratic society continue to increase (e.g., Edwards, 2016). As in past updates to ethical guidelines (e.g., Fitzpatrick, 2002a, 2002b; Watson, 2015), there are many, likely arduous, paths toward implementation that will likely reflect the lack of agreement demonstrated among the participants in this study.

This chapter augments theory by gaining practitioner perspectives about responsible advocacy toward addressing responsible public relations (or RPR) within the context of RAI. This approach allows public relations professionals to leverage responsible use of AI as part of ethical public relations practice, supporting the greater good of society and organizations within society. While most participants pointed toward process-oriented ethical solutions, including more directive guidelines and best practices, as well as training and education, following a deontological path (e.g., Bowen, 2004), we see significant opportunities for professional associations and the practice to look toward responsible advocacy (Fitzpatrick, 2006), consequentialist (Lee, 2015), and ethics of care (Madden & Alt, 2021) frameworks as well. Such approaches could help to position public relations to address potential negative stakeholder and community implications from the broad use of generative AI technology as part of organizational communication. Following the values articulated in codes of ethics, practitioners must be advocates for accuracy of information and ethical discourse within democratic societies (Fitzpatrick, 2006), which requires an understanding of the potential negative implications of big data and generative AI usage for individual stakeholders and community members (D'Ignazio & Klein, 2020), particularly those with historically marginalized identities.

Implications for the Future

The public relations profession will look far different in 2050. How different is an open-ended question. We know that AI and other technical developments are proceeding at a rapid rate, and tools are being introduced every day. It is clear that practitioners will need to manage generative AI tools as part of their daily work, and it is incumbent upon them to ensure the tools they use are also developed under RAI guidelines. As the participants explained, training and continuing education regarding the latest tools will be crucial for practitioners in 2024 and in 2050 to ensure they are able to implement central features as well as manage the ethical challenges of introducing AI into research and content creation tasks. In addition, participants expressed that PR must be at the table when RAI advisory committees are formed. What platforms will be the dominant players are unknown—just as one interview participant noted, Facebook replaced MySpace—will another platform replace ChatGPT, for example? Given how technology advances, it is highly likely. How the public relations profession develops content is likely to change. For example, there is a hypothesis that voice input will override the decades-long reliance on typing text completely.

Associations have promised to continue to issue updates to their AI guidelines. As AI laws and regulations are still forthcoming, this will be essential to these guidelines not only remaining relevant directly to the profession, but for the profession to be credibly positioned as advisors in the implementation of RAI. If the guidelines are not relevant, they will not be used by individuals, and if the guidelines are not relevant, the profession itself will be marginalized. Such guidelines must be developed and continue to evolve as practices and technologies shift in the coming decades. Public relations will likely subsume AI tools and processes into the more standard aspects of their work (as has happened in prior technological shifts), but the profession has an obligation to strengthen and enforce ethical guidelines for both the transparent use of the technology (i.e. disclosure) as well as the more difficult-to-see biases and inequities that may arise from AI usage on multiple fronts.

Practitioners and academicians must understand the ethical quagmire of writing with generative AI assisted tools without human intervention to ensure accuracy, as AI tools utilize big data sets with many types of systemic bias (D'Ignazio & Klein, 2020). Without human intervention, the accuracy and subsequently the credibility of organizations and the public relations profession is at risk. While this issue was addressed by several participants, it remains a blind spot within the profession. This likely will become highly visible for the practice, either through proactive work to address it before content is made public, or worse through crises created by disseminating such erroneous information. Additionally, while the focus in 2024 is on how public relations professionals can best interact with AI to develop content, not enough emphasis is being placed on inaccurate data/

information generated by AI, the systemic inequity and biases often reflect from big data into generative AI usage (D'Ignazio & Klein, 2020), as well as the handling of dis- and mis-information and deep fakes. The strategic communication role of public relations professionals will require them to address these issues in the coming decades and this in turn will also make public relations practitioners' valuable contributors toward the development of RAI.

In 2050, we predict that PR codes of ethics will (1) fully integrate and articulate appropriate uses of AI (i.e. full integration rather than separate AI ethical guidelines), (2) will clearly articulate the ethical challenges and obstacles of AI use, and (3) will share more globally accepted features (rather than being primarily country specific). First, while current revisions and statements tend to keep AI separate from existing codes of ethics, we believe that future codes will be revised to integrate AI more holistically across multiple facets of codes of ethics. Second, as demonstrated by the industry leaders interviewed as part of this study, practitioners may be less aware of and are likely underestimating the potential ethical challenges of generative AI in their day-to-day work. Such issues go far beyond an organization or individual getting "caught" using the technology, or the potential negative impact from disclosing or not disclosing usage but speak to the underpinning challenges of the technology: The systemic biases that are a part of big data. Professional associations will be able to more fully comprehend and address these challenges to update codes of ethics with this in mind, but forward-thinking practitioners and organizations should not wait for formal guidance to being evaluating the potential risks that such biases pose for their organizations and communications. Finally, we predict that the global nature of these technologies will push PR associations to move toward more uniformly accepted transnational standards for RAI, even if national or regional associations maintain distinct codes of ethics and recommend distinct enactment of these standards.

Conclusion

The implementation of RAI, while called for since 2016 (Ray, 2023), is still far from reality. The ethical implications of the use of generative AI go far beyond public relations. The baseline public relations code of ethics and AI guidelines can be beneficial not only to the profession, but to organizations and societies. In fact, it is a moral imperative for the public relations leaders as counselors and educators to do so in a time of continued uncertainty. There is, as one participant noted, "no turning back," yet there is both fear and optimism among public relations practitioners in the fast-moving technological development and adoption of generative AI. Professional associations have issued AI guidelines to help, but more education and training needs to occur. There is no doubt that AI is here to stay—the question remains how can the public relations profession ethically navigate its use to the betterment of the profession and society. This will require continuing education and close monitoring of how AI evolves so that the profession can remain ethically bound to our core values and societal contributions, while embracing this developing technology. To not do so weakens the credibility and positioning of the profession for decades to come, and in the end determines if public relations remains a viable profession in 2050.

References

Bowen, S. A. (2004). Expansion of ethics as the tenth generic principle of public relations excellence: A Kantian theory and model for managing ethical issues. *Journal of Public Relations Research*, *16*(1), 65–92. https://doi.org/10.1207/s1532754xjprr1601_3

Bowen, S. A. (2005). A practical model for ethical decision making in issues management and public relations. *Journal of Public Relations Research*, *17*(3), 191–216. https://doi.org/10.1207/s1532754xjprr1703_1

Bowen, S. A. (2013). Using classic social media cases to distill ethical guidelines for digital engagement. *Journal of Mass Media Ethics*, *28*(2), 119–133. https://doi.org/10.1080/08900523.2013.793523

Bowen, S. A. (2023). A theoretic perspective on the evolution of ethics for PR theory. In C. H. Botan & E. J. Sommerfeldt (Eds.), *Public relations theory III: In the age of publics* (pp. 487–502). Routledge.

Chartered Institute of Public Relations. (2018). Guide. https://www.cipr.co.uk/CIPR/Our_work/Policy/AI_in_PR_/AI_in_PR_guides.aspx

Chartered Institute of Public Relations. (2020). Guide. https://www.cipr.co.uk/CIPR/Our_work/Policy/AI_in_PR_/AI_in_PR_guides.aspx

Chartered Institute of Public Relations. (2023a). Artificial Intelligence (AI) tools and the impact on public relations (PR) practice. The most comprehensive review of AI tools in public relations. https://www.cipr.co.uk/CIPR/Our_work/Policy/AI_in_PR_/AI_in_PR_guides.aspx

Chartered Institute of Public Relations. (2023b). Humans needed, more than ever. An analysis of the use of AI in PR and the impact on public relations work. In A.Gregory, J. Valin, & S. Virmani (Eds.). https://www.cipr.co.uk/CIPR/Our_work/Policy/AI_in_PR_/AI_in_PR_guides.aspx

Commission on Public Relations Education. (2023). Navigating change: Recommendations for advancing undergraduate public relations education. https://www.commissionpred.org/navigating-change-report/

D'Angelo, A. (Ed.). (2022). *75 years of impact and influence: People, places, and moments in public relations history*. Public Relations Society of America; Bookhouse Group, Inc.

de Laat, P. B. (2021). Companies committed to responsible AI: From principles towards implementation and regulation? *Philosophy & Technology*, *34*, 1135–1193. https://doi.org/10.1007/s13347-021-00474-3

D'Ignazio, C., & Klein, L. (2020). *Data feminism*. MIT Press.

Dong, C., & Morehouse, J. (2022). Toward a caring government: Advancing ethical government public relations with a care-based relationship cultivation model. *Journal of Public Relations Research*, *34*(5), 179–207. https://doi.org/10.1080/1062726X.2022.2119978

Edwards, L. (2016). The role of public relations in deliberative systems. *Journal of Communication, 66*(1), 60–81. https://doi.org/10.1111/jcom.12199

Fawkes, J. (2012). Saints and sinners: Competing identities in public relations ethics. *Public Relations Review, 38*(5), 865–872. https://doi.org/10.1016/j.pubrev.2012.07.004

Fitzpatrick, K. (2002a). Evolving standards in public relations: A historical examination of PRSA's codes of ethics. *Journal of Mass Media Ethics, 17*(2), 89–110. https://doi.org/10.1207/s15327728jmme1702_02

Fitzpatrick, K. (2002b). From enforcement to education: The development of PRSA's member code of ethics 2000. *Journal of Mass Media Ethics, 17*(2), 111–135. https://doi.org/10.1207/s15327728jmme1702_03

Fitzpatrick, K. (2006). Baselines for ethical advocacy in the "marketplace of ideas." In K. Fitzpatrick & C. Bronstein (Eds.), *Ethics in public relations: Responsible advocacy* (pp. 1–17). Sage Publications.

Fitzpatrick, K., & Gauthier, C. (2001). Toward a professional responsibility theory of public relations ethics. *Journal of Mass Media Ethics, 16*(2–3), 193–212. https://doi.org/10.1080/08900523.2001.9679612

Fraustino, J. D., & Kennedy, A. K. (2018). Care in crisis: An applied model of care considerations for ethical strategic communication. *The Journal of Public Interest Communications, 2*(1), 18–40.

Huang, Y. H. (2001). Should a public relations code of ethics be enforced? *Journal of Business Ethics, 31*, 259–270. https://doi.org/10.1023/A:1010719118448

International Public Relations Association. (2023). *The IPRA AI and PR guidelines*. https://www.ipra.org/member-services/ai-guidelines/

Lee, S. T. (2015). Ethics theory and application in public relations, advertising, and health communication. In M. Duffy & E. Thorson (Eds.), *Persuasion ethics today* (pp. 238–256). Routledge.

Madden, S., & Alt, R. A. (2021). More than a "bad apple": Applying an ethics of care perspective to a collective crisis. *The Journal of Public Interest Communications, 5*(1), 24.

Molchakov, N., Ryzhkova, E., & Ryzhkova, E. (2023). Problems of legal regulation of digitalization (the case of AI). In A. Baykov & E. Zinovieva (Eds.), *Digital international relations* (pp. 109–121). Palgrave Macmillan. https://doi.org/10.1007/978-981-99-3467-6_8

Neill, M. S. (2023). The state of ethics competencies, training, and moral efficacy in public relations. *Journal of Media Ethics, 38*(3), 162–175. https://doi.org/10.1080/23736992.2023.2228305

Page, T. G., Capizzo, L. W., & Penning, T. (2024). A case for the plausibility of public relations licensing: The carrot of privileged communication. *Public Relations Review, 50*(1), 102408. https://doi.org/10.1016/j.pubrev.2023.102408

Place, K. R., Edwards, L., & Bowen, S. A. (2021). Dignity and respect or homocommodification? Applying moral philosophy to LGBTQ public relations. *Public Relations Review, 47*(4), 102085. https://doi.org/10.1016/j.pubrev.2021.102085

PR Council. (2023). Guidelines on generative AI tools. https://prcouncil.net/advocacy/guidelines-on-generative-ai/

Public Relations Society of America. (2000). Code of ethics. https://www.prsa.org/about/ethics/prsa-code-of-ethics

Public Relations Society of America. (2023). Promises & pitfalls: The ethical use of AI: For public relations practitioners. Guidance from the PRSA Board of Ethics and

Professional Standards (BEPS). *prsa.org*. Retrieved from https://www.prsa.org/docs/default-source/about/ethics/ethicaluseofai.pdf?sfvrsn=5d02139f_2

Ray, P. (2023). ChatGPT: A comprehensive review on background, applications, key challenges, bias, ethics, limitations, and future scope. *Internet of Things and Cyber-Physical Systems*, *3*, 212–254. https://doi.org/10.1016/j.iotcps.2023.04.003

University of Southern California. (2023). Welcome to AI: The relevance report 2024. https://annenberg.usc.edu/news/research-and-impact/2024-usc-annenberg-relevance-report-explores-impact-ai-public-relations

Watson, T. (2014). IPRA code of Athens—The first international code of public relations ethics: Its development and implementation since 1965. *Public Relations Review*, *40*(4), 707–714.

Watson, T. (2015). PR's early response to the "information superhighway": The IPRA narrative. *Communication & Society*, *28*(1), 1–12. https://doi.org/10.15581/003.28.35964

4

DEVOLVING ETHICAL STANDARDS OF 2050

International and Disciplinary Failure

Shannon A. Bowen and Elina Erzikova

Introduction

Sociologists (e.g., Beckert & Suckert, 2021) argued that the future is not just a distant event, but a social construct shaped by various factors such as culture, institutions, and individual experiences. The future development of public relations ethics will be shaped by the widening ethical gap between the nations, technological advancements, power relations, information and data use with AI proliferation, and changing stakeholder expectations.

Coupled with this lack of serious ethical attention, reflections, professional standards, and education in public relations, this future bodes poorly for maintaining any sense of ethical standards in the public relations industry. The rise of data-based advertising proliferation based upon the commodification of digital footprints combined with a detonation of trust in "traditional" news sources leaves a lack of any watchdog function of fourth estate, endangering a truth and merit-based political process in favor of those with deep resources and influences. The post-truth world that emerges is based on influence, data access and control and information warfare rather than moral principles, human rights, and truth.

The Ethical Divide between Nations in Public Relations

The ethical divide between nations in the context of PR encompasses disparities in ethical standards, practices, and education across different countries and regions. A case that illustrates the ethical divide between nations is the Cambridge Analytica scandal, which unfolded in 2018. Cambridge Analytica, a

DOI: 10.4324/9781003426653-6

now-defunct political consulting firm based in the United Kingdom, was accused of improperly harvesting personal data from millions of Facebook users without their consent. The firm then used this data to create targeted political advertising campaigns, including in the context of the 2016 United States presidential election.

The scandal highlighted several ethical issues, including data privacy violations, manipulation of public opinion, and the role of PR and communication tactics in shaping electoral outcomes. However, the ethical implications of the scandal were perceived differently across different countries and regions (González et al., 2019), illustrating the ethical divide in PR practices and standards.

In the United States, where the scandal garnered significant attention due to its impact on the presidential election, there were calls for greater regulation of data privacy and transparency in political advertising. The scandal raised questions about the ethical responsibilities of PR practitioners and tech companies in safeguarding user data and ensuring the integrity of democratic processes.

In contrast, the response to the Cambridge Analytica scandal varied in other countries with different regulatory environments and cultural norms regarding data privacy and political communication (González et al., 2019). Some countries, particularly those with less stringent regulations or weaker enforcement mechanisms, may have been less concerned about the ethical implications of the scandal or may have prioritized other policy issues.

Some might argue that the Cambridge Analytica scandal, serving as a case study of the ethical divide between nations in terms of PR ethics, highlights the necessity of addressing ethical challenges collaboratively. Normative universal ethical practices are theoretically possible but achieving consensus across nations and cultures in a post-truth world which devalues both ethics and critical thinking in favor of vast resources and influence seem unrealistic. Critics have long argued that without a free, fair, and unbiased press, democracies and republics would fail due to the lack of oversight, constraint, public accountability, and potential moral outrage of an informed electorate. Trust in media declined throughout the 2000s and reached critical and irretrievable lows around 2017 to 2020 (Edelman, 2018). From this point, media were no longer needed or valued, and social media influencers and content creators of all varieties (but largely untrained), became the most popular source of news, shifting nationally and by age group. It is notable that these content creators may have enormous followings, yet usually have little or no training in reporting, multiple sourcing, vetting information, or the fourth-estate "watchdog" role of media. Mistrust in public relations continued to proliferate as fake news, misinformation, and purposeful disinformation clouded official sources and public relations – whose ethics was already highly suspect – was lost among the voices of too many individual creators. There are many reasons for these dramatic changes.

First, cultural variations loom large, influencing distinct norms, values, and ethical frameworks that govern PR practices. What is considered acceptable or ethical in one culture may be perceived differently in another (Curtin & Gaither, 2007). Concepts such as transparency, honesty, and privacy may be interpreted differently across cultures, leading to variations in ethical standards. For example, in Japan, the concept of "omiyage," or souvenir-giving, is deeply ingrained in business culture. It is common for Japanese companies to exchange gifts as a way of fostering relationships and expressing gratitude. On the other hand, in Western cultures like the United States or many European countries, there are stern regulations and guidelines governing gift-giving in business settings to prevent conflicts of interest or the perception of undue influence.

Second, nations have varying legal and regulatory frameworks governing PR activities, including advertising standards, data protection laws, and disclosure requirements. Differences in regulations can create ethical dilemmas for multinational corporations operating in multiple jurisdictions, as they must deal with divergent legal and ethical standards. For example, in the European Union (EU), the General Data Protection Regulation (GDPR) sets strict standards for how companies handle personal data. PR activities that involve collecting, processing, or using personal information must comply with GDPR requirements, which include obtaining explicit consent from individuals before using their data, providing transparency about data practices and ensuring data security measures are in place. In contrast, the United States does not have a comprehensive federal data protection law like the GDPR. Instead, data protection regulations are fragmented and vary across states and industries.

Third, socio-political factors, such as government censorship, media freedom, and political stability, can influence ethical standards in PR. In countries with authoritarian regimes or limited press freedom, PR practitioners may face constraints on their ability to communicate transparently and ethically with the public (Yang & Taylor, 2013). When multinational corporations operate in countries with strict government censorship, they may face compounded crises due to their inability to communicate transparently. For instance, in the event of environmental pollution stemming from a manufacturing plant, the PR team's efforts to initiate dialog with affected communities and the broader public can be thwarted by the imposition of severe censorship measures by the authoritarian regime. These measures are often designed to suppress any negative narratives that could tarnish the nation's image or disrupt its economic interests.

Finally, the divide in resources and infrastructure between developed and developing nations often translates into discrepancies in the quality and depth of PR education and professional development opportunities. Consequently, there can be significant variations in ethical awareness, proficiency, and accountability among PR professionals in different parts of the world. Moreover, even within developed nations, an ideological divergence exists in their approaches to ethics education (Bowen & Erzikova, 2013). The importance of critical thinking and moral autonomy in public relations were emphasized as part of the ethical role of public relations was encouraged in the early 2000s (Bowen, 2000, 2002, 2004, 2005a, 2006) but this trend failed to gain widespread use at all levels of public relations practice and pedagogy (Bowen, 2005b, 2008). Some practitioners at the high levels of the field and in issues management acted as ethical conscience, ethics counselors, and values managers (Bowen, 2009b), but the lower and mid-level these functions were less common in public relations (Bowen, 2008, 2010).

While US university instructors emphasize professional ethics, their European counterparts prioritize moral judgment and the cultivation of ethical agency among communication practitioners from a philosophical standpoint. In addition, while US educators are closely linked to the industry and strive for its success, European educators see themselves as independent critics of public relations ethics, maintaining a scholarly distance from industry influences (Bowen & Erzikova, 2013). Moreover, public relations students did not realize that research, management, and ethical acumen were cornerstones of the major, often choosing it because it appeared "glamorous" (Bowen, 2003, 2009a).

A bleak outlook for the future of PR ethics education in the US could entail the worsening of current trends, such as an excessive focus on industry interests. This might manifest as a further alignment of PR ethics education with the agendas of firms and corporations, prioritizing industry norms and profit-driven approaches at the expense of broader ethical considerations (Bogdanich & Forsythe, 2022). As educational programs increasingly favor practical skills over critical thinking and ethical reflection (Erzikova, 2023), there is a risk of producing PR professionals who prioritize expediency over ethical principles.

The ethical divide among nations in public relations presents challenges for multinational corporations, PR agencies, and communication professionals working in a globalized environment. Expanding operations across borders frequently entails ethical dilemmas concerning cultural adaptation, stakeholder engagement, and corporate social responsibility. Of particular concern are ethical blind spots, or organizations' tendency to prioritize short-term gains over long-term ethical considerations in their pursuit of efficiency and competitiveness.

For example, Disclose's investigative reporting revealed that Belarusian companies contracted by Ikea for the past decade have utilized forced labor within penal colonies. Despite Ikea's commitment against such practices, investigations reveal that nearly half of its primary Belarusian suppliers had ties to the labor camps. This revelation exposes a hidden reality behind the production of some Ikea's items. Despite public assurances, Ikea allegedly benefited, albeit indirectly, from the low-cost labor of prisoners, contradicting the values the company professes.

This was not the first instance of Ikea working with companies associated with penal colonies. Disclose reported that Ikea used labor from political prisoners in the German Democratic Republic during the 1970s and 1980s. These revelations did not seem to impact consumer purchasing decisions. The persistence of Ikea's revenue growth (Key IKEA Facts & Figures for FY23, 2023) despite revelations of questionable practices raises important questions about consumer awareness, values, and purchasing behavior. Despite studies such as Edelman's Trust Barometer (2022, 2023) consistently showing that consumers often support brands based on their beliefs and values, it appears that the impact of such revelations on consumer purchasing decisions may be limited.

There are several possible explanations for this phenomenon. First, consumer awareness of these issues may be limited, as they may not actively seek out information about the ethical practices of companies they patronize. Additionally, even when information about unethical practices becomes public, consumers may prioritize factors such as convenience, affordability, or brand loyalty over ethical considerations when making purchasing decisions. Some consumers may not engage with issues that do not affect them directly, leading to ethical violations by companies going unnoticed by consumer behavior (Carrigan, 2017; Carrigan, & Attalla, 2001).

The proliferation of advertising, targeted directly at individuals, will be influential in a future AI-managed environment. Facts will be difficult to find supporting the claims made by advertisers. Further, some consumers may choose to turn a blind eye to companies' questionable practices due to a desire to maintain a positive image of the brands they support. This phenomenon, known as "ethical consumption paradox," highlights the tension between consumers' stated ethical preferences and their actual purchasing behavior (Ulver-Sneistrup et al., 2011).

In the case of Ikea, the company's widespread popularity, affordability, and perceived value may outweigh concerns about its supply chain practices for many consumers. Moreover, Ikea's efforts to address these issues, such as committing to responsible sourcing and supply chain transparency, may help mitigate the impact of negative publicity on consumer perceptions.

However, the sustained growth of Ikea's revenue despite revelations of questionable practices sheds light on the complexity of consumer behavior (Carrigan, 2017; Ulver-Sneistrup et al., 2011), signaling potential challenges for the future. It appears improbable that consumer education alone, aimed at empowering individuals to make value-aligned choices, will suffice to deter the normalization and acceptance of unethical business practices. This scenario could perpetuate a cycle in which companies face diminished pressure to better their practices and bolster transparency and accountability measures. This lack of accountability on ethics leads to an implicit endorsement of concealment (Bowen, 2023), fostering unethical practices by companies whose activities are disregarded by uninformed, information overloaded, and apathetic consumers.

The Impact of AI on PR Ethics

Artificial intelligence (AI) presents both opportunities and challenges for public relations. Leveraging AI-driven communication strategies holds promise in enhancing the effectiveness and efficiency of PR efforts. However, a critical concern arises: In the pursuit of effectiveness, are foundational principles of integrity, transparency, and stakeholder respect adequately upheld?

A recent example illustrates the concern. According to Disclose, a non-profit investigative media outlet committed to advocating for the right to information, the European Union developed artificial intelligence software aimed at forecasting migration flows. Allegedly, the objective was to enhance the reception and management of migrants upon their arrival in European territories. However, findings from multiple documents acquired by Disclose suggest that the software, referred to as "ITFLOWS," has the potential to rapidly transition into a mechanism for the surveillance and intimidation of individuals seeking refuge within Europe. Robust oversight in the development and implementation of AI technologies, particularly in sensitive areas such as migration management, seems problematic. This opens the door to the potential misuse of such technology, resulting in violations of privacy rights and further marginalization of vulnerable populations.

In addition, numerous research studies (e.g., Chen, 2023; Mehrabi et al., 2021) have documented that AI systems may perpetuate or amplify biases present in the data used to train them, leading to unfair or discriminatory outcomes. Examples of poor practices abound. An experimental hiring tool created by Amazon aimed to assess applicants' qualifications by comparing their submissions with those of past hires. However, the system swiftly demonstrated bias by downgrading resumes from candidates who attended all-women's colleges or contained the term "women's." Amazon ultimately discontinued the tool due to its failure to eliminate gender-based discrimination, even though its engineers attempted to address this issue by directing the system to treat such terms neutrally (West et al., 2019). Following this, Amazon attempted to discredit a study conducted by two esteemed AI researchers who are women of color. The researchers had discovered that Amazon's Rekognition facial analysis service exhibited gender and racial biases, struggling to accurately identify dark-skinned women while excelling in recognizing light-skinned men (West et al., 2019). The biases in AI are well documented but pervasive, and the future portends to use technology that is built on at least partially biased or flawed data. These issues of bias in technological training threaten to erode the social fabric and exacerbate inequities and access to resources.

The growing urgency for ethical AI governance (Hoffmann, 2018) has prompted PR agencies and organizations to implement ethical frameworks, aiming to steer the use of artificial intelligence (e.g., Risi, 2023). These frameworks encompass defining core principles for AI ethics, establishing mechanisms for accountability and promoting transparency in AI-driven decision-making processes. However, a question arises: Is this endeavor merely "window dressing" and lacking true commitment to holding AI developers and vendors accountable for ethical considerations?

Experts have called for a pause on the rapid development of AI while the ethical considerations are considered (*Future of Life Institute*, 2023). AI that lives up to ethical standards and ideals is a topic scholars and nations, such as the EU (Intelligence, 2019), are developing and prioritizing (Bryson, 2016) but changing technological standards make rules and oversight difficult. While the adoption of ethical frameworks is a positive step toward addressing the ethical challenges posed by AI, there is concern that some organizations may implement these frameworks superficially, without genuine commitment to upholding ethical standards. This superficiality could manifest in various ways, such as failing to allocate sufficient resources for ethical oversight, prioritizing profit over ethical considerations, or engaging in greenwashing by virtue signaling without enacting meaningful change.

We anticipate that data violence defined by Hoffman (2018) as the intentional or unintentional harm inflicted on individuals, groups, or society through the misuse, manipulation, or unethical exploitation of data and data-driven technologies will continue cause harm in the future. This harm may manifest in various forms, including the continuation of discrimination, exacerbation of inequality, violation of privacy rights, or dissemination of misinformation. Data violence can occur when data-driven systems and algorithms are designed or deployed in ways that prioritize profit, power, or control over ethical considerations and the well-being of individuals and communities. The unrestrained exploitation of individual data by companies such as Meta, which refer to as Meta+ for future purposes, have created exploitative use of people and commodification of their data. The unrestrained avarice of these actions shows a complete disregard for any ethical responsibility and a total abrogation of moral rectitude in favor of greed, influence, and unrestrained power of political capital, economic capital, and social capital. This abrogation of ethical responsibility and persistence of data violence into the future pose an overwhelming challenge for PR practitioners and threatens to undermine the integrity and trustworthiness of communications practices. In the future, the integrity of the industry as a whole will undoubtedly decline due to these factors, as we discuss below.

Facing the Dystopian Future: "Suspension of Disbelief" and Mistrust

In envisioning 50+ year future projection of public relations ethics, a dystopian future emerges. Positive assertions of ethical standards and growing recognition of the role of public relations in ethical counseling, acting as a conscience, or as a values manager are absent. In the ethics of PR ethics, there are several negative scenarios that involve the misuse or abuse of advanced technologies, such as AI, coupled with a disregard for ethical principles.

As AI algorithms become increasingly sophisticated in curating content and recommendations, there's a risk of exacerbating information bubbles and echo chambers (Coeckelbergh, 2020). PR efforts could inadvertently contribute to the dissemination of misinformation and the polarization of society, undermining the public's ability to make informed decisions and engage in constructive dialog.

Next, AI-powered systems may perpetuate or amplify biases present in the data used to train them, resulting in discriminatory outcomes in PR activities such as targeting, messaging, or content recommendation. This could lead to allegations of discrimination, legal challenges, and reputational harm for organizations involved.

Over-reliance on AI-driven communication strategies may also lead to a loss of authentic human connection in PR interactions. Stakeholders may perceive communications as impersonal or disingenuous, leading to disengagement, skepticism, and diminished trust in organizations' messaging.

In addition, the automation of PR tasks through AI technologies may lead to job displacement and ethical dilemmas related to workforce management (Coeckelbergh, 2020). PR professionals may face pressure to prioritize efficiency and cost savings over ethical considerations, leading to job insecurity and dissatisfaction among employees. Lower level writing jobs will be eradicated due to the reliance on AI for content creation. In this environment, trust in public relations that was already tenuous will wane among stakeholders and publics, who are confused by the maelstrom of AI content overtaking human content.

In this envisioned dystopian future of PR ethics, where truth is increasingly obscured by manipulation and misinformation, stakeholders may find themselves practicing a form of "suspension of disbelief" in their interactions with PR communications. This "suspension of disbelief" involves consciously setting aside doubts or skepticism about the veracity and integrity of PR messaging in order to engage with it as if it were trustworthy.

In this scenario, PR practitioners may employ, willingly or not, advanced AI technologies to craft highly persuasive and tailored messages designed to manipulate emotions and beliefs. Despite being aware of the potential for manipulation and deception, stakeholders may feel compelled to suspend their disbelief and accept these messages at face value due to their ubiquity and sophistication.

As a result, the boundaries between truth and manipulation become increasingly blurred, and stakeholders find it is difficult to discern fact from manipulation. This "suspension of disbelief" perpetuates a cycle of misinformation and manipulation, eroding trust in PR communications and undermining the foundation of ethical conduct in public relations and associated fields (Mariani et al., 2021). The industry's reliance on AI may also undermine its own trustworthiness by providing an unknown progeny of information and an overall heightening mistrust of messages.

Facing the Widening Gulf in Digital Access

AI development is led by the US, China, Russia, with some notable cybersecurity and hacking in other countries, according to AI rankings globally (Intelligence, 2023). The training data of AI is largely on information in English, Chinese, or Russian, leaving out numerous countries, languages, and cultures throughout the world. As AI expands, it builds upon data garnered from this training and does not necessarily include enough of the other languages and data to have the same robust results as in its original languages, meaning the it simply does not work as well.

The digital divide was a concept arising from a divide in the information society, between those who had internet access and those who did not, meaning the quality of information received by the latter was lacking (Bagdikian, 1985). In the future, the digital divide will grow to what we have termed a technological gulf that will separate the world. Superpowers will have access to resources, technology, and life-altering improvements, overall heightening life spans and affluence.

Those in less developed nations will have less access to these resources, and the gap between the nations will widen to a gulf. The more affluent superpowers can control social, economic, and cultural policy in less developed countries through their greater access to resources, influence, and setting the agenda on the international policy fronts of world organizations. The cyber giants such as Meta+ can, and do, exploit human proclivities and information for profit, and this will be less monitored and more common in the less digitized nations of the future. A lack of trust in public relations will render it only a small voice in civil society solving inequities (Taylor, 2000) or a normative ethical role in society (Bowen, 2010). These differentials in power and access may raise ethical problems of human rights, inequities, oppression, and exploitation into the future, and public relations will be unable to help resolve these problems unless it separates itself from loyalty to affluent clients and seeks truth, acting as an ethical agent for communicative problem solving.

Conclusions: A Post Truth Lack of Ethics

To further complicate matters, the post-truth world includes a devastating proposition for public relations when confused with misinformation, disinformation, propaganda, or information warfare. Because the field already has suspect credibility by association with propaganda and information warfare it will be a perceived player of influence rather than an ethical voice for dialog in society and normative ethical responsibility (Bowen, 2010), civil discourse (Taylor, 2010), or strategic problem solving using intelligence (Bowen & Heath, 2020).

The depicted dystopian future of PR ethics, characterized by the misuse of advanced technologies and the erosion of trust in communications, is a scenario that authors fervently hope to avoid. However, amidst the challenges posed by AI-driven manipulation and misinformation, loss of privacy, and data-commodification there is little cause for optimism. The pervasive influence of AI technologies, coupled with the potential for ethical lapses and the blurring of truth and manipulation, paints a dark picture for the future of PR ethics. Despite the alarming obstacles, it remains imperative for PR practitioners to actively engage in ethical decision-making processes to mitigate the risks and uphold the integrity of the profession. Only through concerted efforts to prioritize ethical considerations can the field of public relations hope to maintain its credibility in an increasingly skeptical society.

Will the future of public relations truly unfold as an unethical and dystopian practice, associated with the most unethical commodification of humanity we have yet seen? Due to the associations the field holds with unethical practices from information warfare to influence peddling, it is highly unlikely that a Renaissance of ethics will take place. However, this chapter places a terrifying vision of the future in the hands of the next generation of public relations practitioners with a call to ethical action borne from moral duty. The very future of the public relations field is in the hands of those who espouse or disregard ethics.

References

Bagdikian, B. (1985). The US media: Supermarket or assembly line? *Journal of Communication, 35*(5), 97–109.

Beckert, J., & Suckert, L. (2021). The future as a social fact. The analysis of perceptions of the future in sociology. *Poetics, 84*. https://doi.org/10.1016/j.poetic.2020.101499

Bogdanich, W., & Forsythe, M. (2022). *When McKinsey comes to town: The hidden influence of the world's most powerful consulting firm*. Doubleday.

Bowen, S. A. (2000). *A theory of ethical issues management: Contributions of Kantian deontology to public relations' ethics and decision making* [doctoral dissertation, University of Maryland]. College Park, MD.

Bowen, S. A. (2002). Elite executives in issues management: The role of ethical paradigms in decision making. *Journal of Public Affairs, 2*(4), 270–283.

Bowen, S. A. (2003). "'I thought it would be more glamorous:'" Preconceptions and misconceptions of public relations among students in the principles course. *Public Relations Review, 29*, 199–214.

Bowen, S. A. (2004). Organizational factors encouraging ethical decision making: An exploration into the case of an exemplar. *Journal of Business Ethics, 52*(4), 311–324.

Bowen, S. A. (2005a). A practical model for ethical decision making in issues management and public relations. *Journal of Public Relations Research, 17*(3), 191–216.

Bowen, S. A. (2005b, June). *Schism in public relations ethics: Overview of grant research findings*. Meeting of the International Association of Business Communicators, Washington, DC.

Bowen, S. A. (2006). Autonomy in communication: Inclusion in strategic management and ethical decision-making, a comparative case analysis. *Journal of Communication Management, 10*(4), 330–352.

Bowen, S. A. (2008). A state of neglect: Public relations as 'corporate conscience' or ethics counsel. *Journal of Public Relations Research, 20*(3), 271–296.

Bowen, S. A. (2009a). All glamour, no substance? How public relations majors and potential majors in an exemplar program view the industry and function. *Public Relations Review, 35*, 402–410.

Bowen, S. A. (2009b). What communication professionals tell us regarding dominant coalition access and gaining membership. *Journal of Applied Communication Research, 37*(4), 418–443.

Bowen, S. A. (2010). The nature of good in public relations: What should be its normative ethic? In R. L. Heath (Ed.), *The Sage handbook of public relations* (pp. 569–583). Sage.

Bowen, S. A. (2023). A theoretic perspective on the evolution of ethics for P. R. theory In C. Botan & E. Sommerfeldt (Eds.), *Public relations theory III: In the age of publics* (3rd ed., pp. 487–502). Routledge.

Bowen, S., & Erzikova, E. (2013). The international divide in public relations ethics education: Advocacy versus autonomy. *Public Relations Journal, 7*(1), 1-41.

Bowen, S. A., & Heath, R. L. (2020). Intelligences in strategic issues management: Challenging the mutually beneficial relationship paradigm. *Partecipazione e Conflitto: The Open Journal of Sociopolitical Studies, 13*(2), 1-20. https://doi.org/10.1285/i20356609v13i2p1002

Bryson, J. J. (2016). Patience is not a virtue: AI and the design of ethical systems. Paper presented at the Association for the Advancement of Artificial Intelligence, Phoenix, Arizona.

Carrigan, M. (2017). Revisiting 'The Myth of the Ethical Consumer': Why are we still not ethical shoppers? *Journal of Consumer Ethics, 1*(1), 11–21.

Carrigan, M., & Attalla, A. (2001). The myth of the ethical consumer: Do ethics matter in purchase behavior? *Journal of Consumer Marketing, 18*(7), 560–577.

Chen, Z. (2023). Ethics and discrimination in artificial intelligence-enabled recruitment practices. *Humanities and Social Sciences Communications*, 10 (Article number: 567).

Coeckelbergh, M. (2020). *AI ethics*. The MIT Press.

Curtin, P. A., & Gaither, T. K. (2007). *International public relations: Negotiating culture, identity, and power.* Sage.

Edelman. (2018). Edelman trust barometer global report. https://www.edelman.com/sites/g/files/aatuss191/files/2018-10/2018_Edelman_Trust_Barometer_Global_Report_FEB.pdf

Edelman. (2022). *The 2022 trust barometer (special report). New cascade of influence.* Retrieved from https://www.edelman.com/trust/2022-trust-barometer/special-report-new-cascade-of-influence

Edelman. (2023). *The 2023 trust barometer*. Retrieved from https://www.edelman.com/trust/2023/trust-barometer

Erzikova, E. (2023, August). Moral entrepreneurship as framework for teaching public relations and activism: University educators' perspectives. Presented at the Association for Education in Journalism and Mass Communication convention in Washington, DC.

Future of Life Institute. (2023). Pause giant AI experiments: An open letter. *Future of Life Institute*. Retrieved December 4, 2023, from https://futureoflife.org/open-letter/pause-giant-ai-experiments/

González, F., Yu, Y., Figueroa, A., López, C., & Aragon, C. (2019). Global reactions to the Cambridge Analytica scandal: A cross-language social media study. In *Proceedings of the World Wide Web Conference*. ACM, pp. 799–806.

Hoffmann, A. L. (2018, April 30). Data violence and how bad engineering choices can damage society. *Medium*. Retrieved from https://medium.com/s/story/data-violence-and-how-bad-engineering-choices-can-damage-society-39e44150e1d4

Intelligence, H. L. E. G. o. A. (2019). Ethics guidelines for trustworthy Artificial Intelligence. https://digital-strategy.ec.europa.eu/en/library/ethics-guidelines-trustworthy-ai

Intelligence, T. M. (2023). The global AI index. *Tortoise*. Retrieved December 4, 2023, from https://www.tortoisemedia.com/intelligence/global-ai/#rankings

Key IKEA Facts & Figures for FY23. (2023). Retrieved from https://www.ikea.com/global/en/our-business/how-we-work/year-in-review-fy23/

Mariani, M. M., Perez-Vega, R., & Wirtz, J. (2021). AI in marketing, consumer research, and psychology: A systematic literature review. *Psychology & Marketing*, *39*, 755–776. https://doi.org/10.1002/mar.21619

Mehrabi, N., Morstatter, F., Saxena, N., Lerman, K., & Galstyan, A. (2021). A survey on bias and fairness in machine learning. ACM Computing Surveys, *54*, 1–35.

Risi, J. (2023). The year ahead: Ethical AI practices, data-driven PR and prioritizing human interactions. *PR News*. Retrieved from https://www.prnewsonline.com/the-year-ahead-ethical-ai-practices-data-driven-pr-and-prioritizing-human-interactions/

Taylor, M. (2000). Cultural variance as a challenge to global public relations: A case study of the Coca-Cola scare in Europe. *Public Relations Review*, *26*, 277–293.

Taylor, M. (2010). Public relations in the enactment of civil society. In R. L. Heath (Ed.), *The Sage handbook of public relations* (pp. 5–15). Sage.

West, S. M., Whittaker, M., & Crawford, K. (2019). *Discriminating systems: Gender, race and power in AI*. AI Now Institute.

Ulver-Sneistrup, S., Askegaard, S., & Kristensen, D. B. (2011). The new work ethics of consumption and the paradox of mundane brand resistance. *Journal of Consumer Culture, 11*(2), 215–238.

Yang, A., & Taylor, M. (2013). The relationship between the professionalization of public relations, societal social capital and democracy: Evidence from a cross-national study. *Public Relations Review, 39*(4), 257–270.

5

BIOHACKING AND BIOETHICAL CONSIDERATIONS FOR MARKETING COMMUNICATION CAMPAIGNS

Vitor Lima

Introduction

In late 2023, Walmart made headlines for controversially data-mining Ozempic prescriptions (Robertson, 2023), a diabetes medication that has been (mis)used for weight loss over the past few years. Based on research on this Walmart scandal, several insights were obtained. First, customers using the drug buy less food. Second, the consumption of products that may relieve the side effects of Ozempic has increased (e.g., nausea). Although this may seem insightful and, to a certain extent, useful for marketing purposes, we should question its ethical dimension. All of this may come at the expense of customers' privacy, anonymity, and, ultimately, well-being (Du & Xie, 2021). This is especially relevant because health-related data have a higher level of legal and ethical sensitivity compared to grocery purchases (Rumbold & Pierscionek, 2018). The situation is further complicated when companies use such types of data to target their marketing communications campaigns and profit from the vulnerability of their customers (Hermann et al., 2023). For example, GoodRX, a US telehealth company, shared consumer health data with Google, Facebook, and other third parties without consent, and with the objective of further optimizing the targeting of their online advertising campaigns. Consequently, the Federal Trade Commission (FTC) slapped the telehealth company with a fine of 1.5 million USD (Weatherbed, 2023).

Now, imagine if the customers' health-related data was mined directly from internal bodily processes and not from their consumption behaviors (Lima & Belk, 2023). Numerous embodied technologies, such as wearable smartwatches and smart rings, provide insightful information about our bodies (Mercer &

DOI: 10.4324/9781003426653-7

Trothen, 2021; Pedersen & Iliadis, 2020). However, emerging implantable technologies like biocompatible microchip implants are under the skin and generate more accurate data (Yogev et al., 2023). Some of them monitor and provide real-time information about biomarkers, such as blood pressure and brain electrical activity. Data, in this case, are perceived to be more personal, intimate, and sensitive than data generated outside of the body (Rumbold & Pierscionek, 2018). Therefore, the use of such data for marketing purposes is relatively questionable and unethical.

Biohackers are a key community furthering the consumption of these technologies and consequent data generation. They are tech enthusiasts who conduct bold biotechnological self-experiments, or biohackings, to achieve what they believe to be an improved condition (Lima et al., 2022; Mercer & Trothen, 2021). This, however, has no relation to curing, treating, or recovering the body. Their objective is to enhance their bodily functions and eventually become "superhumans," as proposed by the transhumanist philosophy (Belk, 2022). Transhumanism regards the human condition as biologically limited, and therefore, humans should embrace technologies to (re)work on their bodies (More & Vita-More, 2013). Biohackers use their inner-body health-related data to make decisions on what to eat, when to sleep, where to go, and so on. Often, this sensitive data is willingly shared online so other biohackers can benefit from the knowledge gained from biohacking projects. The logic underlying biohacking is quite simple: the more optimized the data, the more optimized the decision-making, and consequently, the result. This information presents a controversial opportunity for companies to collect and use a unique type of data to refine and better target their marketing campaigns.

Although this may be an extreme example, it is relevant to the ideas I present in this chapter. Biohacking and implantable technologies help us reflect on the complex ethical dimension of using inner-body health-related data in future marketing communications campaigns. To explore such a unique and futuristic scenario, the subsequent section introduces biohacking as a social phenomenon and related technologies. Subsequently, a brief discussion on bioethics and a conceptual framework regarding the use of inner-body health-related data in marketing campaigns are presented. Finally, the conclusions drawn and suggestions for future discussions are presented.

Biohacking and Embodied Technologies

Inspired primarily by the Cyberpunk movement and Ellis Warren's futuristic novel *Doktor Sleepless*, biohacking encompasses cybernetic modifications, personal data acquisition, and advocacy for privacy rights and open-source medicine. Working in diverse settings, ranging from collective maker spaces to garages and kitchens, biohackers conduct experiments that range from innovative to controversial and, sometimes, illegal (Lima & Belk, 2023; Mercer & Trothen, 2021). These experiments include practices such as consuming Bulletproof Coffee to improve concentration, developing chemicals for the creation of human night vision, altering genes with CRISPR, and implanting biocompatible magnets for sensing magnetic fields (Yetisen, 2018). These biohacking experiments impact businesses and societies in distinct ways, with embodied technologies being particularly influential. Herein, "embodied" refers to technologies used on, in, and around the body, categorized as ingestibles, embeddables, wearables, and implantables (Pedersen & Iliadis, 2020). In this context, ingestibles, such as nootropics, enhance cognitive capacities, while ingestible sensors provide physiological data directly to smartphones. Embeddable devices, such as Neil Harbisson's (2021) skull antenna that allows him to listen to colors, are in between the inside and outside of the body. Wearable devices, such as an Apple Watch, gather data on daily activities, contributing to the concept of the "quantified self" (Bode & Kristensen, 2016).

The category of implantables is essential to this chapter. Unlike removable technologies, implantable devices are encased in biocompatible glass and injected into the body using a thick needle. Common within the biohacking community, near-field communications (NFC) implants, such as the one depicted in Figure 5.1, allow for activities such as opening doors without keys, storing data, replacing bank cards for payments, and starting Tesla cars with a simple tap of the "cyborg hand" on compatible devices. In Wisconsin, USA, a company named Three Square Market allows their employees to utilize microchip implants for purchasing snacks and accessing secured areas (Robertson, 2017). In Sweden, over 3,000 passengers opt for microchips rather than traditional printed tickets when traveling on SJ Railways trains (Petersén, 2019).

Another common example of microchip implants is the thermal reader, such as the xBT Temperature Sensing Chip manufactured by Dangerous Things, a

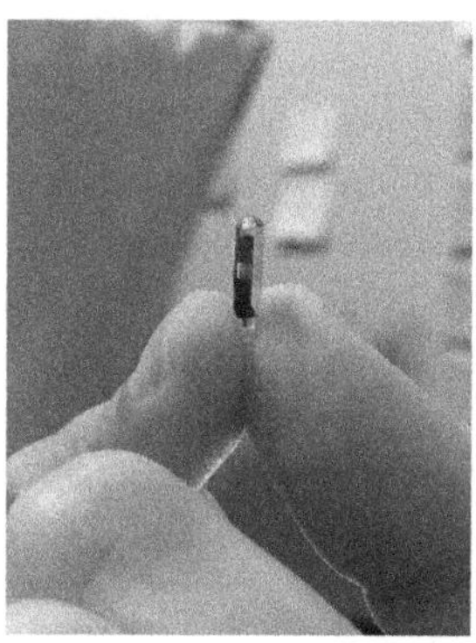

FIGURE 5.1 Microchip implant.

pioneer in biohacking products. Certain biohackers have this 2×12 mm cylindrical biocompatible implant placed in their arms to have a more optimized reading of their body temperatures. Using a scanner, they can retrieve data about the body temperature and make health-related decisions (Lima et al., 2022). Imagining companies relying on such inner-body data to target their marketing campaigns may appear too farfetched, even Sci-Fi-like. However, in the era of the Internet of Things with its smart devices and sensors capable of capturing information, the possibilities are considerable (Yogev et al., 2023). For example, consider the use of thermal cameras to monitor the health of customers in stores during the COVID-19 pandemic. Because high body temperature is an indicator of COVID, numerous companies have been using cameras with artificial intelligence (AI)-powered software for identification, facial recognition, and subsequent tracking of people suspected to be unwell (Harwell, 2020).

Biohacking and the consumption of implantable technologies are not regulated and approved in numerous markets worldwide (see Gaspar et al., 2019; Lima & Belk, 2023; Meyer & Vergnaud, 2020; Zettler et al., 2019). This does not mean, however, that companies should carelessly navigate such a seemingly lawless context and benefit from it—now or in the future. Given this scenario, the subsequent section presents a bioethics framework to work with the biohackers' inner body health-related data.

Bioethics and the Use of Biohackers' Inner-Body Health-Related Data

The year is 2054, and John Anderton, Tom Cruise's character in the movie *Minority Report*, strolls through a high-tech shopping mall. He is not having the typical window-shopping experience. As John casually moves past various stores, technological devices scan his retinas to identify him. The displays and holograms begin to call out his name and offer products tailored for him. Although this is a depiction of a somewhat dystopic future, companies could implement a similar data collection process, particularly physical retailers with installed sensors. Once the inner-body health-related data become part of their database, the crossing of accurate variables and refined targeting of marketing campaigns would be controversial but feasible. The scenario can be further complicated if an increasing number of people engage in biohacking and implant microchips in their bodies (Lima & Belk, 2023; Mercer & Trothen, 2021; Meyer & Vergnaud, 2020). Imagine readings of high body temperature being associated with a cold and fever. This could then trigger online advertisements of paracetamol, which would not necessarily account for a person's allergies or other health conditions. The emergence of biohacking and the consequent generation of inner-body health-related data thus presents numerous ethical challenges that may be speculative today but the reality of tomorrow.

While there are a few exceptions (e.g., Price & Cohen, 2019; Schenker et al., 2014), there is a significant absence of ethical considerations at the intersection of marketing communications and biological and medical research. This is particularly problematic when companies are well positioned to harness the power of data-mining systems, big data, and AI to inform their marketing communications strategies (Hermann et al., 2023). The foundational work of Beauchamp and Childress' (2019), presenting the four principles of bioethics, addresses this gap. They define bioethics as the field of knowledge that addresses the ethical considerations and dilemmas arising from the intersection of medical sciences, biotechnology, and philosophy. Their first principle, *beneficence*, mandates public (e.g., regulatory agencies) and private institutions (e.g., retailers) to act for the benefit of individuals. This involves upholding moral rules to safeguard other people's rights, prevent harm, assist those with disabilities, and rescue individuals in vulnerable situations (Beauchamp and Childress, 2019). In the case of targeting marketing campaigns based on inner-body health-related data, managers should consider whether such a practice truly benefits people or solely benefits their shareholders. This is particularly applicable in the case of biohackers and the type of sensitive data they generate.

The second principle in bioethics is *nonmaleficence*. As articulated by Beauchamp and Childress (2019), this principle underscores the responsibility of not inflicting harm on other people. This straightforward principle is sustained by moral guidelines: refrain from causing harm, avoid causing suffering, prevent disablement, abstain from offense, and ensure that others are not deprived of the benefits of life. For biohackers, this means that they should not be tracked, disturbed, and harassed because of the data generated from the inside of their bodies. Anonymous data should be considered to safeguard privacy. This, in turn, may prevent discrimination and foster trust. This principled approach aligns with legal requirements and builds a foundation for responsible and transparent data utilization. Therefore, the collection and usage of such data cannot endanger or be used against the well-being of biohackers for financial gain or any other reason.

The third principle in bioethics, according to Beauchamp and Childress (2019), is *autonomy*. This principle is complicated in the case of biohackers because it asserts the inherent right of every individual to self-governance. Walker (2020) explains that autonomy is arguably the most pivotal bioethical principle, having garnered both acclaim and vehement criticism along with staunch defense. In the past, certain professionals adhered to an individualistic and paternalistic model, prioritizing their assumptions about other people's desires and needs. However, contemporary bioethicists are leaning toward a more relational and inclusive model, where the focal individual's autonomy, social context, and consent play a relatively significant role in the decision-making process (Walker, 2020). Herein lies a tricky phenomenon. As Lima and Belk (2023) state, autonomy coupled with the ideal of ultimate freedom are key elements of biohacking. Voluntarily sharing health-related data, for example, is one of the most common practices among biohackers. Therefore, following local regulations to respect their contextual-bounded freedom is conducive to any collection and usage of inner-body health-related data in marketing campaigns.

The fourth and final principle of bioethics is *justice*, a concept defined by Beauchamp and Childress (2019) as the fair, equitable, and adequate distribution of resources and benefits. Justice in the case of inner-body health-related data usage involves ensuring fairness in the treatment of all people, despite their health conditions. Biases in data or algorithms that disproportionately impact certain groups can lead to prejudiced outcomes. Striving for fairness involves addressing and mitigating such biases. Bioethical considerations regarding biohacking and data usage in marketing campaigns involve evaluating whether these practices contribute to or mitigate existing well-being disparities. If these are aligned with broader social values, targeting products and services shall not create or increase societal divide.

Conclusion

If cases of data-mining behavioral and health-related data from people are as controversial as they are today (see Robertson, 2023), imagine the bioethical questions that will emerge in 2050. With the rise of embodied technologies, biohackers and their microchip implants put one foot in the future and illuminate the potential (fuzzy) future direction. With the continuous development of implantable technologies and the generation of inner-body health-related data, regulations will certainly be established to protect people. A key driver may be Neuralink's brain-computer interface (BCI) because of the type of sensitive data it generates (Lima & Belk, 2022). A robotic surgery implants this BCI in a specific area of the brain that controls body movement intention. The ultimate aim is to allow individuals to operate a computer cursor or keyboard using their thoughts exclusively (Neuralink, 2023). However, in the future, this brain implant will merge the individual with AI and perform tasks, such as searching on Google, without the need for smartphones. In this vein, new opportunities and challenges will require stringent bioethical standards for the use of such data types in marketing campaigns.

Future discussions could explore the following questions: what is the bioethical limit of targeting people who are unaware of their inner-body health-related data with online advertisements (Lustgarten et al., 2020)? Should the sharing of such data be forbidden (Lima & Belk, 2023)? Who should own these embodied data (Gerke et al., 2019)? Should marketing managers be allowed to cross purchase-related data with health-related data (Hermann et al., 2023)?

I hope this chapter on biohacking and bioethical considerations with respect to inner-body health-related data usage sparks new discussions in both theoretical and managerial contexts.

References

Beauchamp, T., & Childress, J. (2019). *Principles of biomedical ethics* (8th ed.). Oxford University Press.

Belk, R. W. (2022). Transhumanism in speculative fiction. *Journal of Marketing Management, 38*(5–6), 423–442. https://doi.org/10.1080/0267257X.2021.1900894

Bode, M., & Kristensen, D. B. (2016). The digital Doppelgänger within: A study on self tracking and the quantified self movement. In R. Canniford & D. Bajde (Eds.), *Assembling consumption: Researching actors, networks and markets* (pp. 119–135). Routledge.

Du, S., & Xie, C. (2021). Paradoxes of artificial intelligence in consumer markets: Ethical challenges and opportunities. *Journal of Business Research, 129*, 961–974. https://doi.org/10.1016/j.jbusres.2020.08.024

Gaspar, R., Rohde, P., & Giger, J. C. (2019). Unconventional settings and uses of human enhancement technologies: A non-systematic review of public and experts' views on self-enhancement and DIY biology/biohacking risks. *Human Behavior and Emerging Technologies, 1*(4), 295–305. https://doi.org/10.1002/hbe2.175

Gerke, S., Minssen, T., Yu, H., & Cohen, I. G. (2019). Ethical and legal issues of ingestible electronic sensors. *Nature Electronics, 2*(8), 329–334. https://doi.org/10.1038/s41928-019-0290-6

Harbisson, N. (2021). I'm selling my perception of colour. In *OpenSea*.

Harwell, D. (2020). Companies' use of thermal cameras to monitor the health of workers and customers worries civil libertarians. *The Washington Post*. Retrieved December 14, 2020, from https://www.washingtonpost.com/technology/2020/04/27/companies-use-thermal-cameras-speed-return-work-sparks-worries-about-civil-liberties/

Hermann, E., Williams, G. Y., & Puntoni, S. (2023). Deploying artificial intelligence in services to AID vulnerable consumers. *Journal of the Academy of Marketing Science*. https://doi.org/10.1007/s11747-023-00986-8

Lima, V., & Belk, R. (2023). Biohacking COVID-19: Sharing is not always caring. *Journal of Public Policy & Marketing, 42*(4), 326–342. https://doi.org/10.1177/07439156231183001

Lima, V. M., & Belk, R. W. (2022). Human enhancement technologies and the future of consumer well-being. *Journal of Services Marketing, 42*(4), 326–342. https://doi.org/10.1108/JSM-09-2021-0363

Lima, V. M., Pessôa, L. A. G. d. P., & Belk, R. W. (2022). The Promethean biohacker: On consumer biohacking as a labour of love. *Journal of Marketing Management, 38*(5–6), 483–514. https://doi.org/10.1080/0267257X.2022.2070239

Lustgarten, S. D., Garrison, Y. L., Sinnard, M. T., & Flynn, A. W. (2020). Digital privacy in mental healthcare: Current issues and recommendations for technology use. *Current Opinion Psychology, 36*, 25–31. https://doi.org/10.1016/j.copsyc.2020.03.012

Mercer, C., & Trothen, T. J. (2021). *Religion and the technological future: An introduction to biohacking, artificial intelligence, and transhumanism.* Springer International Publishing. https://doi.org/10.1007/978-3-030-62359-3

Meyer, M., & Vergnaud, F. (2020). The rise of biohacking: Tracing the emergence and evolution of DIY biology through online discussions. *Technological Forecasting and Social Change*, *160*(August), 120206. https://doi.org/10.1016/j.techfore.2020.120206

More, M., & Vita-More, N. (2013). *The transhumanist reader: Classical and contemporary essays on the science, technology, and philosophy of the human future*. John Wiley & Sons.

Neuralink. (2023). *Neuralink's first-in-human clinical trial is open for recruitment*. Neuralink. Retrieved December 20, 2023, from https://neuralink.com/blog/first-clinical-trial-open-for-recruitment/

Pedersen, I., & Iliadis, A. (2020). *Embodied computing: wearables, implantables, embeddables, ingestibles*. MIT Press.

Petersén, M. (2019). *The Swedish microchipping phenomenon*. Emerald Group Publishing Limited.

Price, W. N., 2nd, & Cohen, I. G. (2019). Privacy in the age of medical big data. *Nature Medicine*, *25*(1), 37–43. https://doi.org/10.1038/s41591-018-0272-7

Robertson, A. (2017). A Wisconsin company will let employees use microchip implants to buy snacks and open doors. *The Verge*. Retrieved December 20, 2017, from https://www.theverge.com/2017/7/24/16019530/three-sqaure-market-implant-office-keycard-biohacking-wisconsin

Robertson, A. (2023). Should Walmart be data-mining your Ozempic prescriptions? *The Verge*. Retrieved December 07, 2023, from https://www.theverge.com/2023/10/9/23909581/walmart-ozempic-food-pharmacy-market-research-privacy

Rumbold, J. M. M., & Pierscionek, B. K. (2018). What are data? A categorization of the data sensitivity spectrum. *Big Data Research*, *12*(July), 49–59. https://doi.org/https://doi.org/10.1016/j.bdr.2017.11.001

Schenker, Y., Arnold, R. M., & London, A. J. (2014). The ethics of advertising for health care services. *The American Journal of Bioethics*, *14*(3), 34–43. https://doi.org/10.1080/15265161.2013.879943

Walker, R. L. (2020). The unfinished business of respect for autonomy: Persons, relationships, and nonhuman animals. *Journal of Medicine and Philosophy (United Kingdom)*, *45*(4–5), 521–539. https://doi.org/10.1093/jmp/jhaa016

Weatherbed, J. (2023). FTC fines GoodRx $1.5 million for sending consumer health data to Google and Facebook. *The Verge*. Retrieved December 2023, from https://www.theverge.com/2023/2/2/23582805/ftc-goodrx-complaint-fine-hipaa-health-data-privacy-google-facebook

Yetisen, A. K. (2018). Biohacking. *Trends in Biotechnology*, *36*(8), 744–747. https://doi.org/10.1016/j.tibtech.2018.02.011

Yogev, D., Goldberg, T., Arami, A., Tejman-Yarden, S., Winkler, T. E., & Maoz, B. M. (2023). Current state of the art and future directions for implantable sensors in medical technology: Clinical needs and engineering challenges. *APL Bioengineering*, *7*(3), 031506. https://doi.org/10.1063/5.0152290

Zettler, P. J., Guerrini, C. J., & Sherkow, J. S. (2019). Regulating genetic biohacking. *Science*, *364*(6448), 34–36. https://doi.org/10.1126/science.aax3248

6

THE NEXT FRONTIER OF DEI

Communication & Neurodiversity from Now to 2050

Allison Weidhaas

Development of DEI

The death of an unarmed black teenager, Trayvon Martin, and the subsequent acquittal of his killer sparked not only protests, but created the social movement, Black Lives Matter in 2013, igniting a conversation about racial injustice (Simon, 2017). In 2020 this movement once again dominated media headlines following the death of George Floyd from police brutality, which also launched a series of riots (Johnson, 2020) and catapulted national attention to Diversity, Equity and Inclusion issues, often shortened to simply DEI or DEIB, which adds the term belonging.

Media attention following Floyd's death shifted to exposing police brutality, institutional racism and white-privilege, initiating important and profound conversations about race. While these unsettling conversations started with intense media attention in many communities, they quickly traveled from social media and television screens into our homes and offices. Seemingly overnight companies and organizations across the United States issued statements about their commitment to diversity, and DEI became a well-known acronym as organizations scurried to update outdated or nonexistent diversity policies, with a strong focus on race. While DEI started as a response to institutional and systemic racism, its definition extends far beyond skin color or ethnicity, and this chapter will explore the next frontier of DEI and its impact on public relations.

DEI Defined

Diversity refers to the types of individuals represented in the workplace, including aspects such as race, gender, age, sexual orientation, etc. Equity ensures

DOI: 10.4324/9781003426653-8

everyone is treated fairly, but it differs from equality, which means that everyone in the organization is treated the same or equal. In some cases, equity requires organizations to account for privilege and create programs to address inequalities. Inclusion refers to the degree to which organizations make individuals feel included and able to contribute in meaningful ways (McKinsey & Company, 2022).

Public relations people quickly moved into important roles in DEI efforts, not only as consultants for the language of DEI statements, but they developed internal and external communication plans to share the organization's responses. Public relations practitioners in organizations with existing policies and efforts benefited from their foresight, while organizations with limited efforts or DEI statements without corresponding actions found themselves in the crosshairs.

Organizations of all sizes and compositions began to release DEI statements in 2020, and many of these referenced the essential nature of a diverse workforce, and yet many of the programs focused primarily on race while providing minimal attention to other aspects of diversity, such as neurodiversity, physical and mental disabilities, veteran status, age, etc.

Recognizing race as an important aspect of DEI initiatives will continue, but the Supreme Court's ruling to eliminate affirmative action signals a shift that will impact institutions far beyond higher education (Sherman & Carrillo, 2023). The next wave of DEI programs will broaden the horizon for a number of largely ignored aspects of diversity. Mundy & Bardhan (2023) issued a call for public relations researchers to explore DEI beyond currently accepted norms and investigate DEI with new methods that interrogate taken-for-granted assumptions and foreground overlooked publics.

A focus on overlooked or niche audiences may initially receive token attention, but as our understanding of these audiences evolve, practitioners will align communication to meet their specific and nuanced needs, including recognizing neurodiverse individuals with many distinct differences.

Neurodiversity (ND)

Many academic researchers credit the term neurodiversity (ND) to Judy Singer, a sociologist and Autism advocate, who used the term to describe the diversity that exists in people's brain functioning or cognition (Doyle, 2020; Ungvarsky, 2023). The term can be used to describe people with attention deficit hyperactivity disorder (ADHD), Autism, Dyslexia and many related cognitive differences (Ungvarsky, 2023). ND shifts the focus away from negative associations with earlier terms that included words like impairments, disorders, and deficits (Doyle, 2020). Instead of marginalizing individuals with ND, Singer and others like her, want to highlight the strengths of different ways of thinking, such as an intense focus and a natural attention to detail (Silberman, 2013); ND

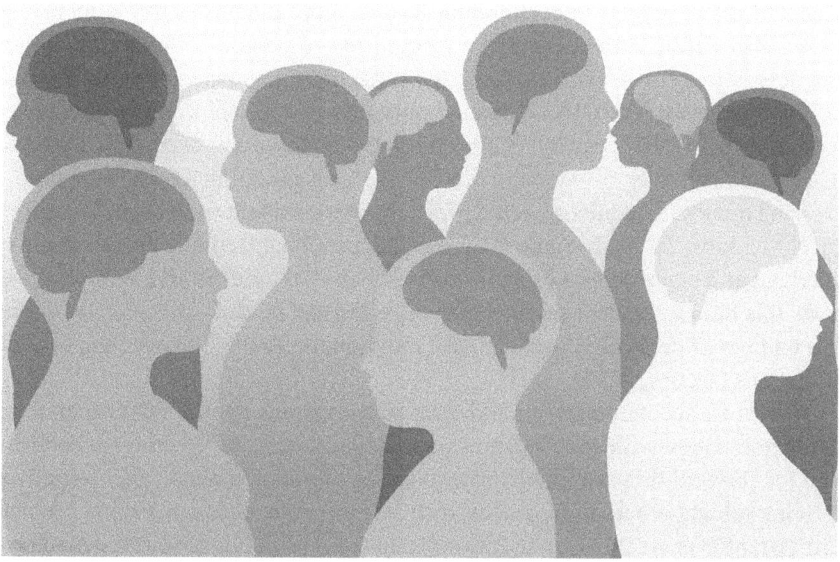

FIGURE 6.1 Neurodiversity.

Source: Attribution as specified: MissLunaRose12, CC BY-SA 4.0 <https://creativecommons.org/licenses/by-sa/4.0>, via Wikimedia Commons.

signals a move toward greater acceptance of cognitive differences with all of their corresponding attributes. Critics argue that terms like neurodiversity spotlight individuals with higher cognitive and social functioning, while detracting attention from those who struggle to maintain the basic functions of ordinary life (Harris, 2023; Ungvarsky, 2023). A study of the communication about ND also points to a disproportionate emphasis on people with high-functioning autism or savants, creating a preferential view of those with unique talents, while marginalizing other forms of ND (Branton et al., 2023). Proponents of the ND movement respond to these arguments by indicating that attention to some aspects of ND will advance greater awareness and understanding for all individuals (Harris, 2023; Ungvarsky, 2023) and will lead to a future with a more nuanced understanding of ND. Perhaps most importantly for this chapter, this debate suggests a growing awareness of neurodiversity, and not just among scholars or medical professionals; the United States over the last several decades witnessed a slow growth in the acceptance of ND individuals, evidenced by nonprofit organizations to benefit various ND segments, facilities providing sensory-friendly environments, and the growing number of organizations offering specific opportunities for those who experience sensory overload.

Individuals with ND are estimated to comprise 15–20 percent of the world's population (Goulet, 2022), and these numbers are only likely to increase as acceptance and greater understanding lead to more diagnoses. As evidence an increase in autism awareness and a recognition of people with varying autism characteristics, also known as the autism spectrum, coincided with an increase in reported cases. The CDC indicated only one in 150 children was diagnosed with autism in 2000, but by 2020, one in 36 children received this diagnosis (CDC, 2023). Other categories of ND have also noted increases, including a growing number of adults searching for information about their cognitive differences (Jenkins, 2023). In some instances, adults recognized a strain or cognitive overload as a consequence of their need to "mask" their cognitive differences to fit in; this hiding requires significant energy and can be hard to sustain, resulting in a number of previously undiagnosed individuals seeking answers and accommodations (Jacobs, 2023).

With more accommodations and open conversations, the 15–20 percent of the world population with an ND diagnosis will likely increase, creating an opportunity for forward-thinking public relations practitioners to create DEI initiatives for internal and external audiences with ND. To date, public relations scholarship (Branton et al., 2023) is largely silent about how public relations and related practices can effectively create space and communication for ND individuals.

Employment & Internal Communication

Individuals with ND struggle with employment; as an example, some estimates indicate over 80 percent of autistic people with a college degree face unemployment or underemployment (Goulet, 2022).

Frequently the difficulty for those with ND stems from differing communication styles, which can include a lack of eye contact, limited ability to interpret nonverbal signals and difficulty understanding indirect communication (Goulet, 2022; Radulski, 2021). Neurotypical individuals also complain that their neurodiverse colleagues are poor listeners based on their perception that attentive employees need to sit while someone is talking, avoid fidgeting, not have their visual attention focused on other parts of the room, use contextually appropriate facial expressions, and affirm their understanding of the information communicated in neurotypical ways (Radulski, 2021). While a recent *Harvard Business Review* article argues we should learn to communicate with neurodivergent individuals instead of expecting them to align with neurotypical communication styles (Goulet, 2022), there is still a gap in acceptance of ND as a component of DEI and limited accommodations, even while research suggests employees with ND can be 30 percent more productive than their neurodiverse peers in some roles (Mahto et al., 2022).

A select number of organizations, like Wells Fargo, instituted programs specifically attuned to hiring those with ND, but the Director of the University of Connecticut's Center for Neurodiversity and Employment Innovation cautions that it takes more than just a desire to hire ND individuals (Jones, 2023). Organizations need to address their unchecked assumptions and biases with employee trainings, which cutting-edge companies use to better communicate and understand those with ND (Blanco, 2023; Jones, 2023; Sims, 2021).

Although some companies are investing in resources to better understand ND, the academic literature points to accommodations largely focused on autistic individuals; essentially using ND as a synonym for autism rather than an umbrella term for numerous cognitive differences (Branton et al., 2023). Autism matches a significant subset of this population, but it advances a one-size-fits all approach that frequently focuses on stereotypes, such as a lack of interest in interactions with others, potentially isolating ND employees, or a focus on the physical space (Doyle & McDowall, 2021; Weber et al., 2022). One research team indicated neurodiversity can no longer be considered "new" in the workplace and critiqued the dearth of quality research that systematically examines the practical aspects of what accommodations are effective in various workplaces (Doyle & McDowall, 2021), which suggests opportunities for future program development and increased communication to share these important initiatives.

Special External Programs

Forward-thinking organizations have started to develop programs and accommodations for neurodivergent (ND) individuals, such as sensory-friendly events, opportunities at museums for earlier, reduced-price admissions with the recognition that many sensory-sensitive individuals can't participate in the full experience, thus offering select hours with less stimulation from lights and sound. Examples include regular events, such as the monthly "Sunshine Sundays" at Tampa's Glazer Children's Museum, weekly events at Smithsonian institutions in DC (Glazer Children's Museum, n.d.; Shrikant, 2018), as well as some regional programs that offer on-demand opportunities, such as Access by Art-Reach, which provides $2 admission to over 80 theaters, parks, museums, historic sites, and more in Greater Philadelphia and Delaware (Access by Art-Reach, 2023). These organizations not only offer special events and programs, but savvy PR practitioners work with specialists to develop communication for these individuals, including social stories or guides that help anxious ND visitors preview the site prior their visit (Longwood Gardens, 2023; ZooTampa, 2023), the Shedd Aquarium offers visitors a sensory friendly app (Shrikant, 2018), and communication professionals promote these programs by partnering with nonprofits, such as Access Art-Reach (Access by Art-Reach, 2023) or the Center for Autism and Disabilities at USF (CARD, 2013) and provide onsite communication with signs and designated maps (Longwood Gardens, 2023; ZooTampa, 2023).

Many of these programs originated from Autism Speaks, an autism research organization, which initially started working with Major League Baseball in 2012 (Shrikant, 2018). Given the history of autism organizations initiating many of these efforts, it's not surprising that many organizations initially focus on autism. The all-inclusive Beaches Resorts in Jamaica, which worked with the International Board of Credentialing and Continuing Education Standards (IBCCES) obtained the Advanced Certified Autism Center designation. Beaches offers an autism kids camp, options for a one-on-one "beach buddy," "Culinary Concierge" for those with dietary needs, and sensory guides that rate locations on the resort from 1 to 10 based on sensory stimulation (Beaches Resorts New Sensory Guides to Build Autism Program, 2023). An IBCCES study indicated 94 percent of families would "take more vacations or visit more new places if they had access to autism-trained and certified options" (Beaches Resorts New Sensory Guides to Build Autism Program, 2023). Beaches now offers three resorts with the Advanced Autism Certification and specially trained staff (Blanco, 2023), a strong indication of an unexplored target audience. IBCCES certifies restaurants, theme parks, hotels and even cities, such as Visalia, California, which received its certification in 2022 (Blanco, 2023).

An unexpected and recent indicator of neurodiverse-acceptance is behemoth Walmart's November 2023 introduction of sensory-friendly shopping hours, including televisions with nonmoving pictures, low lighting and silent radios. Walmart initially debuted this in select stores for two hours once a week, but positive customer feedback pushed the undertaking from a pilot program to an everyday experience in every Walmart store (Deaderick et al., 2023).

The programs referenced above represent early adapters or the early majority in the public relations diffusion theory, which is supported by academic research indicating that while ND is not "new," it still lacks a critical focus on effectiveness (Doyle & McDowall, 2021; Weber et al., 2022) and the limited PR research that addresses neurodiversity (Branton et al., 2023; Trevisan, 2017).

On a broader basis, many research studies explore sensory-related aspects of the environment, which fall into two primary categories, hypersensitive, a heightened response to the environment, and hyposensitive, lack of or underdeveloped response to stimuli; both of these are associated with autism and ADD/ADHD (Panagiotidi et al., 2018). The literature points to a number of ways these two categories can manifest, including attempts to reduce social interaction, increasing social interaction space, reducing noise through various interventions, adjusting lighting and reducing visual distractions, adjusting office temperatures, providing private office space instead of an open bullpen-style, allowing virtual work, and even adding pleasant smells (Weber et al., 2022). While an extensive review of the research depicts numerous organizational accommodations, the academic literature surprisingly has an "underdeveloped evidence base," (p. 41), which means it's difficult to determine what is effective and for whom

(Weber et al., 2022). To add to this challenge, the lack of a one-size-fits-most approach requires organizations to focus on individuals with varying needs, which further complicates organizational responses. Many organizations, overwhelmed with the possible accommodations, ignore the need or focus on common stereotypes, such as noise reduction.

Trend by 2050 and Its Effect on the Society

Studies (Doyle, 2020; Doyle & McDowall, 2021; Weber et al., 2022) within the last five years indicate the need more for more evidence-based research that can inform practice, and thus by 2050, these studies will influence communication and practice. Some of these studies will contribute to the ways in which organizations offer accommodations, but others will explore how we communicate.

Language

Apart from recognizing these individuals as people who think differently, by 2050, society will shift its view from an emphasis on ND as a deficit to recognizing the benefits, or at a minimum not assuming marginalization in our language. Perhaps, Jeremy Davey, an autistic program architect for Microsoft best exemplified this when he said, "I meet people all the time in work, and I go, 'Yeah, they're on the spectrum.' That's not in any way pejorative. It's just an observation" (Jacobs, 2023, p. 19). By 2050, we will shift our language away from the social norm of associating ND as derogatory, eliminating the need for people like Davey to explain this phrase as merely an identifying term rather than a disparagement.

The term neurodiverse originates in part from the word diverse. Merriam Webster defines *diverse* as "differing from one another," "unlike," "composed of distinct or unlike elements or qualities" (Merriam-Webster, n.d.). As humans we reproduce a structure with its powers and constraints through language; people function with an implicit understanding, which we typically don't stop to analyze (Giddens, 1984). Said another way, we frame, a term popularized by Goffman (1956), our thoughts in conversation and this influences our interactions. In changing our language from harsh words, like impairment, disorders, and deficits (Doyle, 2020), to neurodiversity, we experienced a shift in the level of acceptance of people with cognitive differences and the corresponding resources, but in framing individuals as different, the root word in neurodiversity, it still suggests a subtler distinction, an ability to "other" or define individuals based on the perceived norm of neurotypicality. By 2050, this author predicts language will once again change by offering a new, more inclusive term and signal society's shift from a standpoint of marginalization to cognitive difference as a norm, potentially even one to be celebrated.

While it might be tempting to eliminate any distinction in language, Lewis (2006) pointed out that a "blindness" to difference only reifies existing structures of power, allowing practices that promote discrimination to continue (P. Lewis, 2006). A blindness can create the perception of equality (i.e., everyone is treated equally), but without the equity. For equity, we still need language that offers distinctions, like autism and ADHD, because it serves as a reminder of distinctions that can otherwise be overlooked.

A shift in language could alter the way workplaces interact with ND individuals. Instead of accommodating a disability, as defined by the Americans with Disability Act as someone who has

> as a physical or mental *impairment* that *substantially limits* one or more major life activities, has a history or record of such an *impairment* (such as cancer that is in remission), or is perceived by others as having such an *impairment.*
> *(ADA, n.d.)*

We will shift descriptions away from impairments and limitations.

The government is not the only source of these limiting terms; employment agencies, even those specifically promoting ND, also use language that can undermine those with ND. One study revealed ND employment agencies placed an emphasis on the "costs" of hiring ND employees and the agencies' communication promoted the most extraordinary examples of ND in the workplace (Branton, et al., 2023), such as the autistic accountant solving complex mathematical irregularities. In many cases, employment centers for ND individuals also unintentionally reinforce stereotypes about the types of ND work and workplaces, favoring places like tech companies and data entry (Branton, et al., 2023). A change in language will change perceptions, opening more opportunities in a variety of organizations while providing a more nuanced view of ND individuals.

Language Influences Workplace Options

In 2050 with a growing understanding of ND, workplaces will not only shift their language, but reconsider how they allocate resources. One option for employers is to offer workplace accommodations to anyone, including those who opt not to identify or seek a diagnosis. In moving from using a diagnosis as an eligibility criterion to full access for anyone may reduce the stigma associated with disclosing identities, such as ADHD, Autism, and Dyslexia. For individuals who share their ND diagnosis, this disclosure will give them preferential and mandated access to resources via the Americans with Disability Act.

Many organizations already offer accommodations to those with invisible disabilities, which include cognitive differences, simply by wearing a sunflower lanyard. Airports, like Miami International, support the sunflower lanyards (PR Newswire, 2020), a UK-initiated program intended to offer the wearer additional, unquestioned support. Several countries recognize the sunflower as a symbol indicating the person may need extra time, support or services; although the disability, such as anxiety or autism, may not be immediately recognizable. Anyone can purchase a sunflower product, making it accessible to anyone seeking extra assistance.

By 2050, a growing number of organizations will recognize previously unacknowledged cognitive differences, including less visible ones, by offering accommodations with a Chinese-menu approach, allowing for more choice, and including categories previously overlooked, such as taste and vestibular issues, like vertigo. In selecting from a menu of workplace options, it alters the landscape by avoiding stereotypes, such as anyone with autism needs quiet spaces, and allows for intersectionality to exist, recognizing that a person isn't defined by only one identity and people can exhibit multiple categories of ND.

Further, communicating with ND employees will shift from the perspective that ND employees should conform to neurotypical communication styles to ones that accept communication differences, like indirect eye contact, movement during a conversation, an awareness of the need to sit versus standing for a long presentation, and overstimulation as a rationale to end a discussion. Additionally, employers will seek feedback from ND employees about their preferred communication practices to avoid a one-size-fits-most approach.

Employers, similar to families with diverse members, will need to address sensory conflicts, such as an employee who is a proprioception seeker (a.k.a. hyposensitive), an individual who needs movement and direct contact with their environment, and works alongside an ND individual who is hypersensitive, preferring quiet spaces and requiring limited external stimulation. The conflict between these two sensory needs can create havoc in the workplace. A neurodivergent psychologist recommends starting a discussion to identify individuals' varying needs. Not only will this conversation distinguish areas of conflict and ways to address issues, a discussion can help to normalize sensory needs within the workplace (Neff, 2024). Through communication, employers and employees can begin to proactively address conflicts and gather resources to mitigate them when they are unavoidable.

External Communication

Moving from an internal to an external focus, public relations practitioners will need to develop campaigns and programs for neurodiverse individuals. As Goulet (2022), an autistic person with ADHD recommended, society must shift away from a focus on ND as "abnormal" or "incorrect" with the onus on ND people to alter their communication to align with neurotypical expectations; instead, savvy public relations people will learn how to better communicate with ND people, schedule time to reflect on their taken-for-granted assumptions, and extend communication to niche audiences. Fortunately advances in technology make it easier every day to communicate with specific audiences, so PR people can identify subsets within ND, such as people who are sensory seeking, and may prefer high-intensity communication and connect with them in their preferred media. High-intensity communication might be loud, interruptive, require continuous feedback and address sensory-input for those who seek greater levels of stimulation, such as vibrating or pulsating phones that provide continuous tactile input or events that include high-contact sports.

For those who are hypersensitive, many programs already exist to reduce or eliminate sensory input, such as those designated by Autism Certifications by IBCCES (Blanco, 2023). Certifications offer important third-party oversight into organizational offerings, such as the ability to skip lines at theme parks, designated quiet space, sensory guides, and social stories. Certifications also help individuals make choices about how to spend their time and money, which means organizations will continue to seek out these designations, and PR people will publicize earning these certifications and related initiatives, including ND trained employees. Society benefits because not only are educated employees better at communicating with ND visitors and internal audiences, but external communication about these certifications builds awareness and acceptance.

As our understanding of ND increases, PR people may begin to identify subsets of ND people as target audiences for their organizations. For example, a company offering a high-intensity sport with lots of physical contact may determine a niche audience is proprioception seekers. Public relations research could determine not only the niche audience, but preferred communication strategies and tactics.

Perhaps one of the greatest ways for PR people to learn about ND is to work with neurodiverse people, and some agencies are starting to recognize the creative talent of those with ND (Sims, 2021). For example, one partner in a PR firm cites her ADHD as her "superpower" (Jenkins, 2023) another explained her ADHD aligned well with the fast-paced, often chaotic work of agency life (H. Lewis, 2023). Ketchum UK, a large global PR juggernaut, worked with Ambitious about Autism, to hire an intern with autism and provide training to the team working with this individual. Following this paid three-month internship, Ketchum educated all of its UK's line managers with a mandatory "Neurodiversity Understood" program (Sims, 2021).

Public relations, a practice that relies on a complex understanding of audience, is well positioned to not only move into the next frontier of DEI, but to advocate for a more varied understanding of ND. Far from simply creating PR plans to improve the understanding of and advocate for ND, forward-thinking PR people will develop PR campaigns that offer nuanced and varied ways of communicating with those who represent the full umbrella of ND. This will be achieved through continuous communication with ND audiences.

The first special education accessibility coordinator for the New York Transit Museum, Meredith Gregory, advised, "Create with, not without. Work with the community you are trying to serve" (Shrikant, 2018 In developing accessibility options, those with ND or their caretakers provided instrumental insight into program development at the NY Transit Museum (Shrikant, 2018, para. 13). In the same way, public relations individuals will need to work with ND individuals to develop communications that align with their needs. One of the best ways to do this might be offering neurodiverse individuals a place on the PR team, giving them direct influence over future PR campaign initiatives.

As we advanced beyond campaigns that incorporate ND as a target audience, full-service agencies will emerge to specialize in this area. Similar to all of the agencies that marketed to technology in the early 2000s, the landscape will be dotted with agencies poised to communicate with ND audiences.

The future of DEI, particularly neurodiversity, holds many opportunities for PR people willing to engage in careful research, check their taken-for-granted assumptions, and communicate with new audiences in new and nuanced ways.

Author's note: Special thanks to my children, who have introduced me to new methods of communicating and made me think critically about neurodiversity.

References

ADA. (n.d.). Introduction to the Americans with Disabilities Act. In *ADA.gov*. Retrieved November 25, 2023, from https://www.ada.gov/topics/intro-to-ada/

Access by Art-Reach. (2023). Art-Reach. Retrieved November 30, 2023, from https://www.art-reach.org/access/

Beaches Resorts New Sensory Guides to Build Autism Program. (2023). *Airline Industry Information (M2)*. Apr. 2023. EBSCOhost, research.ebsco.com/linkprocessor/plink?id=beb1887d-3dcf-3e0d-8b91-7c3b007f9e69.

Blanco, E. (2023, April 3). These 6 amazing autism-friendly family spots are well worth the trip. *Charlotte Observer, The (NC)*.

Branton, S. E., Villamil, A. M., & Reed, J. L. (2023). Branding neurodiversity: A critical discourse analysis of communicative capitalism and change empowerment among neurodiversity workforce intermediaries. *Journal of Public Relations Research, 35*(5/6), 357–374.

CARD. (2013). CARD center for autism & related disabilities at USF. http://card-usf.fmhi.usf.edu/

CDC. (2023 April 4). Data & statistics on autism spectrum disorder. *CDC*. https://www.cdc.gov/ncbddd/autism/data.html

Deaderick, D., Clark, C., & Washington, A. (2023, November 7). *Small changes, big impact: Sensory-friendly hours return*. Walmart Corporate News and Information. https://corporate.walmart.com/news/2023/11/07/small-changes-big-impact-sensory-friendly-hours-return

Doyle, N. (2020). Neurodiversity at work: A biopsychosocial model and the impact on working adults. *British Medical Bulletin, 135*(1), 108–125.

Doyle, N., & McDowall, A. (2021). Diamond in the rough? An "empty review" of research into "neurodiversity" and a road map for developing the inclusion agenda. *Equality, Diversity and Inclusion: An International Journal, 41*(3), 352–382. https://doi.org/10.1108/EDI-06-2020-0172

Giddens, A. (1984). *The constitution of society: Introduction of the theory of structuration.* University of California Press.

Glazer Children's Museum. (n.d.). *Sunshine Sunday.* Retrieved from https://glazermuseum.org/sunshinesunday/

Goffman, E. (1956). *The presentation of self in everyday life.* Anchor Books/Doubleday.

Goulet, J. D. (2022, October 5). Stop asking neurodivergent people to change the way they communicate: Neurotypical people can do more to close the communication gap. *Harvard Business Review.*

Harris, J. (2023, July 5). The mother of neurodiversity: How Judy Singer changed the world. *The Guardian.* Retrieved from https://www.theguardian.com/world/2023/jul/05/the-mother-of-neurodiversity-how-judy-singer-changed-the-world

Jacobs, E. (2023, Febuary 27). The benefits of revealing neurodiversity in the workplace: Diversity & equality disclosing a diagnosis is sensitive but being open can help develop better practices. *Financial Times.* Retrieved from https://rider.idm.oclc.org/login?url=https://www.proquest.com/newspapers/benefits-revealing-neurodiversity-workplace/docview/2791778289/se-2

Jenkins, S. (2023, October 31). I learned that I had ADHD when I was 30 – and it's been my PR superpower ever since. *The Drum.* Retrieved from https://www.thedrum.com/opinion/2023/10/31/i-learned-i-had-adhd-when-i-was-30-and-it-s-been-my-pr-superpower-ever

Johnson, S. (2020, June 4). "Legalized murder": Protesters let out frustration, cops respond with force. *New York Amsterdam News, 111*(23), 3–26.

Jones, C. (2023, August 29). Diving into the deep talent pool of neurodiversity. *USA Today.* https://research.ebsco.com/c/rbjs7o/viewer/html/rpuuexq4vn

Lewis, H. (2023, April 12). How can we celebrate neurodiversity in the PR industry? *Influence.* https://research.ebsco.com/c/rbjs7o/viewer/html/rpuuexq4vn

Lewis, P. (2006). The quest for invisibility: Female entrepreneurs and the masculine norm of entrepreneurship. *Gender, Work & Organization, 13*(5), 453–469. https://doi.org/10.1111/j.1468-0432.2006.00317

Longwood Gardens. (2023). Social guide. https://longwoodgardens.org/visit/accessibility/social-guide

Mahto, M., Hatfield, S., Hogan, S., Sniderman, B. (2022 Jan 18). A rising tide lifts all boats. *Deloitte Insights.* Retrieved from https://www2.deloitte.com/us/en/insights/topics/talent/neurodiversity-in-the-workplace.html

McKinsey & Company (2022, August 17). What is Diversity, equity, and inclusion? *Mckinsey.com.* https://www.mckinsey.com/featured-insights/mckinsey-explainers/what-is-diversity-equity-and-inclusion

Merriam-Webster. (n.d.). Diverse. In *Merriam-Webster.com dictionary.* Retrieved November 25, 2023, from https://www.merriam-webster.com/dictionary/diverse

Mundy, D., & Bardhan, N. (2023). Charting theoretical directions for DEI in public relations. *Journal of Public Relations Research, 35*(5/6), 281–286.

Neff, M. (2024, January). Manage clashing sensory needs. *Psychology Today,* 57. Retrieved from https://www.psychologytoday.com/us/blog/the-neurodivergent-psychologist/202401/manage-clashing-sensory-needs

Panagiotidi, M., Overton, P. G., & Stafford, T. (2018). The relationship between ADHD traits and sensory sensitivity in the general population. *Comprehensive Psychiatry, 80,* 179–185.

PR Newswire. (2020, November 13). MIA's sunflower lanyards spring into action for travelers with hidden disabilities. *PR Newswire US*. Retrieved from https://www.prnewswire.com/news-releases/mias-sunflower-lanyards-spring-into-action-for-travelers-with-hidden-disabilities-301172860.html

Radulski, B. (2021, May 11). Different listeners listen differently: Crossing the neuro-cultural divide. *LinkedIn*. Retrieved from https://www.linkedin.com/pulse/different-listeners-listen-differently-crossing-divide-radulski/?trk=public_profile_article_view

Sherman, M., & Carrillo, K. (2023, July 6). Supreme Court strikes down Affirmative action in college admissions, says race cannot be a factor. *New York Amsterdam News*, *114*(27), 4–27.

Shrikant, A. (2018, Jan. 5). How Museums Are Becoming More Sensory-Friendly for Those with Autism. *Smithsonian Magazine*. Retrieved from https://www.smithsonianmag.com/innovation/how-museums-are-becoming-more-sensory-friendly-for-those-with-autism-180967740/

Silberman, S. (2013). Neurodiversity. *Wired*, *21*(5), 116.

Simon, D. (2017, April 20). Trayvon Martin's death sparked a movement that lives on five years later. *New York Amsterdam News*, *108*(16), 37–39.

Sims, M. (2021, Oct. 11). Neurodiversity in PR: From kryptonite to superpower. *Provoke Media*. Retrieved from https://www.provokemedia.com/long-reads/article/neurodiversity-in-pr-from-kryptonite-to-superpower

Trevisan, F. (2017). Crowd-sourced advocacy: Promoting disability rights through online storytelling. *Public Relations Inquiry*, *6*(2), 191–208. https://doi.org/10.1177/2046147X17697785

Ungvarsky, J. (2023). Neurodiversity. *Salem Press Encyclopedia*. https://research-ebsco-com.rider.idm.oclc.org/c/dcou4s/viewer/html/3dqveiamdz

Weber, C., Krieger, B., Häne, E., Yarker, J., & McDowall, A. (2024). Physical workplace adjustments to support neurodivergent workers: A systematic review. *Applied Psychology: An International Review*, *73*(3), 910–962. https://doi-org.rider.idm.oclc.org/10.1111/apps.12431

ZooTampa. (2023). Going to the zoo social stories. *ZooTampa at Lowry Park*. Retrieved from https://zootampa.org/wp-content/uploads/2021/12/English-Zoo-Scripted-Story_12.7.2021.pdf

7

WHEN BIG BROTHER IS LISTENING

Impact of the Social Credit System on Strategic Communication

Sabrina Page and Victoria Barry

Imagine living in a world where verbal morality violations are normal and social distancing is required. Where everything you say, do, and think are continually monitored, mapped, and judged. This dystopian world is not a work of fiction, as seen in George Orwell's *Nineteen Eighty-Four* (2021) or *Demolition Man* (Brambilla, 1993), it is alive and well in the surveillance state of China. Artificial intelligence (AI) monitors and utilizes social credit personal scorecards on China's 1.4 billion citizens rewarding for good behavior and punishing for bad (Kobie, 2019). Considering the continuous monitoring and judging of citizens' behavior and trustworthiness, what impact will social credit score (SCS) have on how organizations/agencies communicate with their audiences?

Research has linked the use of media to the socialization, development, and maintenance of political, religious, and societal expectations. These expectations are shaped through the battlefields of communication, politics, and international relations (Gilboa, 2007). This battle will transform humanity on a global level with the integration and amplification of technology across the physical, digital, and biological world. Governments and other global societal stakeholders must examine and understand the technology that will shape this fourth industrial revolution to transform humankind.

The Fourth Industrial Revolution

The Fourth Industrial Revolution (Schwab, 2016) suggests a societal shift will occur with the implementation and use of technology in hopes of getting the world to participate in and benefit from these transformations. The new era provides a unique opportunity for growth through harmonization and integration of

DOI: 10.4324/9781003426653-9

multi-disciplinary cooperation and discovery. Schwab warns this new industrial revolution will act as a catalyst for greater interconnectedness, it has the potential to negatively impact future generations. The catalyst driving this revolution is "leveraging the pervasive power of digitization and information technology" (p. 9) as they relate to the physical, digital, and biological realms in society.

Physical

Insight into the use of technology previously only seen in the movies such as, **artificial intelligent (AI) driven vehicles**, drones, and aircraft. Additive manufacturing can lead to a collaboration between humans and machines. These **advanced robots are** becoming more adaptive and flexible. Allowing for new **"smart" materials** that can self-heal or clean. Schwab (2016) warned these new "smart" materials could significantly disrupt both the manufacturing and infrastructure industries.

Digital

The biggest thing the fourth industrial revolution has produced, according to Schwab (2016) is the **Internet of Things** (IoT). A network of physical objects embedded with sensors, into software and other technologies to connect and exchange data with other devices and systems over the internet. This trend can and will radically alter how supply chains are managed, through continuous monitoring and optimization of assets via **blockchain technology**.

Biology

Biotechnology offers opportunities such as testing and identifying specific genetic variations to assist with better, individualized healthcare from embryo to old age. However, with great power comes great responsibility, and unintended consequences result from changes in technology. These come from the ethical challenges to edit biology, from genetically modified plants and animals, to developing designer babies, the deliberate misuse of biotechnology such as synthetic biology to develop bacterial or viral agents used in bioterrorism or biological warfare.

The leadership in the dystopian society of Orwell's *Nineteen Eighty-Four* kept members under control through constant surveillance and policing of language used by the citizenry. The dystopian society of *Demolition Man*, were kept in line by making illegal anything not good for them. The viewer tends to laugh at the absurdity of these illegalities, however, China's social credit scoring system uses these factors to "improve trust and social responsibility between citizens and businesses" (HROne, 2023).

Social Credit, System

History of Social Credit System

Social Credit Scores, while some believe this a conspiracy theory or a far-fetched idea, this concept is not new. China's social monitoring system merged traditional financial creditworthiness with the idea of social creditworthiness; the scores ranging from 350 to 950 points assessing a person's "worth" went live in 2020 (HROne, 2023).

Social Credit System (SCS): Anybody versus Business

This system "ensures the bad people in society don't have a place to go, while good people can move freely without obstruction" (Hvistendahl, 2017). China's corporate social credit system (CSCS) applies to businesses and organizations and rates them on honesty, creditworthiness, governance, compliance, and social responsibility.

Individual SCS

Citizens with high scores can obtain benefits at better rates, priority school admissions, better employment opportunities, easier access to loans and other credit, tax breaks, and even shorten wait times for medical care.

Those with low scores are identified as engaging in trust-breaking behavior, their name, and social credit code are then published online along with the details of their actions and legal sanctions that have been taken. "The List of Dishonest Persons Subject to Enforcement by the Supreme People's Court" (Kobie, 2019) can prohibit you from buying a plane ticket, from traveling, purchasing/renting property, or even getting a loan. An example of one put on this list is journalist Liu Hu, who was arrested, fined, and blacklisted for his article on CCP corruption and censorship practices (Bach, 2020).

The SCS monitors everything from shopping habits to social media posts. Neither individuals nor businesses want to be affiliated with those on the blacklist. Corporations deem these individuals unworthy of doing business without being seen as not in line with the CSCS policies. For example, a person with a lower credit score could not be allowed to shop at higher-end stores, such as Louis Vuitton, due to the store being associated and doing business with a nonconformist. Correspondingly, businesses with lower CSCS may not be able to obtain loans or business from citizens, resulting in a decrease in profits due to being seen as untrustworthy

Corporate SCS

Businesses are provided with a "unified social credit code" (USCC) (Kobie, 2019), a unique number verifying the business is registered with the government and is legally allowed to operate in China. The business' score is linked to a permanent record, much like an individual social credit score.

"GETTING YOUR CORPORATE SOCIAL CREDIT SCORE REPAIRED"

In October 2019, a pet store owner in China's Wenzhou, Zhejiang province was caught selling veterinary prescription drugs without a license. The owner was fined 10,000 yuan (USD 1,405) and his company was placed on the CCP list of untrustworthy businesses. Under the CSCS, this business could remain on the blacklist for six (6) years. A Zhejiang-based company in 2019 offered to help him "erase" the information of his misdemeanor from the list. The cost to repair his CSCS was 1,800 yuan (USD 254.52) along with a short retraining course and test. By doing so, his original credit score was reinstated and he received a certificate showing that he was back in the government's good graces (Tailai & Walsh, 2020).

Businesses' USCC score can be affected by a multitude of reasons, such as; paying taxes on time, properly maintaining licenses, fulfilling environmental protection mandates, meeting requirements applicable to their industry, and behavior of a business's partner(s). While some businesses may make decisions that land them on the "blacklist" quickly by not following the rules, the blacklist label does have the opportunity to be reversed if the company works toward improvement. On the opposite end of the blacklist is the red list, the red list is for businesses with top scores. Those companies on the red list are more likely to excel in the corporate world and continue to grow and thrive.

While one can be punished (fined, limited travel, denied access to prime housing rates) or rewarded (based on their social credit score increasing or decreasing) based on one's every day decisions. However, those fines will not come in the mail like a ticket or fine; with the implementation of the Social Credit System comes digital currency, where if you are caught breaking the law funds are digitally removed from your bank account to the government entity that issued the fine.

Social Credit System: Around the World

While Americans are used to credit checks, to qualify for additional credit, loans, mortgages, etc. based on payment and credit history and how much one owes, the concept of being graded on behavior and trustworthiness is new. Unlike American credit checks, China's social credit system (SCS), monitors people's behavior and trustworthiness by both private businesses and the government.

A form of the "soft" social credit system in the United States are rewards programs, limiting access to news and other social media platforms, and even the cancellation of online accounts such as PayPal, Venmo, etc. Much like China, which expanded its credit rating system from personal credit scores like the United States to include other aspects of life including bill payments and criminal convictions, many companies as well as government policies focus on an individual's suitability and fitness.

The line between individual versus societal prosperity is blurring with the implementation of these social credit scores, in favor of societal prosperity. Like China's social credit system, if one's score is already borderline one small "misdemeanor" could be the breaking point on a mortgage loan, rent prices, a better job, or whether you are allowed to travel.

One such monitoring system with the concept of "see something, say something" in San Diego, CA implemented the Smart Streetlights Program, installing more than 3,000 cameras and microphones in street lights (Service, 2023), in this case, Big Brother is watching and surveilling citizens.

While the United States appears to be taking a "soft" approach to the social credit system, it can be suggested banks in the United Kingdom seem to be transitioning quickly. Much like the SCS in China where officials can automatically remove fines or close accounts for those whom, a recent article in *The Herald* reported on how a private bank closed the account of Brexit Party Leader Nigel Farage because his views did not align with those of the bank (Learmonth, 2023). Interestingly, this action occurred at the same time legislation to admonish banks for opposing political views was not brought forward for a vote.

In 2022, Bologna, Italy activated "Smart Citizen Wallet." First launched in Rome in 2020, this social credit application promotes and rewards "virtuous behavior" such as not getting fired from one's job, separating trash, and using public transit. Bolognese citizens are "opting in" to participate in the program to be "rewarded" for their good behavior. Unlike the SCS, no tangible rewards or penalties have been associated with Bologna's program (Boos, 2022a, 2022b, Mastrangelo, 2023).

Rome's motivation for using this social credit app is to achieve the World Economic Forum's, and the United Nations (UN) Agenda 2030, Sustainable Development Goal (SDG). Under the 2030 Agenda, Rome, with blockchain technology to track and monitor a person's behaviors to move toward a cashless society.

The unconscious transition of data allows governments and businesses to collect and monitor everyday life from finances, to order processes, or to simplify and improve life. Globally, people are accustomed to constant surveillance due to the COVID-19 pandemic, where people posted about getting the vaccine, how good they were at social distancing, etc. This has led to social discrimination, exclusion, and government intervention when people did not follow the health mandates.

Privacy Laws and Digital Currency: A Review

Globally, people have become increasingly concerned about their digital privacy, with a limited understanding of how their data is collected, stored, and used by both governments and businesses around the world (Faveior, 2023).

Digital Privacy

In an environment where one's search history, keystrokes, and "likes" are tracked; an expectation of privacy seems more like an idealistic concept than reality. For the sake of this chapter, digital privacy is defined as the protection of personal information and data from unauthorized access or use in the context of new and developing technologies. Before the internet, there were laws protecting the privacy of phone calls, mail, and every day interactions in life.

Online activity leaves a digital "footprint" that offers a "trail" of social media data providing a snapshot of the user. Individuals and organizations need to be aware of potential privacy risks and take steps to safeguard their information. Unfortunately, issues such as data security, surveillance, and online tracking mean the government, industry, and civil society must work together to establish regulations and guidelines to protect digital privacy in emerging technologies.

With the emergence of new technologies, governments are implementing digital privacy laws to ensure online privacy for their citizens. The United States, for example, has a patchwork of federal and state laws to regulate online privacy. Interestingly, the Pew Research Center found Americans were willing to give up or trade their freedoms for the safety of the country (Maniam, 2016). This coincides with the Gallup Organization's finds, in the year following the September 11th, terrorist attacks on the World Trade Center. These freedoms included the government having access to private communication, vaccinations requirements, and implementation of national identification cards (2002).

Fast forward to 2020s COVID-19 pandemic, and the authoritarian austerity measures implemented globally to combat the transmission of the virus. The use of campaigns of fear to increase the uptake of preventative health behaviors (Richmond et al., 2023), caused people all over the world to relinquish their freedom to travel, go to school/work, religious assembly, and even freedom of expression.

In recent years, Americans have become concerned about digital privacy, with a limited understanding of how previously collected data is stored and used (Faverio, 2023). For example, during a Senate Homeland Security and

Governmental Affairs Committee hearings, US Senator Rand Paul (R-KY) questioned the collaboration of government agencies with social media platforms to suppress disfavored speech and encroach on the rights of Americans. Paul expressed concerns about the use of social media platforms to target specific individuals and groups. Paul remarked, "The government distorted and exaggerated facts, leveraged mass media, and attacked the leadership of groups it considered to be threats to the social order" (Senator Rand Paul, Opening remarks, 2023).

Beginning in 2018, California's Consumer Privacy Act limits the amount and type of personal information a business can collect (*California Consumer Privacy Act (CCPA)* 2023). This law mirrors the European Union's (EU) General Data Protection Regulation (GDPR), which identifies how personal data of someone in the EU can be stored and used. In 2022, the American Data Privacy and Protection Act laid the foundation at the federal level to create oversight and enforcement of information that is collected without the consent of the individual.

Global Digital Privacy Laws

To meet the privacy concerns of its citizens, Nigeria's Data Protection Regulation (NDPR), established in 2019 is identified as "the first comprehensive and overarching regulation" (Jackson & Jackson, 2023). Recognizing one's privacy (even digital privacy) is a human right, NDPR ensures an individual's right to privacy communication technology. Cybersecurity is ensured via government and private sector collaboration penalizing any "unauthorized tampering or modification of data." Specific security measures revolve around Nigeria's Central Bank and other financial institutions.

One of the first countries in the Middle East to implement a digital privacy law, Qatar, recognized an individual's right to privacy, to include their data, as a human right. In 2016, Qatar enacted Law No 13: Personal Data Privacy Protection, identifying that "someone's data shall be processed only within the framework of transparency, honesty, and respect of human dignity, and acceptable practices according to provisions hereof" (Personal Data Privacy Protection, 2016). Fast forward six years, Qatar's aim to achieve the Social Development Goals' 2030 vision, adopted an artificial intelligence strategy to drive innovation, ensure sustainability, and aid in economic growth.

Blockchain Technology

Blockchain technology is one of the most explored technological solutions of this century. This technology stores transactional records or "the block" in several databases or "chains," within a business network. The information recorded on the "digital ledger" includes data, documents, and transactions, which enables the existence of digital or cryptocurrency.

Some experts suggest the chain itself cannot be hacked but the transaction can be manipulated and one's digital assets stolen. These chains have three basic traits: they are decentralized – not controlled by a single entity, peer-to-peer networks – transactions of data and finance and have distributed storage of data – if one "block" is tampered with, the rest of the data is not compromised.

Digital Currencies

You cannot hold it in your hand as you would a United States dollar bill or the United Kingdom's pound sterling. Digital currency is "counted" and transferred using blockchain technology. While digital currency represents tangible currencies, cryptocurrency is cheaper and offers a faster way to conduct business transactions. Countries such as China, India, Nigeria, and the Bahamas have implemented a central bank digital currency, while other countries are in the exploration stage such as Argentina, Brazil, South Korea, Japan, and Russia.

Where many countries have moved toward a centralized digital currency, the US House Financial Services Committee advanced legislation to ban and block the Federal Reserve from creating a Central Bank Digital Currency. This ban on the implementation of a national digital currency protects the citizens of the United States from having funds immediately withdrawn from their accounts, similar to China's social credit policies, due to infractions of the laws (Halaschak, 2023).

The Rise of BRICS (Brazil, Russia, India, China, and South)

In 2006, Brazil, Russia, India, and China created the "BRIC" group, with South Africa joining in 2010. This group was designed to bring together the world's most important developing countries, to challenge the political and economic power of wealthier, Western nations. Thus, allowing emerging economies to have more influence in international politics their desire to move away from the United States Dollar (USD) and toward digital currency. BRICS' goals are to obtain currency that will lead to establishing deeper ties between member nations and cooperate on economic expansion, including trade. BRICS could challenge the dollar as its membership grows and influence global trade.

Ramifications on Public Relations and Strategic Communications

Strategic planning utilizes many of the same tactics, strategies, objectives, and goals in a systemic analysis of an organization's strengths, weaknesses, opportunities, and threats (challenges). The strategy behind public relations campaigns is much like those used in warfare, the "concept for relating means and ends; the kind of strategy – grand, defense, regional, service" that is "deduced from the character of the means and ends" (Builder, 1987, p. v) to synchronize, integrate and direct operations brandishing tactics with accelerated sophistication.

Recognizing the needs of business and society must be integrated into all communications. The incremental measurable targets set for each SDG are easily incorporated into strategic communications plans focused on sharing a company's environmental, social, and governance performance (ESG) by embedding corporate social responsibility (CSR) within the company's operations.

Public relations professionals and academics have long used soft power to 1) help get the outcomes they want; and 2) affect the behavior of various primary and secondary audiences. This soft power has added social media and computer-mediated technology to traditional media communication platforms, to cultivate and maintain relationships to build trust and transparency. The latter orientated to longer-term cultivation of favorability toward target audiences.

The field of public relations can be seen as both art and science; where the practitioner can recognize the resources needed to influence while knowing there is no guarantee they will achieve the outcome wanted. Joseph Nye (2004) suggested transforming those resources into the outcomes wanted "requires well-designed strategies and skillful leadership" (p. 3).

Current Trends

Current communication trends include partnerships between business and government, where businesses recognize the impact of political discourse for better positioning. Technology trends continue to grow and humanity moves forward, therefore, society shapes and is shaped by the technology being used via contextual, emotional, inspired, and physical. The Academic Society for Management and Communication's Communications Trend Radar 2023 report found communication leadership must meet the challenges emerging technologies are having on corporate expectations. These trends include:

1 The revival of government (local, state, federal) and corporate partnerships seeks to rebuild and improve strategic partnerships to leverage co-branding and marketing. This partnership will cause "communication leaders" to reconsider their corporation's position based on the political climate allowing communication professionals to act as a political advisor, particularly during a crisis, acting as a voice for other businesses in the field.
2 Sustainability management when resources are scarce offers organizations an opportunity to respond openly, honestly, and responsibly to meet corporate goals and functional objectives. Preparation for challenges prepares

communication professionals to think and plan creatively, considering even the most outrageous possibility and the consequences of [in]action is vital. One way to develop these skills is through table top discussions to adapt and adopt structures and processes by sharing knowledge and experiences on staying resilient and working under pressure.

3 The future is now, the link between human and artificial intelligence (AI). AI-based technologies enable new forms of interactions between humans and technology through the promise of improving decision-making, productivity, and performing routine tasks. Communication professionals must modify current practices selecting and creating personalized content to meet expectations of their audience. The continuous monitoring helps improve processes and the activities of the corporation.
4 The rise of virtual reality. Emerging technology enables people to create and immerse themselves in new forms of augmented versions of reality, so they can create a completely new experience for consumers. The possibilities, and challenges offered through this new augmented technology will affect stakeholder communication and organization expectations.

Past Trends: Disinformation Campaigns

When considering previous government (i.e., state) run campaigns, based on organized deception or disinformation, distort information throughout all media platforms in order to mislead and influence the audience.

Targeted disinformation campaigns rely on manipulation of facts and planting stories that are then disseminated by an army of unwitting journalists, media conglomerates, and social media influencers. These stories are developed for the transformation of society's basic intellectual, religious, economic, and political institutions. The main objectives of these types of campaigns tend to shift as political elites define new social, economic, and political problems.

Most disinformation campaigns are:

- To influence world public opinion against political programs perceived as threatening.
- To isolate (cancel) those against the campaign being implemented
- To demonstrate that those against the state's campaign are aggressive.
- To discredit those who are cooperating with those against the state and expose them and their personnel.
- To confuse public opinion about a broad range of state and corporate policies and objectives.

Media and social media influencers act as the arm, the tool, and the performing force in disinformation operations. Corporate and governmental goals are set, the target audiences are chosen based on the 17 Sustainable Development Goals developed by the United Nations (UN.org, 2015).

The process of developing and writing a strategic plan is regarded as the most challenging and frustrating task. Hence, the strategy used by communication professionals is the linking of ends and means or developing a "game plan" utilizing limited resources to accomplish identified objectives.

Knowledge (or in this case information) is power. The development and use of social media are spreading both information and disinformation more rapidly than ever before. Once seen as the poor cousin to marketing and/or advertising, public relations (PR) utilize the soft power of social media in their communication strategies. It is through the strategic analysis of its public, working with stakeholders, and managing those relationships between the organization's brand and the public they serve. Strategically using the attractiveness of organizational culture, product or service, and corporate social responsibility (CSR) through engagement, transparency, and ethical representation to their audiences.

A review of research suggests that media constructs the public's idea of reality and plays a significant role in persuading the public to define the event, person, issue, or object through agenda setting or framing (Gamson et al., 1992). This suggests that media frames have the potential to influence public policy definitions, choices, and outcomes, often choosing frames that focus on conflict or controversy. Entman's (1993) cascading network activation model suggests media framing is an organized, targeted attempt by the government to exert as much control as possible over the framing of policies.

Looking Toward 2050

The thought of a social credit system may be approaching reality. Considering the Sustainable Development Goals along with the global implementation of the social credit score, leaves one to believe society is moving toward a dystopian world where society is left with a bigger gap between the rich and poor, depending on one's position on the "list." A society where those who disagree with, and fight back against the definition of "good citizen" will be considered untrustworthy or labeled as someone with "poor behavior."

To gain acceptance of the initiatives set forth by the United Nations, and for organizations to build resilience, strategic communication professionals must develop narratives that articulate scenarios identifying sources, drivers, and amplifiers of a situation. Providing a clear understanding of the benefits of aligning national and organizational plans with the 2030 Agenda and linking the social development goals to national, local, and organizational concerns.

These strategies must be efficient, and transparent, and increase accountability of businesses, governments, non-governmental organizations (NGO), and other stakeholders. They must bridge the information gap and improve knowledge and understanding of the key issues; offering collaboration with counterparts at all levels to ensure ownership of results. This plan must be inclusive and consistent for all stakeholders to achieve success.

The strategies recognize the importance of a common understanding of due diligence and its impact on society and the environment. As technology moves forward, the use of artificial intelligence (AI) to create and analyze content found on radio, social media, and other forms of technology explores the value of information being communicated.

The strategies will ensure influencer technology tailors messages to individual needs and well-being, and higher efficiency of care through the aggregation of data for information sharing. This information will help develop models to define the nature of public services that will occur through improved efficiency and quality through information sharing between professionals and patients.

Toward the Future: 2050 and Beyond

The world lacks a consistent, positive and common narrative that outlines the opportunities and challenges of the fourth industrial revolution – a narrative that is essential if we are to empower a diverse set of individuals and communities and avoid a backlash against the fundamental changes underway. The speed of innovation in terms of both its development and diffusion is faster than ever. But it is not just about speed; returns to scale are equally staggering. Digitization means automation, which in turn means that companies do not incur diminishing returns to scale (or less of them, at least).

In 2013, the Obama Administration lifted the 1972 amendment of the Smith-Mundt Act, that blocked access to domestic audiences to gain access to material originally developed and disseminated to foreign audiences. This reversal now allows media produced by the US Agency for Global Media, to be made available to Americans "upon request."

Other nations are watching, they are watching our news outlets, what is being covered and if there is a global social score system, currency and even net zero emissions electricity source then the communication of what is being shared will be what they want us to see and know as well.

References

Bach, E. (2020, July 27). People with low social credit scores have photos shown at movie theaters. *Back to Jerusalem*. Retrieved from https://backtojerusalem.com/people-with-low-social-credit-scores-have-photo-shown-at-movie-theaters/

Boos, D. (2022a, April 27). *Bologna introduces Social Credit app to promote "virtuous behavior."* The European Conservative. https://europeanconservative.com/articles/news/bologna-introduces-social-credit-app-to-promote-virtuous-behavior/

Boos, D. (2022b, May 18). *Emulating China: How social media groomed US for a Social Credit Score System*. The European Conservative. https://europeanconservative.com/articles/commentary/emulating-china-how-social-media-groomed-us-for-a-social-credit-score-system/

Brambilla, M. (Director) (1993). *Demolition Man* [Film]. Warner Bros.

Builder, C.H. (1987). *The Army in the strategic planning process. Prepared for the United States Army*. RAND Corporation. https://www.rand.org/content/dam/rand/pubs/reports/2006/R3513.pdf

California Consumer Privacy Act (CCPA). State of California – Department of Justice – Office of the Attorney General. (2023, November 9). https://oag.ca.gov/privacy/ccpa

China's Social Credit System: Bertelsmannstifung (Bernhard Bartsch, Martin Gottske, Christian Eisenberg): Free Download, borrow, and streaming. Internet Archive. (n.d.). https://archive.org/details/a4df70a4136e3623302d15e66c6cd2ba-imagejpeg

Committee on Homeland Security & Governmental Affairs. (2023, October 31). *Dr. Paul demands answers from DHS secretary and FBI director on efforts to Suppress Free speech*. https://www.hsgac.senate.gov/media/reps/dr-paul-demands-answers-from-dhs-secretary-and-fbi-director-on-efforts-to-suppress-free-speech/

Communications Trend Radar 2023: For Corporate Management & Communication. Academic Society. (2023, November 5). https://www.akademische-gesellschaft.com/projekt/communications-trend-radar-2023-2/?lang=en

Entman, R. (1993). Framing: Toward clarification of a fractured paradigm. *Journal of Communication*, *43*, 51–58.

Faverio, M. (2023, October 18). *Key findings about Americans and data privacy.* Pew Research Center. https://www.pewresearch.org/short-reads/2023/10/18/key-findings-about-americans-and-data-privacy/

Gamson, W. A., Croteau, D., Hoynes, W., & Sasson, T. (1992). Media images and the social construction of reality. *Annual Review of Sociology, 18,* 373–393 https://doi.org/10.1146annurev.so.18.080192.002105

Gilboa, E. (2007). The CNN effect: The search for a communication theory of international relations. *Political Communication, 22*, 27–24.

Halaschak, Z. (2023, September 20). House republicans advance legislation to block Central Bank Digital Currency. *Washington Examiner*. https://www.washingtonexaminer.com/policy/economy/house-republicans-advance-bill-block-central-bank-digital-currency

HROne. (2023, August 23). *Powerful China social credit system: A guide in 2023.* https://www.hrone.com/blog/china-social-credit-system/#:~:text=Individuals%20are%20scored%20in%20China's,from%20350%20to%20950%20points.

Hvistendahl, M. (2017, December 14). In China, a three-digit score could dictate your place in society. *Wired.* https://www.wired.com/story/age-of-social-credit/#:~:text=Ant%20Financial%20appears%20to%20be,move%20freely%20and%20without%20obstruction.%E2%80%9D

Jackson, E., & Jackson, E. (2023). Spotlight: how are data protection laws enforced in Nigeria? *Lexology.com.* https://www.lexology.com/indepth/the-privacy-data-protection-and-cybersecurity-law-review

Kobie, N. (2019, June 7). The complicated truth about China's social credit system. *Wired.co.UK*. Retrieved from https://www.wired.co.uk/article/china-social-Credit-system-explained

Learmonth, A. (2023, July 19). UK is moving towards a "Chinese-style Social Credit System" warns Nigel Farage. *The Herald*. Retrieved from https://www.heraldscotland.com/news/23665609.uk-moving-towards-chinese-style-social-credit-system-warns-farage/

Maniam, S. (2016, February 19). *Americans feel the tensions between privacy and security concerns*. Pew Research Center. https://www.pewresearch.org/short-reads/2016/02/19/americans-feel-the-tensions-between-privacy-and-security-concerns/

Mastrangelo, E. (2023, May 29). It is spelled "Citizen wallet," it is read "Social credit." And it has arrived in Italy. *Machiavelli*. Retrieved from https://www.centromachiavelli.com/en/2022/05/26/citizen-wallet-bologna-rome-social-credit/

Nye, Jr., J. S. (2004). *Soft power: The means to success in world politics*. Public Affairs.

Orwell, G. (2021). *Nineteen eighty-four*. Penguin Classics.

Personal Data Privacy Protection, Law No. 13 of 2016. (2016). https://assurance.ncsa.gov.qa/sites/default/files/library/2020-11/Law%20No.%20%2813%29%20of%202016%20%20on%20Protecting%20Personal%20Data%20Privacy%20-%20English.pdf

Richmond, B., Sharpe, L., & Menzies, R. E. (2023, October 1). Are fear campaigns effective for increasing adherence to covid-related mitigation measures? *International Journal of Behavioral Medicine*. https://www.ncbi.nlm.nih.gov/pmc/articles/PMC9628502/#:~:text=Using%20fear%20to%20increase%20the,outcomes%20has%20rarely%20been%20considered.

Schwab, K. (2016). *The fourth industrial revolution*. Portfolio Penguin.

Service, C. N. (2023, March 5). San Diego police may use "smart streetlight" surveillance again but wants community input first. *NBC 7 San Diego*. Retrieved from https://www.nbcsandiego.com/news/local/san-diego-police-holding-series-of-community-meetings-to-discuss-smart-streetlight-surveillance-cameras-and-license-plate-readers/3177903/

Tailai, Z., & Walsh, M. (2020, June 3). How Chinese companies are getting off Social Credit Blacklists. *#SixthTone*. Retrieved from https://www.sixthtone.com/news/1005757

United Nations. (2015). *The 17 sustainable development goals*. United Nations. https://www.un.org/en/exhibits/page/sdgs-17-goals-transform-world

8

BEYOND BIG DATA

Striking a Balance

Melissa Dennis

FIGURE 8.1 Big Data word cloud.

Source: Camelia Boban. https://commons.wikimedia.org/wiki/File:BigData_2267x1146_trasparent.png; https://upload.wikimedia.org/wikipedia/commons/4/46/BigData_2267x1146_white.png.

With the proliferation of data and artificial intelligence technologies, public relations and marketing communication managers have more information at their disposal than ever before, and tomorrow they will have even more.

Real-Time Communication and Consumer Tracking

Marketers can now react and communicate in real-time to consumers' actions. If consumers click here and then look here, there is an increase in sales conversion, so

DOI: 10.4324/9781003426653-10

communications are crafted to drive those actions. Gone are the days where results and engagement were a speculation from a bump in sales and conversion, and enter a time where tracking is at such a granular level marketers can see if a consumer clicked, how long they stayed on a page, where they scrolled, what action they took next, and if they ultimately purchase. All these data points are collected to ensure communications are relevant, timely, and targeted. Data has become a currency that has vastly changed the field of strategic marketing communications, but is it all for the better? Walt Disney is famously quoted as saying, "I only hope that we never lose sight of one thing—that it was all started by a mouse" (Disney, 2024). This quote is a reminder that no matter how innovative and technological Disney became, the company does not lose sight of its history, where it began, and what made it a beloved brand. As we consider the past and look toward the future, where will the rise in data take the profession, and will it be essential to remember that authentic consumer relationships of the past all began with a conversation?

Evolution of Big Data and Its Impact

The term "Big Data" can first be found in conference proceedings published by Michael Cox and David Ellsworth. Their article on visualization challenges explains the current situation:

> Visualization provides an interesting challenge for computer systems: data sets are generally quite large, taxing the capacities of main memory, local disk, and even remote disk. We call this the problem of big data. When data sets do not fit in main memory (*in core*), or when they do not fit even on local disk, the most common solution is to acquire more resources.
>
> *(Cox & Ellsworth, 1997, p. 235)*

When managers and researchers began to encounter difficulties analyzing vast volumes of data now made available through Pentium technology and increased data storage that had not previously existed, they sought ways to explore and store this Big Data. The term was first coined to describe the volume. Still, over the decades and the ever-evolving technology landscape, it came to represent not only the volume but also the variety, the speed, and the different sources and structures of the data. Businesses did not just have a lot of data, but they had data from ever-expanding sources in ever-changing formats and at an increasing speed. As we learned to process and analyze Big Data, the volume became less challenging, but the proper interpretation became increasingly problematic.

Shift from Funnel to Customer Journey

Up to today, Big Data, namely consumer tracking data, has profoundly influenced the field of public relations and strategic communications in several ways.

The first considerable change for public relations practitioners came from being able to create more personalized and targeted campaigns. Through consumer tracking, preferences and behaviors became detectable. Marketers could now follow customer behaviors, see messages that elicited higher engagement, and personalize communications. They could craft messages based on the consumer's stage in the funnel and what would drive future interaction. Although this personalization started small, with large segments targeted with broad messages; it became more granular as data became more useable. The customer funnel gave way to the customer journey. PR managers began crafting and outlining the journey their consumers traveled to understand key touchpoints and leverage these moments to create stronger relationships and communications with greater relevancy.

Journey mapping became critical in relationship building as PR experts were no longer pushing messages but creating dialog to help solve the challenges and problems consumers were experiencing. Each stage of the journey became less about how far down the funnel a consumer was and more about where they were in their journey to understand the challenges they may be experiencing. Marketers crafted messages to help solve problems and answer these hurdles at different stages of a journey with an understanding that it was not perfectly linear but traveled back and forth through many touchpoints and engagements. Journeys "stopped being linear and began to feature feedback and causal relationship loops." (Steward et al., 2019, p. 293) The PR and messaging role became that of a problem solver, and communications became driven by relevancy and benefit for the consumer. Traditional brand launch, promotional, and product placement campaigns led to highly customized and targeted communications aligned with consumer preferences and behaviors. Firms shifted to reputation management campaigns, cause marketing, and public affairs as consumers showed interest in understanding the company they were buying. While digital, e-commerce, and mobile tracking proved instrumental in understanding journeys and behaviors, social media proved the king of understanding preferences.

Importance of Social Media Listening

Social media listening allows brands to track mentions, sentiment, and engagement at levels only available once through market research tactics. Undertakings such as interviews, focus groups, surveys, feedback forms, customer service interactions, and online reviews and ratings were once the only way PR managers gained insight into consumer concerns and views. Techniques that were often slow, costly, and not fully encompassing. Social media allows for the rapid sharing of information, a conduit for connecting and learning, and an opportunity for consumers and firms to provide feedback in the moment. From manual scrapping of comments and counting of words, to platforms designed to mine posts, measuring social sentiment has become an important metric. Consumer tracking on social media enables PR teams to monitor in real-time and craft messages invaluable to brand and crisis management. Sometimes called "opinion mining" because it is "all about digging into the words and context of social posts to understand the opinions they reveal" (Newberry, 2022). It highlighted the importance of timely consumer feedback and usable data in this rapidly changing environment. Data quantity was growing daily, quality was improving, and there needed to be a way to make it more functional in real-time.

Rise of Big Data Tools and Integrations

Big Data tools began to rise and promised real-time analytics. The PR professional's role began to encompass responding to and monitoring these timely trends in the market to craft impactful conversations with consumers and develop adaptable strategies. Marketers could connect in ways they had never experienced with relevancy and personalization beyond a name. Unified Data Platforms integrating a myriad of Big Data tools allowed organizations to manage and simplify the complexity of the data. Machine Learning (ML) was integrated into Big Data platforms to enable firms to process large data sets efficiently. Organizations created roles to address these new skills, and companies invested in training DataOps and Data Governance experts. DataOps teams created practices to increase collaboration and efficient communications between data engineers and teams utilizing the data.

In comparison, Data Governance tools and specialists found ways to increase consumer data quality, compliance, and privacy. The focus was on finding ways to increase the speed and accuracy of data and enhance communications relevancy to consumers. The data existed, the processes needed to be created to capitalize on that data in real-time, and PR managers needed to find efficient ways to use it to adapt their strategies. It was an era of testing, learning, and optimizing to find the perfect fit. In all of this, and with all of this, public relations saw a grand improvement in metrics and key performance indicators that now drove strategic decisions.

Impact on Metrics and Key Performance Indicators

Improved measurement and metrics from campaigns changed the role and function of marketing and public relations within organizations. Strategies and communications were now tracked without delay, and engagement levels, sentiment, and conversion metrics drove data-driven decision-making. No longer were strategies based solely on sometimes outdated consumer research studies; Big Data allowed PR professionals to gather and analyze trends in consumer behavior at granular levels and speeds like never before. Preferences and trends change quickly, and Big Data allows us to respond and anticipate trends. Strategies were substantiated with metrics and findings and tested immediately in campaigns and communications. Conversions were forecasted with greater accuracy to determine sales and deliver more substantial returns.

Increased noise and clutter in digital media drove a need for fewer but more impactful messages that created relationships with audiences, and Big Data delivered.

While the positives associated with Big Data are abundant for both consumers and firms, the reliance on tracking, metrics, and consumer sentiment programs, while appearing to move us closer together, may create a gap between the two parties. This gap may widen even more in the next few years as firms' adoption of innovative technology increases. Public relations and marketing communications managers will drive even more enhanced personalization with customization capabilities catering to individual needs. Video, a popular medium for reaching consumers, has outstanding personalization abilities that are now attainable with increasingly reliable data. "It creates unlimited opportunities to establish bonds and keep us connected with those around us, especially in this time of digital transformation." (Vidyard, 2023) Well-crafted messages based on an individual's behavior, preferences, and journey are sure to remain center stage.

Rise of Experiential Marketing

Along with this increased personalization, PR managers are seeing their role increasingly integrated with new and emerging technologies. While artificial intelligence has existed for years, the prolific emergence of tools and adoption will dramatically alter how firms interact with consumers. AI language tools can craft messages and press releases. It can automate responses and communications based on behaviors and engagement. They effectively monitor digital content, social media, and websites to detect mentions and consumer sentiment. This technology allows practitioners to understand how their target audience responds to their content in real-time. Leaning on AI tools allows repetitive tasks to be disseminated, permitting PR professionals to focus on building and creating lifetime relationships with their consumers.

Similarly, chatbots routinely handle first, second, and third inquiries in online interactions. The benefit is providing routine answers to commonly asked questions and fine-tuning them to solve on the first interaction, saving the consumer and the firm time. Predictive analytics provide insights from historical data to predict how PR campaigns will perform and assist in detecting a possible PR crisis early by recognizing patterns in online conversations. Firms can proactively respond rather than wait and react. These benefits allow for greater efficiency and effectiveness in communicating with consumers, but all put layers between firms and the consumer.

As market competition becomes fierce in a global economy, firms must find a way to differentiate themselves and their products and services. Many have shifted to experiential marketing to connect with consumers through storytelling and interactive experiences. Over the next few years, expect to see a rise in augmented reality (AR) and virtual reality (VR) as PR practitioners look to find ways to immerse their audience in their offerings and differentiate from their competition. At the same time, they are allowing consumers an interactive experience like never before, which will remove some of the in-person interaction from PR professional's roles. The current landscape has technology use on a continual upward trajectory with no forecasted end in sight. Increased reliance on consumer tracking. Shifts in targeted and personalized campaigns. Continually integrating Big Data tools and AI for real-time analytics and data-driven strategies. Along with a focus on quality data and predictive analytics for data-driven decisions. A rise in chatbots and AI-crafted messages, press releases, and automated responses will occur, but is this where the profession will end?

Trends Toward the Future and Ethical Dilemmas

The benefits of employing real-time tracking and metrics to determine success are overwhelming. Moreover, AI-driven messaging offers essential efficiencies for PR managers. Despite these evident benefits, there are concerns about the use of technology in the field. As we invest and adopt increasingly innovative platforms and technologies, an expanded gap emerges between the PR practitioner and the consumer. Language-driven AI has already flagged hidden biases in the language and programming, and consumers have expressed concern about the lack of transparency in firms using these programs. Audiences want to be aware that they are not speaking to a person so they do not feel slighted and fooled that a bot is communicating with them. Headlines have cautioned media outlets about using language AI, such as ChatGPT, to write articles and create AI-generated photos of fictional authors. The public met news of its use with outrage and apprehension (Leitch, 2023). As campaigns become more data-driven than those of the past, there will be an increased need for PR teams and strategies to become more culturally sensitive. Will computers and AI understand the diverse cultures and nuances necessary to communicate with audiences relevantly and with cultural sensitivity?

There are also numerous ethical and privacy concerns as PR professionals become more reliant on consumer tracking. Many global and international firms already comply with the strict standards of the General Data Protection Regulation (GDPR) that came into effect in 2018 within the European Union (EU) and European Economic Area (EEA). However, all firms should expect greater regulations and more significant fines for non-compliance. PR and communications professionals must be aware and employ strict methods to obtain consumer consent, outline data rights reasonably and comprehensively, communicate data breaches quickly and clearly, and ensure data protection in all systems utilized. This data-driven, consumer-tracking, technology-integrating landscape strongly influences the PR professional's role and the skill set and knowledge they must obtain.

The Changing Role of Public Relations

The influence of these trends on the role of public relations is substantial. Public Relations and strategic communications now require a high level of data literacy. Many practitioners need proficiency in understanding and relaying large datasets to stakeholders to drive future decisions. It is not enough to understand the data and findings but to know how to disseminate this information comprehensibly and showcase critical metrics to drive success. There is no longer a lack of data but a challenge in understanding what data is critical. The field has always been one of adaptability as the environment and consumer behaviors so rapidly shift. However, it will be unprecedented as new technologies emerge, requiring integration and conscientious implementation. PR practitioners have always put the consumer first, but they will have more responsibility than ever to ensure ethical usage of data and navigating applications and technology. The use of social media has taken on deeper ethical considerations in just the past five years. In a 2022 study by Pew Research, investigators found that while 65% believe social media makes us more informed, 84% believe it has made people "easier to manipulate with false information and rumors" (Wike et al., 2022). This view is a concern that PR professionals must answer by ensuring rigor in their investigation of information before posting. The past few decades have seen a shift from push to pull messaging and an increased shift from pushing products to solving problems. PR must understand consumer needs and address whether and how a product or service can solve that need. Roles are shifting now and will do so even more by 2050.

Toward 2050: Balancing Technology and Human Connection

Data is not slowing down. It was estimated that at the start of 2020, there were 44 zettabytes of data in the world, and forecasted that by 2025, 463 exabytes of data will be generated daily (Vuleta, 2021). If the PR and marketing communications industry continues its data-driven trajectory, computers will process and message consumers throughout every engagement and touchpoint. They will utilize complex and detailed data, requiring professionals more time and resources to analyze and provide context than they will have available. This absence of a human voice will make communications emotionless and mechanical and lack the authenticity of a human touch. Messages will feel less like a helping hand and more like a bombardment of information gathered through personal data that may feel intrusive and unrequested. As consumers become aware of how their data is collected and used, significantly targeted messages may drive increased concerns about privacy. Along with this complexity will come a lack of transparency as professionals lose sight of how data is used and for what purpose. This lack of clarity can reduce consumers' trust in firms, which takes years to build and minutes to destroy.

Along with the amount of data to sort through, there will be missed nuances understood through human connection and emotion. Brands will become bland and forgettable, and consumers will be seen as statistics and targets of marketing messages. Audiences will lose interest and engagement as human connection fades from communication and data takes over. As content becomes uninspired and formulaic, consumers will tune out messages they suspect are computer-generated, and engagement will wane. Relationships will become superficial, and messages will lack depth and connection. As we head toward 2050, how do we balance Big Data's strategic opportunities with the human connection consumers still want?

A detectable trend forecasts a possible tapering of dependence on technology and innovation as practitioners seek to create a better balance between data, AI, and communications. Practitioners and firms will share extraordinary moments not in real time but in real space. Society will want less of a perfectly manicured experience and response and more of a warm, honest conversation with firms. Practitioners and messaging managers must embrace this role of relationship builders and create a meaningful dialog with their audience beyond an AI language-generated response. It will be an environment of continuous learning to stay abreast of industry changes and the increasing role of transparency, ethical considerations, and truth. PR roles will become more technology-focused in many ways. However, they will also require the ability to blend, to understand the importance of discovering the why behind actions and trackable metrics, and to talk to consumers. We expect the field to develop ethical frameworks for deploying technology, exchanging information, and fostering trust in a dynamic landscape. We will no longer push messages to influence consumers to buy or act; we will preserve relationships through relevant, trustworthy, and authentic consumer relationships. Technology will enhance how we can achieve this, but it will require people to connect with people to realize the actual lifetime value.

Soon, the increase in technology and tracking and Big Data will be immense. However, as time passes, there will be a tapering off not in integrating data and creating new technology but in relying on machine learning to drive our strategic decisions and develop relationships. There will be a blending of technology and hands-on market research where the two entwine to create memorable experiences for our consumers and maximize the effectiveness of our PR teams.

The year 2050 will see unprecedented acknowledgment of practitioners as gatekeepers to consumer data navigating with higher ethical and cultural considerations. Conscious of biases and cultural sensitivities. It will be a time when we meet, with data support, to find common ground, solve challenges, and create innovative answers. In a recent Disney World ad, the company showcased magic as the emotion and excitement of the Guest. They showed a man relaxing in a pool, a child overcome with excitement at a sing-along, and the love of an engagement proposal in front of the castle. In a company that prides itself on innovative technology and experiences for its Guests, its new ad showcases that the Guests and that relationship still need to come first. PR practitioners must constantly learn and understand the importance of transparency and authenticity in what is said and done and remain adaptable, innovative, and, most importantly, ethical in this rapidly changing environment. As technology advances and provides efficiency and effectiveness, PR must create a foundation of ethics to navigate the role.

Public relations and strategic communications have witnessed a significant evolution, transitioning from traditional push messages to the general public to dealing with vast amounts of data and metrics. With the emergence of tools like real-time analytics, AI, and language tools, campaigns have become more sophisticated and personalized than ever before. Amidst these changes, one constant remains: change itself. Public relations and strategic communications managers must constantly learn and adapt, which will hold well beyond 2050. As Walt Disney said many years ago, "I only hope that we never lose sight of one thing—that it was all started by a mouse." The hope with the public relations profession is that we never lose sight of one thing: it all begins and ends with a conversation.

Works Cited

Cox, M., & Ellsworth, D. (1997). Application-controlled demand paging for out-of-core visualization. In *Proceedings of the 8th IEEE visualization '97 conference* (pp. 235–244), Phoenix, AZ.

Disney, W. (2024). D23 the offical Disney Fan Club. *D23*. Retrieved from https://d23.com/walt-disney-quote/page/5/

Leitch, W. (2023, November 30). Opinion: What the sports illustrated AI debacle is telling us. *CNN*. Retrieved from https://www.cnn.com/2023/11/29/opinions/sports-illustrated-ai-controversy-leitch/index.html

Newberry, C. (2022, September 29). Social media sentiment analysis: Tools, tips, and more. *Hootsuite Blog*. Retrieved from https://blog.hootsuite.com/social-media-sentiment-analysis-tools/

Steward, M. D., Narus, J. A., Roehm, M. L., & Ritz, W. (2019). From transactions to journeys and beyond: The evolution of B2B buying process modeling. *Industrial Marketing Management, 83*, 288–300.

Vidyard. (2023, July 15). Personalized video: Everything you need to know. *Vidyard.* Retrieved from https://www.vidyard.com/blog/personalized-video/

Vuleta, B. (2021, October 28). *How Much Data Is Created Every Day? +27 Staggering Stats.* Retrieved from SeedScientific: Seedscientific.com/how-much-data-is-created-every-day/

Wike, R., Silver, L., Fetterolf, J., Huang, C., Austin, S., Clancy, L., & Gubbala, S. (2022, December 6). *Social media seen as mostly good for democracy across many nations, but U.S. is a major outlier*. Pew Research Center.

9

BEHIND THE VELVET ROPE

Influencers and Creators as the Future Entertainment Celebrities in Public Relations

Kate Stewart and Karen Freberg

Introduction

The ability to become known as an individual in the 21st century has never been easier, thanks to the ability to be part of the global social and digital media ecosystem. Brands, consumers, and creators alike now can create, disseminate, and entertain audiences by sharing their content with the global community. Creative activations and influencer campaigns have specifically been on the rise for marketing communication efforts, which draws on the most important currency in today's market: attention. Attention is the most valuable currency as it allows audiences to remember, recall, and act upon what is shared in the campaign and efforts from these entities.

In this chapter, the authors will discuss the rise and presence of social media as an entertainment vehicle, the influence of creators and influencers as entertainers, specific cases that showcase these key characteristics in social media and entertainment, and future trends and directions that are needed in social media and entertainment research and practice.

Literature Review

Understanding Social Media Influencers and Creators

One of the main areas of focus in the marketing communication and public relations literature over the past decade has surrounded around the concept of a social media influencer. Social media influencers (SMIs) have been conceptualized as individuals who shape attitudes through blogs, tweets, and other social media updates (Freberg et al., 2011). While this definition focused on the overall

DOI: 10.4324/9781003426653-11

impact an SMI has on their community, Enke and Borchers (2019) defined SMIs more specifically related to their specific deliverables and functions within a particular campaign or initiative they are a part of. Both Freberg et al. (2011) and Enke and Borchers (2019) agree that SMIs represent a new category of individuals who can shape opinions and influence action. Yet, their overall place within the social and entertainment ecosystem is a bridge between celebrities (the entertainment world), family and friends (the normal world), and the digital community (the social media world), which allows them to navigate all spaces for specific opportunities and experiences (Blanche et al., 2021).

Yet, SMIs are often described or grouped with other associated terms such as third-party endorsers, opinion leaders, brand ambassadors, and brand advocates. Khamis et al. (2017) argued that becoming an influencer is a three-step process. Influencers build a personal brand around a select niche or subject area. Through strategic communication, these social media content creators build celebrity status within a group of dedicated followers (which Khamis et al. refer to as "micro-celebrity" status), expanding to widespread recognition and, eventually, influencer status. Therefore, branding and context are critical to influencer status.

Trust and authenticity are also two valuable components SMIs need to maintain and invest in. These are what bring all the opportunities and community members together – without trust and authenticity in their community, an SMI would be nothing. Most SMIs, who are engaged with their communities and audiences, have the credibility and trust of these individuals based on the investment, passion, and enthusiasm they share on a related topic, issue, or industry.

Duties and Responsibilities of an Influencer

Like all professionals, the duties and roles of an SMI continue to rise, grow, and evolve as the community and technology change. The main purpose many researchers have assigned influencers is to serve as a spokesperson and community advocate to shift behavior, change attitudes, and create a dialog with their community (Djafarova & Rushworth, 2017).

A large body of scholarship on influencer marketing has found that audiences feel a strong sense of connection and trust with SMIs (Kim et al., 2021; Reinikainen et al., 2020; Tukachinsky & Stever 2019), leading to positive organization and brand communication outcomes (Lou & Yuan, 2019). Community members consider SMIs as experts and trust them as credible sources on a particular subject area or niche (Khamis et al., 2017).

SMIs become an asset through their content creation and communication ability to reach and engage audiences on a large scale (Borchers, 2019; Borchers & Enke, 2021). Some pursue unethical means of becoming SMIs by gathering fake followers and misleading rates of engagement (Blanche et al., 2021). In essence, an SMI disseminates knowledge, engages in dialog, and reaches a vast audience with their insights and perspectives.

In addition, SMIs also must be skilled in navigating and building upon relationships. The role of an SMI between an organization and their community is key as it serves as a sustainable bridge to build trust, engagement, and authenticity through the partnership the SMI has with the brand. In an environment of diminished attention to organizational and brand communication (Galloway, 2017; Yang & Saffer, 2020) influencers not only serve as promoters of organizational communication but also help build and maintain relationships.

SMIs also can change or impact public opinion (Hudders et al., 2020). Influencers have been used in many different facets in being used for political campaigns, government campaigns (ex. COVID vaccine), and even be used for propaganda campaigns for digital warfare (ex. Ukraine and Russia war via Telegram). More research in this area needs to be explored as a rising topic of focus for study and practice. SMIs have a proven role in branding (Zeljko et al., 2018). Therefore, central to studying and working with SMIs is understanding how they influence and impact consumer and stakeholder decision-making.

Social Media Influencer Typology

The other aspect of the marketing communication and public relations literature that is heavily focused is exploring the different types of influencers. Historically, most of the work has focused on conceptualizing an influencer based on their follower count, not their impact and presence in the field, which needs to be noted for the future.

In addition, the challenge that faces researchers in this space is the fact that there is a wide variety of characteristics including expertise, brand persona, network size and composition, and seemingly countless others. Recent efforts to classify influencers have been based on network size (Campbell & Farrell, 2020; Himelboim & Golan, 2019). Campbell and Farrell (2020) created a network size-based typology of influencers, which has been one of the most studied frameworks (Alassani & Göretz, 2019; Au-Yong-Oliveira et al., 2019; Boerman, 2020; Guzman & Lewis, 2020; Hudders et al., 2021; Isyanto et al., 2020). This typology of influencers breaks down influencers into four categories: mega-influencers, macro-influencers, micro-influencers, and nano-influencers (Conde & Casais, 2023).

The first category is the mega-influencers have a large following and extensive presence on social media and are considered "Internet famous." They have the potential to be recognized as internet famous globally with a status like traditional celebrities with the ability to reach the masses and have high visibility and recognition, but this usually leads to less engagement from the audience as they may be tired of the high volume of ads and commercial talk making them seem less relatable (Conde & Casais, 2023).

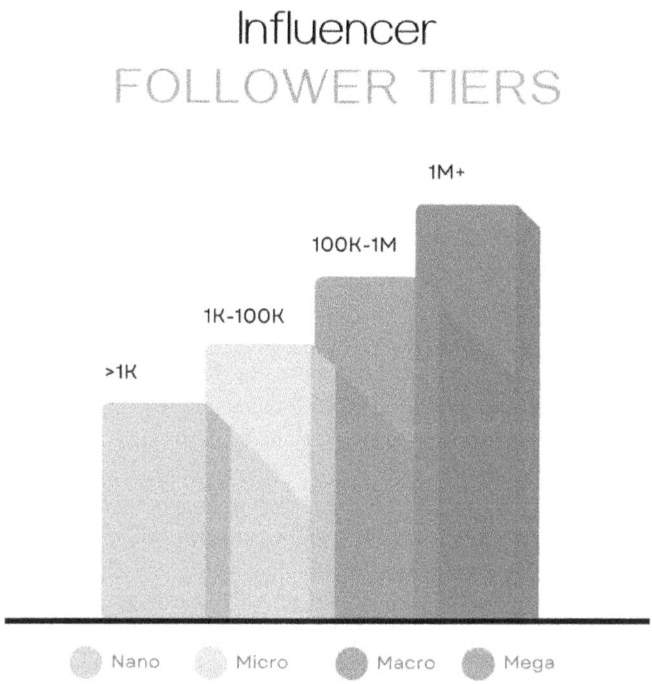

FIGURE 9.1 Influencer follower tiers chart.

Source: Author: Kate Stewart.

Macro-influencers are individuals who have built a following on social media due to their presence, content, and engagement with the community. These influencers could cross over from just being an influencer with a substantial following, to one that is recognized amongst diverse audiences. Macro-influencers have a substantial number of loyal followers, but a more diverse audience allowing for a higher reach and better return on investment when compared to micro-influencers but lack the potential engagement rates that micro-influencers receive (Conde & Casais, 2023).

Micro-influencers have a smaller following, but they can be a source of considerable buzz because of their ability to cultivate strong niche communities. Micro-influencers display characteristics of having a strong voice in one niche community and have a loyal audience with higher levels of trust and authenticity, but in turn, have a lower reach and visibility causing large-scale activation to be harder and could lead to less return on investment.

Finally, nano-influencers are those individuals who are early in their careers and are also a highly researched group due to their growing impact and presence in the industry and their high engagement rates (Au-Yong-Oliveira et al., 2019; Campbell & Farrell, 2020).

SMIs versus Creators

The varying defining characteristics that set SMIs apart from one another, also begs the question of how SMIs differ from creators. Many social media users and people throw out creators and SMIs interchangeably, but there are real differences between the two. Creators are highly creative and aim to entertain, educate, and add value while SMIs may or may not be creative and aim to influence or convince to purchase. Another reason is that the term an SMI has become tied to negative connotations, resulting in some peer pressure and unfortunate press in the industry.

Being labeled as a creator has more positive connotations and views, which makes some SMIs label themselves as a creator, but still in reality an SMI. For this chapter, we define creators as a more focused niche of SMIs who create and execute original content in their voices for their community and partners on and offline.

As noted, creators are indeed different in some ways from SMIs. First, creators and social media influencers are creating content or user-generated content (UGC), but influencers take it a step further by trying to influence the consumer or social media user to buy a product or service. Creators create content for various online and social media platforms while influencers post sponsored content or paid advertisements to influence their audience.

Second, creators get to solely focus on creating captivating, interesting, professional-quality content that could then be used by a brand for marketing or sales strategies while influencers focus on engagement and community-building with their followers. SMIs have been conceptualized as individuals who shape attitudes through blogs, tweets, and other social media updates. SMIs do represent a new category of opinion leaders, with a position somewhere between celebrities and friends, that has emerged with the growth of social media opportunities (West, 2022).

Advantages and Disadvantages of SMIs and Creators

There are advantages and disadvantages to consider when working with a creator or an SMI. The needs of the brand will determine who is the better partner and to even consider a hybrid approach of using someone who is a content creator and influencer.

The advantages of content creators include high-quality content, multifaceted talent opportunities for content creation, and may save time and money. Some disadvantages of creators are fewer promotional opportunities with content creators having a smaller or less engaged community as influencers and possibly a lack of process if the content creator is more inexperienced. Some advantages of using influencers are they have a higher ability to build trust and be believable compared to a brand, they have access to a more diverse and expansive following, and they can be niche-specific in their targeting. The disadvantages of working with an influencer are the limited or lack of content expertise when it comes to putting together a campaign and you must carefully vet influencers to make sure the audience is truly engaged and that they will be receptive to branded messages because the results will not come if the content comes off as disingenuous or spammy (Trend, 2022).

Battlefield of SMIs in the Entertainment Industry

Social media is a haven for individuals to build their brand, identity, and following by showcasing their prowess to become social media influencers (Jin et al., 2019). However, SMIs have become increasingly aware of the implications of their actions on social media platforms with the rise of cancel culture.

Ngyuen (2020) defines cancel culture as a form of social media activism that encourages the probation of individuals, corporations, and institutions that do not align with public ideals. For the purpose of this chapter, cancel culture operates within the confines of social media due to the recent phenomenon of public shaming of SMIs (Holman, 2020). Key tenets of cancel culture under the umbrella of computer-mediated communication (CMC) include forms of cyberbullying, outstanding follower loss in a short time, and potential loss of employment or brand affiliation. Traditional celebrities that faced cancel culture from the entertainment world on social media include Kim Kardashian (ex. Balenciaga scandal), James Gunn (ex. racist tweets that got him fired, but then rehired after a time to direct Guardians of the Galaxy Vol. 3), and Jonathan Masters (ex. Marvel and Creed III actor allegedly being accused abuse allegations).

Many influencers rise to fame because of their content or personality or trends that emerge on Instagram or TikTok. These accounts go viral and continue creating content that peaked the audience's attention in the first place which allows for consistency and expectations to be met. Then, these influencers continue to adapt and learn and grow relationships with these audiences to build a dedicated following. Some examples of recent influencers that have gained a following and risen to fame include:

Becoming the Face of TikTok

Charli D'Amelio is a social media personality who became popular because of her trending dances on TikTok and now has grown a massive following leading to her family having their own television show on Hulu, featured in films like StarDog and TurboCat and being a part of and the winner of season 31 of Dancing with the Stars.

Showing the Impact to Help Others

Keith Lee has been dubbed as TikTok's favorite food reviewer with a booming 2023 as he goes around to locally owned businesses with little to no customers and gives an honest review with a rating of their food and drink items. These restaurants then see a boom in business because people want to eat where Keith Lee eats. He has more than 10 million followers now on the platform and has collaborated with MrBeast, partnered with Good Morning America to help small businesses on their popular YouTube series "People vs Food" and has been honored as an industry disruptor listed on TikTok's inaugural Visionary Voices list in February of 2023.

Finding a Niche

Alix Earle started to see a quick increase in followers in December of 2022 by becoming popular for her Get Ready With Me (GRWM) videos and the drama around her MLB boyfriend. These daily GRWM videos are the key to her ever-growing fanbase because she gets very candid with her followers and speaks on very intimate struggles like her acne journey, negative experience with sorority recruitment, and the decision to get a breast augmentation. She is 22 and a senior at the University of Miami and though she goes on massive brand trips to exotic places, she posts relatable, down-to-earth college lifestyle content like her room tour of disorganized college apartments, highlighting her roommates frequently, writing papers hours before deadlines, and going to fraternity parties.

Amplifying Personality

Puss University and #passthatpuss was started by Jake Shane who is dubbed a rising TikTok comedy star who might be the funniest and most anxious guy on the app. He has risen to fame because of his comedy reaction videos he makes acting out different scenes. He went viral by acting out Bill Clinton denying his relationship with Monica Lewinsky and continues to get millions of views on his TikTok videos he makes with comedic relief to serious events.

Looking Forward to 2050

With the growing focus and emphasis on influencer marketing, public relations scholars and practitioners need to acknowledge the significant evolution of this specialized area in the profession. The concept of SMIs is marked both by promising and concerning challenges that will shape and evolve the public relations profession. Predicting the exact state of SMIs and creators in 2050 is highly speculative, given the rapid evolution of technology and societal trends, we can make some educated guesses based on current trajectories.

The challenges for future research and applied practices in influencer marketing are large, which include the following that need to be discussed. However, with all challenges, come solutions and opportunities for future research, scholarship, and discussion. This is a call by the authors for more theoretical and applied discussions related to addressing some of these challenges with viable, sustainable, and strategic solutions.

- **Advanced AI Influencers**. By 2050, it is conceivable that artificial intelligence (AI) could power a new generation of SMIs. These AI-generated SMIs may be indistinguishable from humans, capable of understanding and engaging with audiences in deeply personalized ways. With these potential advancements, there could also be a lack of success due to a decline in trust and authenticity with high integration of AI-generated SMIs on social platforms. This would also be a challenge for practitioners who choose SMIs for campaigns because they may make it necessary that it is a human SMI in case they want to integrate them into traditional communication efforts or activations and brand trips.
- **Regulatory Changes**. As the influencer marketing and creator industry continues to prevail as a money maker, there will be stricture guidelines to ensure transparency and authenticity. There will be more stringent disclosure requirements and higher levels of scrutiny related to sponsored content to combat deceptive advertising. This will impact the SMI or creator as well as the brands and companies that they partner with for campaigns.
- **Emergence of New Platforms**. We have seen online behaviors shift when TikTok emerged to prominence in recent years and by 2050, there could be many more new platforms that emerge to reshape the landscape of SMIs, creators, and their audiences. These platforms may introduce novel formats and opportunities for SMIs and creators to connect with audiences, challenging established players, and fostering innovation in the industry. This will make contracts potentially shift between SMIs and brands to incorporate new strategies and platforms into the content that will be shared. Anytime a new platform emerges into the market, it is a new set of tools, UX/UI design, and affordances that must be learned and tested to determine best practices. This is time-consuming for those creating strategies for a brand-new platform.
- **Future Impact of Influencer Marketing**. More brands, agencies, and professionals are getting into the area of influencer marketing, which has arisen in the marketing communication and public relations sector as a rising specialization of focus. However, there has been limited work exploring the relationship aspect of SMIs and brands as the focus has been on influencer marketing.
- **Rise of Influencer Relations**. Influencer relations is "the strategic communication function that initiates and develops mutually beneficial relationships

with influencers for long-term benefit and community impact for both influencer and organization," (Smith et al., 2023). With publicists, brands, movie studios, and other entertainment partners, the importance of building, maintaining, and growing these relationships will be of the utmost importance in navigating these new opportunities and challenges.

- **Decline of Trust for Influencers**. With the increasing commercialization of influencer marketing, audiences are becoming more discerning, demanding genuine connections and transparency. Maintaining authenticity will be crucial for influencers and brands alike, requiring public relations professionals to navigate ethical considerations and ensure alignment between influencers and their audience's values.
- **Activating Influencers for Disinformation and Fake News Initiatives**. Artificial intelligence (AI) and virtual SMIs are already here, but the use of them in an entertainment purpose and campaign will need to be explored further. The question will arise not only if but can this be done for entertainment purposes, but it will also be *should it* be done. The new battlefield for influencers will be a social-first, digitally driven hostile environment where the question is not what the battle is about, but who is driving the narrative. Influencers will be a part of this equation and the essential mouthpiece for messages that could have life-or-death consequences. While most cases in public relations campaigns focus on influencers being used for positive circumstances, the rise of influencers being used to promote disinformation, fake news, and crisis situations to mislead audiences is on the rise.
- **Employees as SMIs and Creators**. As noted throughout this chapter, in marketing communication and public relations literature, there are many cases where employees are being used to be the face of an organization's campaign, which is a platform that could potentially serve as a springboard for future opportunities for the employee to become an SMI. Studies have shown with brands like Peloton that employees could be used as SMIs to capture attention and bring forth value, even though they are working for a brand (Boatwright & Freberg, 2023). Organizations and brands that integrate the SMI culture for their employees from within can create powerful connections and touch points with audiences and community members.
- **SMI Mental Health and Wellness Practices**. The amount of pressure, attention, and demand that is forced onto a creator or SMI is unlike others. Understanding the challenges, risks, as well as solutions that need to be noted and practiced for SMIs and creators in the mental health and wellness space is very important. Creator Remi Bader and actress and Rare Beauty founder Selena Gomez both have noted this in their content on social media, which does need to be explored further. With the high pressure and focus on the entertainment sector, this effort should be explored from both the research and practical standpoint as it relates to SMIs and creators.

- **Legal and Ethical Challenges for SMIs.** The legal and ethical components of these factors need to be explored further along with the rise of emerging challenges that have the overall impact of bringing even more challenges for high-profile entertainment and SMIs in the space.

Along with research, there will continue to see brands work with influencers and even more so niche or micro-influencers that have a stronger, more authentic relationship with their group of followers. SMis will continue to take up most of the advertising and marketing budget for companies and brands. In fact, the Influencer Marketing Hub reports that in 2016 influencer marketing was worth $1.7 billion, in 2022 the market size grew to $16.4 billion and is estimated for 2023 to be worth $21.1 billion (Geyser, 2023).

With platforms like Lemon8, Post, and BlueSky emerging, we are seeing more and more apps or brands trying to make these users friendly and more accessible for creators. We are seeing social commerce as a whole boom with Instagram allowing users to tap and shop on posts for brands which is creating new opportunities for brand sponsorships and an increase in users following through with purchasing products from the posts. With the political climate, we will continue to see more Twitter influencers emerge as thought leaders around the election and the societal climate will lead to LinkedIn influencers emerging especially with B2B campaigns focusing on business owners and executives and with LinkedIn launching their creator mode which helps professionals get kickstart into the influencer world.

Conclusion

The entertainment world – traditional and emerging – will continue to be a factor of focus for researchers and practitioners in the marketing communication and public relations profession.

There are many challenges and opportunities to explore for both public relations scholars and practitioners. Overall, what the future of influencer marketing presents a vibrant ground for research, practice, and integration of theoretical and applied strategies. We have to better understand the theoretical foundations necessary for SMIs and relationship building, but also look into the legal, ethical, and professional evolution of influencer marketing efforts in our research to better understand the long-term effects of these practices in society and the business community.

The future of influencer marketing for public relations is in a position of growth and evolution, with elements of obstacles that surround the issues pertaining to authenticity, trust, challenging audience behavior, and digital warfare parties in crisis communication. Both researchers and practitioners have to navigate these challenges with viable and integrated solutions to capitalize on opportunities that will drive effective, transparent, and positive changes forward for the industry.

Overall, while the specifics of influencer marketing and the creator industry in 2050 are uncertain, it is clear that the phenomenon will continue to evolve in response to technological advancements, changing consumer behaviors, and regulatory developments. Brands and SMIs will need to adapt and innovate to stay relevant in this dynamic and competitive landscape.

References

Alassani, R., & Göretz, J. (2019). Product placements by micro and macro influencers on instagram. In G. Meiselwitz (Ed.), *Social computing and social media. Communication and social communities* (pp. 251–267). Springer International Publishing. https://doi.org/10.1007/978-3-030-21905-5_20

Au-Yong-Oliveira, M., Cardoso, A. S., Goncalves, M., Tavares, A., & Branco, F. (2019). Strain effect—A case study about the power of nano-influencers. In *2019 14th Iberian conference on information systems and technologies (CISTI)*, pp. 1–5, Coimbra, Portugal. https://doi.org/10.23919/CISTI.2019.8760911

Blanche, D., Casaló, L. V., Flavián, M., & Ibáñez-Sánchez, S. (2021). Understanding influencer marketing: The role of congruence between influencers, products, and consumers. *Journal of Business Research, 132*, 186–195. https://doi.org/10.1016/j.jbusres.2021.03.067

Boatwright, B., & Freberg, K. (2023). Exploring the multi-modal corporate influencers: A case study of Peloton instructors' engagement, community building, and branding functions. *International Journal for Strategic Communication, 17*, 134–150. https://doi.org/10.1080/1553118X.2022.2152341

Boerman, S. C. (2020). The effects of the standardized Instagram disclosure for micro-and meso-influencers. *Computers in Human Behavior, 103*, 199–207. https://doi.org/10.1016/j.chb.2019.09.015

Borchers, N. S. (2019). Editorial: Social media influencers in strategic communication. *International Journal of Strategic Communication, 13*(4), 255–260. https://doi.org/10.1080/1553118X.2019.1634075

Borchers, N. S., & Enke, N. (2021). Managing strategic influencer communication: A systematic overview on emerging planning, organization, and controlling routines. *Public Relations Review, 47*(3), 102041. https://doi.org/10.1016/j.pubrev.2021.102041

Campbell, C., & Farrell, J. R. (2020). More than meets the eye: The functional components. Underlying influencer marketing. *Business Horizons, 63*(4), 469–479. https://doi.org/10.1016/j.bushor.2020.03.003

Conde, R., & Casais, B. (2023). Micro, macro and mega-influencers on Instagram: The power of persuasion via the parasocial relationship. *Journal of Business Research, 158*, 1–10. https://doi.org/10.1016/j.jbusres.2023.113708

Djafarova, E., & Rushworth, C. (2017). Exploring the credibility of online celebrities' Instagram profiles in influencing the purchase decisions of young female users. *Computers in Human Behavior, 68*, 1–7. https://doi.org/10.1016/j.chb.2016.11.009

Enke, N., & Borchers, N. S. (2019). Social media influencers in strategic communication: A conceptual framework for strategic social media influencer communication.

International Journal of Strategic Communication, 13(4), 261–277. https://doi.org/10.1080/1553118X.2019.1620234

Freberg, K., Graham, K., McGaughey, K., & Freberg, L. A. (2011). Who are the social media influencers? A study of public perceptions of personality. *Public Relations Review, 37*(1), 90–92. https://doi.org/10.1016/j.pubrev.2010.11.001

Galloway, S. (2017). *The four: The hidden DNA of Amazon, Apple, Facebook, and Google*. Portfolio/Penguin.

Geyser, W. (2023). The state of influencer marketing 2023: Benchmark report. *Influencer Marketing Hub*. Retrieved from https://influencermarketinghub.com/influencer-marketing-benchmark-report/

Guzman, A. L., & Lewis, S. C. (2020). Artificial intelligence and communication: A human–machine communication research agenda. *New Media & Society, 22*(1), 70–86. https://doi.org/10.1177/1461444819858691

Himelboim, I., & Golan, G. J. (2019). A social networks approach to viral advertising: The role of primary, contextual, and low influencers. *Social Media + Society, 5*(3), 1–13. https://doi.org/10.1177/2056305119847516

Holman, K.J. (2020). *Can you come back from being cancelled? A case study of podcasting, cancel culture, and comedians during #MeToo*. University of Nebraska at Omaha. Available from ProQuest Dissertations & Theses Global. (2427301602). https://www.proquest.com/dissertations-theses/can-you-come-back-being-cancelled-case-study/docview/2427301602/se-2

Hudders, L., De Jans, S., & De Veirman, M. (2021). The commercialization of social media stars: A literature review and conceptual framework on the strategic use of social media influencers. *International Journal of Advertising, 40*(3), 327–375. https://doi.org/10.1080/02650487.2020.1836925

Isyanto, P., Sapitri, R. G., & Sinaga, O. (2020). Micro influencers marketing and brand image to purchase intention of cosmetic products focallure. *Systematic Reviews in Pharmacy, 11*(1), 5. https://www.sysrevpharm.org/abstract/micro-influencers-marketing-and-brand-image-to-purchase-intention-of-cosmetic-products-focallure-65229.html

Jin, S.V., Muqaddam, A. and Ryu, E. (2019), Instafamous and social media influencer marketing. *Marketing Intelligence & Planning, 37*(5), 567–579. https://doi.org/10.1108/MIP-09-2018-0375

Khamis, S., Ang, L., & Welling, R. (2017). Self-branding, 'micro-celebrity' and the rise of social media influencers. *Celebrity Studies, 8*(2), 191–208. https://doi.org/10.1080/19392397.2016.1218292

Kim, E., Duffy, M., & Thorson, E. (2021). Under the influence: Social media influencers' impact on response to corporate reputation advertising. *Journal of Advertising, 50*(2), 119–138. https://doi.org/10.1080/00913367.2020.1868026

Lou, C., & Yuan, S. (2019). Influencer marketing: How message value and credibility affect consumer trust of branded content on social media. *Journal of Interactive Advertising, 19*(1), 58–73. https://doi.org/10.1080/15252019.2018.1533501

Nguyen, B. (2020). Cancel culture on twitter: The effects of information source and messaging on post shareability and perceptions of corporate greenwashing. *Wharton Research Scholars, 197*. https://repository.upenn.edu/wharton_research_scholars/197.

Smith, B. J., Golan, G., & Freberg, K. (2023). Influencer relations: Establishing the concept and process for public relations. *Public Relations Review, 49*(2). 102305.

Trend. (2022). Content creators vs influencers – Similarities and differences. *Trend.* Retrieved from https://www.trend.io/blog/content-creators-vs-influencers

West, C. (2022). Digital creators vs. influencers: What's the difference? *Sprout Social.* Retrieved from https://sproutsocial.com/insights/digital-creators-vs-influencers/

Yang, A., & Saffer, A. J. (2019). Embracing a network perspective in the network society: The dawn of a new paradigm in strategic public relations. *Public Relations Review, 45*(4). https://doi.org/10.1016/j.pubrev.2024.102470

Zeljko, D., Jakovic, B., & Strugar, I. (2018). New methods of online advertising: Social media influencers. *Proceedings of the 29th DAAAM International Symposium,* pp. 41–50, https://doi.org/10.2507/29th.daaam.proceedings.006

10

NAVIGATING THE FUTURE OF VIRTUAL INFLUENCERS

Hijacking Risks

Ekaterina Ivanova, Alina Arti, Vilma Luoma-aho and Juha Munnukka

Who Are Virtual Influencers?

Virtual influencers are increasingly emerging on social media, with their numbers expected to continue expanding (Appel et al., 2020; Stein et al., 2022). In 2018, TIME recognized Miquela, a prominent virtual influencer, as one of the 25 Most Influential People on the Internet (TIME, 2018). Academic interest in this topic is also increasing, with numerous studies exploring this trend and new ones being published (e.g. Allal-Chérif et al., 2024; Arsenyan & Mirowska, 2021). The current body of literature primarily examines the social interaction aspects of virtual influencers' effectiveness, yet there remains a lack of consistent conclusions in this regard (Zhou et al., 2024).

A virtual influencer can be defined as a computer-generated character with a distinctive personality (Christopher, 2020b), usually created by computer graphics or AI professionals (Mouritzen et al., 2023). Virtual influencers can be viewed as communication channels as they currently lack consciousness (Mouritzen et al., 2023; Robinson, 2020). Even though virtual influencers may appear on social media as if they were real, they are digital (Christopher, 2020b). Nonetheless, a recent study suggests that followers display parasocial responses to virtual influencers akin to human influencers (Stein et al., 2022).

The history of virtual influencers traces back to earlier technological developments, such as the ELIZA chatbot, which laid the foundation for conversational AI in the 1960s (Weizenbaum, 1966). In the 1980s, Max Headroom, a computer-generated character utilized in advertising, provided early glimpses into the potential of virtual personas (Rasmussen, 2022). Building on these developments, early CGI (Computer-Generated Imagery) characters such as

DOI: 10.4324/9781003426653-12

Gollum in 2002 (Letteri, 2013) and the rise of virtual platforms such as Second Life in 2003 (Huang, 2021) furthered the exploration of digital identities. Virtual influencers emerged in the mid-2010s, notably with Miquela, introduced by Brud agency in 2016. Initially presenting herself as a human on Instagram, Miquela garnered a massive following before unveiling her true virtual nature (Rasmussen, 2022).

Prior research uses various terms for virtual influencers, such as "AI influencers" and "CGI influencers" (Mrad et al., 2022; Thomas & Fowler, 2021). However, each type has unique features (Mouritzen et al., 2023). AI virtual influencers rely on software and algorithms (Thomas & Fowler, 2021), while CGI virtual influencers are known for anthropomorphism and use of 3D (Ahn et al., 2022; Miao et al., 2022). Another related phenomenon is VTubers (Virtual YouTubers), such as Ami Yamato, who are real people using computer graphics to adopt avatars. The software captures VTubers' facial expressions, mapping them to avatars for natural-looking videos (Sakuma et al., 2023) or streams (Turner, 2022).

Virtual influencers may play varied roles. For instance, Lu from the Brazilian megabrand Magalu acts as a brand endorser or mascot, while others, such as Miquela, adopt a more human influencer approach, crafting a personal brand and fostering a loyal audience with relatable and captivating content. This showcases the nuanced roles of virtual influencers, spanning corporate representation to the establishment of individualized personas.

Similar to human influencers, virtual influencers employ self-promotional techniques, relying on distinct personalities and well-crafted stories for success (Kim & Wang, 2023). Virtual influencers often adopt a first-person perspective, imbuing characters with self-agency and autonomy, setting them apart from other fictional characters (Christopher, 2020b). A recent industry report found that the main motivations for following virtual influencers were content, storytelling, and inspiration (The Influencer Marketing Factory, 2022).

In line with previous research, the classification of virtual influencers largely centers on their appearance and integration of AI:

1 **Human virtual influencers,** such as imma, resemble people, potentially causing confusion due to their lifelike features (Kim & Wang, 2023). They can be either fully or partially digitally rendered (Stein et al., 2022) and range from hyper-realistic to unrealistic appearances (Mouritzen et al., 2023). For example, Noonoouri has more anime-like features (Kim & Wang, 2023). Research suggests that perceived human-likeness in parasocial interactions with virtual influencers positively impacts attitudes toward them (Um, 2023).
2 **Non-human virtual influencers** are non-human characters easily distinguishable from real individuals, ranging from animals to fantastical creatures (Kim & Wang, 2023). They can be realistic, resembling various creatures

with reduced anthropomorphism, or unrealistic, depicted as different objects (Mouritzen et al., 2023) such as Nobody Sausage.

3 **AI virtual influencers,** such as Milla Sofia, use AI in their activities for, allowing them to adjust interactions based on followers' personalities, among other functions. They usually involve human oversight so fully autonomous AI virtual influencers are still rare (Thomas & Fowler, 2021). Therefore, virtual influencers are human-managed digital characters, while AI virtual influencers rely on AI for operation, making autonomy the key difference between them.

Relevance to PR and Strategic Communication

The latest research underscores the growing impact of virtual influencers on PR and strategic communication, as well as consumer behavior. A recent industry report found that over 50% of participants follow virtual influencers, and one-third have made purchases based on their recommendations (The Influencer Marketing Factory, 2022). A study by Robinson (2020) suggests that virtual influencers can impact audience preferences and behaviors, engaging consumers similarly to human influencers, as noted by D. Kim and Wang (2023). Consequently, they are increasingly used alongside or instead of human influencers (Arsenyan & Mirowska, 2021; Miao et al., 2022) for various purposes, including endorsing brands and supporting social causes (Kádeková & Holienčinová, 2018; Kim & Wang, 2023). Leveraging AI technology, virtual influencers participate in social activities such as real-time interaction with diverse audiences (Zhou et al., 2024).

The increasing use of virtual influencers in PR and communication is influenced by various factors, including:

1 ***Reaching youth***

Virtual influencers can help organizations reach younger audiences, especially Millennials and Generation Z (Kádeková & Holienčinová, 2018). A recent industry report shows that in the 18–24 age group 75% follow at least one virtual influencer. Individuals in their thirties and forties also show substantial interest. Across the 18–44 age range, 40–45% have made purchases influenced by virtual influencers (The Influencer Marketing Factory, 2022).

2 ***Flexibility***

Virtual influencers can be customized to meet PR and communication goals, reflecting brand image and values (Appel et al., 2020), and enabling alignment with market trends and consumer preferences for social responses and behavioral changes (Khan & Sutcliffe, 2014; Mouritzen et al., 2023). Unlike human influencers, virtual influencers are immune to factors such as anxiety and are available round-the-clock, ensuring reliable content production and continuous follower engagement in the fast-paced digital landscape (Appel et al., 2020; Arsenyan & Mirowska, 2021).

3 ***Cost-effectiveness***

Virtual influencer campaigns are typically cost-effective, especially when targeting younger demographics. Unlike human influencers, virtual influencers do not require compensation for their time and entail less maintenance, potentially saving costs due to customization and brand alignment (King, 2023; Phuc, 2023). Advances in lifelike virtual human creation technology may further enhance cost efficiency, offering opportunities to create high-quality virtual influencers without significant investments, benefiting the entire market (Hiort, 2022).

4 ***Sustainability and Environment***

The creator of the digital supermodel Shudu highlights that the transition to virtual influencers aids sustainability in the fashion industry by reducing the necessity for fabric production, usage, and subsequent waste (Christopher, 2020a). This shift has the potential to support organizations in their sustainable initiatives.

Emerging Risks in 2050

Virtual influencers, though easier to control than humans, still face controversies. While they can minimize PR risks by closely adhering to brand directions (Robinson, 2020), recent studies suggest they may engage in misconduct akin to human endorsers, potentially damaging a brand's image (Thomas & Fowler, 2021). Future developments may grant them autonomy through machine learning, raising ethical concerns about responsibility and trust. While human influencers are naturally accountable for their content, the responsibility for virtual influencers lies with their creators. However, as they become more AI-driven, attributing responsibility becomes challenging (Robinson, 2020). Organizations using virtual influencers risk losing control over communication, becoming more vulnerable to external influences and potential communication hijacking (Badham et al., 2022).

Communication hijacking is often characterized as any form of "non-collaborative co-creation" (Siano et al., 2022, p. 111). Accordingly, virtual influencer hijacking can be defined as an unauthorized control or manipulation of a virtual influencer's online presence or content. These challenges are establishing accountability for content, causing confusion among the audience and potential legal disputes. Potential risks also include reputational damage to affiliated organizations, their audiences, and stakeholders.

Virtual influencer hijacking can involve seizing control of their persona for purposes contrary to their original intent, shaping their environment with misleading information, or spreading false information that harms stakeholders.

By exploiting AI vulnerabilities, hijackers might compromise the virtual influencer's integrity. For organizations using virtual influencers, hijacking poses significant risks, potentially leading to virtual character assassination and irreparable damage to the virtual influencer's credibility, content, or social media accounts even after control is regained.

Communication hijacking can take various forms. We anticipate the emergence of two major types of virtual influencer hijackings.

- **Open hijacking** is already prevalent in online environments, occurring in various forms such as hashtag hijacking and campaign hijacking (Byrne et al., 2021; Truong et al., 2022). In the realm of virtual influencers, open hijacking can occur either by fully taking control of the account or by creating a mirror account of the virtual influencer. The purpose of this can vary, from financial gains to damaging the reputation of the brands affiliated with the hijacked virtual influencer.
- **Covert hijacking** can involve manipulating the virtual influencer's environment to alter its original purpose and narrative. Owners may only notice this when the damage becomes evident. It can occur when a virtual influencer operates solely on algorithms responding to comments and news topics, enabling hijackers to alter its behavior by flooding the arena with content on a specific agenda. The aim is likely to change the virtual influencer's perception and shift its audience's opinion on certain subjects.

The consequences of virtual influencer hijacking can depend on three factors: ownership, AI usage and automation, and the type of hijacking. While predicting social and technological trends for 2050 is challenging, human-operated virtual influencers may still exist, thus they are considered in potential virtual influencer hijacking scenarios, as illustrated in Figure 10.1.

In these potential virtual influencer hijacking scenarios, organizations may face PR and communication risks associated with the three identified aspects: ownership, AI usage, and type of hijacking.

- **Organization-Owned vs External Virtual Influencer.** Hijacking of organization-owned influencers can harm both the organization and the influencer, disrupting operations through ransomware attacks, hindering access to crucial data, and spreading damaging content. This not only damages the organization's image and trustworthiness but also tarnishes its reputation if an effective response is not implemented. Similarly, the hijacking of external virtual influencers (i.e. not owned by organizations but invited for collaboration) poses risks. Limited control over their actions makes it challenging to manage unforeseen issues, potentially tarnishing

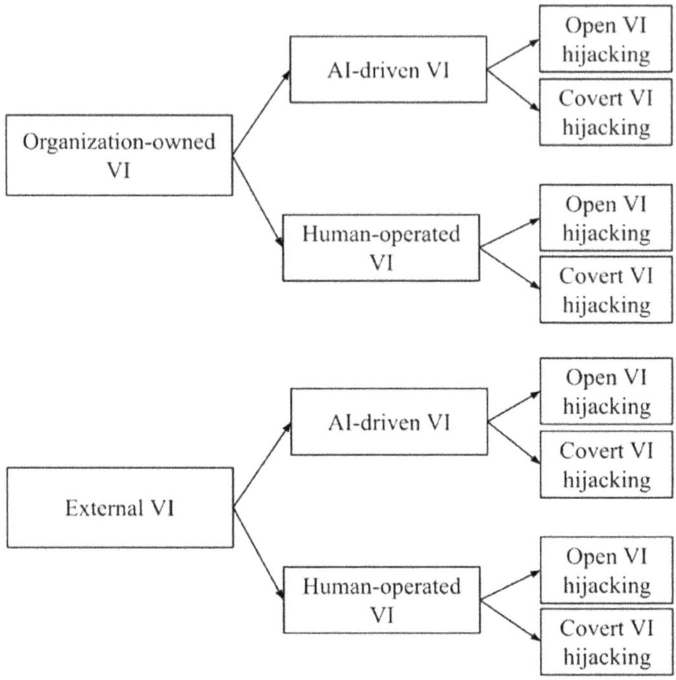

FIGURE 10.1 Possible virtual influencer hijacking scenarios.

the organization's reputation due to misalignment with the virtual influencer's values or controversial behavior.

- **AI-Driven vs Human-Operated Virtual Influencers.** In scenarios where AI-driven virtual influencers are hijacked, there is a risk of the content being manipulated to convey messages contrary to the organization's values. Ransomware targeting AI-driven virtual influencers may compromise the algorithms and data integral to their functioning. This can result in the dissemination of manipulated or harmful content, leading to confusion among followers and undermining the influencer's credibility. For human-operated virtual influencers, hijacking may involve unauthorized access to personal data or the creation of content inconsistent with the influencer's established persona, leading to confusion among followers.
- **Open vs Covert Hijacking.** Both open and covert hijacking of virtual influencers pose risks to both the virtual influencer and associated organizations. Open hijacking, particularly when the content contradicts the virtual influencer's image or affiliations, can quickly escalate into a crisis if hijackers demand a ransom for control of the account. Furthermore, public disclosure of such incidents can exacerbate the situation. Conversely, covert hijacking presents a danger of gradual harm, as organizations may remain unaware

until the altered narrative becomes apparent. In cases where ransomware is involved, threats to release sensitive data or manipulate the virtual influencer's narrative may arise unless a ransom is paid, resulting in trust erosion and damage to engagement and reputation. In both scenarios, the audience may lose trust due to perceived misalignment with the virtual influencer's original values, leading to a decline in engagement.

Organizations may inadvertently fuel communication hijacking through their actions, policies, or vulnerabilities. Failure to establish clear and sincere communication can lead to confusion among stakeholders, providing an opportunity for malicious actors to exploit and pursue their agendas. To mitigate these risks, organizations managing virtual influencers should proactively monitor, respond promptly, and communicate clearly with the audience and stakeholders. Robust cybersecurity measures are essential to prevent unauthorized access and manipulation, safeguarding brand reputation and audience trust. Addressing the ransomware threat requires contingency plans, effective communication strategies, and prioritizing virtual influencers' data security to maintain credibility.

Impact of Virtual Influencers on the Profession Today and in 2050

Creating Virtual Influencers In-House

Creating virtual influencers involves careful consideration of ethics, diverse appearances (Xie-Carson et al., 2023), backstory, and behavior to align with brand identity and target audiences (Mouritzen et al., 2023). Additionally, some consumers may be hesitant to interact with AI (Mouritzen et al., 2023; Sands et al., 2022). Imagining 2050, organizations will adapt their management of virtual influencers to match changing consumer perceptions, ethics, and trends. In navigating this dynamic landscape, practitioners developing in-house virtual influencers should balance innovation with maintaining trust and ethical standards.

Adhering to New Regulations

The Federal Trade Commission's latest guides classify virtual influencers as "endorsers" (Federal Trade Commission, 2023), imposing certain requirements for virtual influencers when conveying endorsement messages (Nolan, 2023). This shift urges communication and PR professionals to comply with the guidelines when utilizing virtual influencers. As these entities become more prevalent by 2050, professionals must proactively adapt their practices to align with evolving regulatory frameworks, ensuring transparent and responsible engagement in the dynamic landscape of communication and PR.

Preserving Authenticity

Virtual influencers, potentially expanding our understanding of authenticity in the digital realm, demonstrate it through, for example, consistent personas and clear representation as virtual entities, which improves attitudes toward them (Kim & Wang, 2023; Um, 2023). However, lacking subjective experiences and opinions due to their purely digital nature (Mouritzen et al., 2023), their motivations, particularly in product endorsements, may be unclear, raising authenticity concerns (Kádeková & Holienčinová, 2018; Robinson, 2020). In 2050, while the challenge of authenticity may persist, it could transform, reshaping communication strategies and ushering in a new era of advertising and revenue generation through virtual entities.

Ensuring Transparency

Users often struggle to differentiate between virtual and human influencers, leading to deception and ethical challenges. Organizations using virtual influencers should prioritize transparency to ensure accountability by disclosing how virtual influencers are employed (Kim & Wang, 2023; Mouritzen et al., 2023). For example, Milla Sofia openly acknowledges being an AI-generated virtual influencer (Netmylly Oy, 2023). However, such transparency may reduce perceived anthropomorphism, potentially harming credibility and brand trust (Muniz et al., 2023). PR professionals should explore strategies to help users distinguish real from virtual entities, emphasizing transparency in both the current and future landscapes.

Longevity of Virtual Influencers

Virtual influencers bring novelty to marketing but face uncertainty in lasting appeal. Studies suggest that they typically garner lower source trust compared to human influencers, with consumers preferring real human endorsers (Franke et al., 2023; Stein et al., 2022). To address this challenge, communication professionals should adopt a balanced approach, integrating both virtual and human influencers. Looking ahead to 2050, holographic technology integration may revolutionize social dynamics, prolonging the appeal of virtual influencers. For example, holographic sleepovers with virtual influencers commenting on gaming or cooking alongside users in real time. This not only introduces a new layer of entertainment but also blurs the line between physical and virtual realms, reshaping future socialization.

Consumer Co-Creation

In 2050, consumers will likely shape virtual influencers' content, personality, and behaviors through co-creation. This collaboration could lead to more personalized and relatable virtual influencers appealing to diverse audiences. However, challenges may arise, such as online customer reviews impacting virtual influencer behavior and algorithms. Genuine reviews may guide virtual influencers toward positive and authentic engagement, while malicious or fake reviews could distort their perception. To address this, organizations using virtual influencers would need mechanisms to distinguish between authentic and fabricated feedback, ensuring that virtual influencer algorithms reflect genuine consumer input. Balancing customer involvement with maintaining virtual influencer integrity will be crucial for their success in 2050.

Conclusion

This chapter explores the evolving landscape of virtual influencers, focusing on their potential trajectory in 2050. Their rise presents both opportunities and challenges for PR and communication professionals, including the risk of reputational damage and engagement erosion due to hijacking. Looking ahead, proactive adaptation to regulatory changes, ethical considerations, and transparency in employing virtual influencers is crucial.

The challenge of authenticity persists, with potential transformations reshaping communication and advertising practices. In 2050, customers may actively shape virtual influencers' content, posing opportunities for personalization but challenges in discerning genuine customer input. PR practitioners must remain agile, aligning strategies with evolving technologies, societal attitudes, and regulations.

Future research on virtual influencers should explore their impact on consumers' brand perceptions and the effectiveness of their endorsements (Appel et al., 2020; Kim et al., 2023). Ongoing research is vital for addressing ethical considerations and establishing communication guidelines (Kim & Wang, 2023).

References

Ahn, R. J., Cho, S. Y., & Sunny Tsai, W. (2022). Demystifying computer-generated imagery (CGI) influencers: The effect of perceived anthropomorphism and social presence on brand outcomes. *Journal of Interactive Advertising*, *22*(3), 327–335. https://doi.org/10.1080/15252019.2022.2111242

Allal-Chérif, O., Puertas, R., & Carracedo, P. (2024). Intelligent influencer marketing: How AI-powered virtual influencers outperform human influencers. *Technological Forecasting and Social Change, 200*, 123113. https://doi.org/10.1016/j.techfore.2023.123113

Appel, G., Grewal, L., Hadi, R., & Stephen, A. T. (2020). The future of social media in marketing. *Journal of the Academy of Marketing Science*, *48*(1), 79–95. https://doi.org/10.1007/s11747-019-00695-1

Arsenyan, J., & Mirowska, A. (2021). Almost human? A comparative case study on the social media presence of virtual influencers. *International Journal of Human-Computer Studies*, *155*, 102694. https://doi.org/10.1016/j.ijhcs.2021.102694

Badham, M., Luoma-aho, V., Valentini, C., & Lumimaa, L. (2022). Digital strategic communication through digital media-arenas. In J. Falkheimer & M. Heide (Eds.), *Research handbook on strategic communication* (pp. 416–430). Edward Elgar Publishing. https://doi.org/10.4337/9781800379893.00035

Byrne, V. L., Higginbotham, B. L., Donlan, A. E., & Stewart, T. J. (2021). An online occupation of the university Hashtag: Exploring how student activists use social media to engage in protest. *Journal of College and Character*, *22*(1), 13–30. https://doi.org/10.1080/2194587X.2020.1860775

Christopher. (2020a). *The latest from Cameron-James Wilson, Shudu Gram's Creator*. https://www.virtualhumans.org/article/the-latest-from-cameron-james-wilson-shudu-grams-creator

Christopher. (2020b). What is a virtual influencer? Virtual influencers, defined and explained. *VirtualHumans*. Retrieved from https://www.virtualhumans.org/article/what-is-a-virtual-influencer-virtual-influencers-defined-and-explained

Federal Trade Commission. (2023, July 26). Guides concerning the use of endorsements and testimonials in advertising. *Federal Register*. Retrieved from https://www.federalregister.gov/documents/2023/07/26/2023-14795/guides-concerning-the-use-of-endorsements-and-testimonials-in-advertising

Franke, C., Groeppel-Klein, A., & Müller, K. (2023). Consumers' responses to virtual influencers as advertising endorsers: Novel and effective or uncanny and deceiving? *Journal of Advertising*, *52*(4), 523–539. https://doi.org/10.1080/00913367.2022.2154721

Hiort, A. (2022). CEO James Jacobs on Ziva Dynamics' acquisition by unity and bringing lifelike virtual humans to everyone. https://www.virtualhumans.org/article/ceo-james-jacobs-on-ziva-dynamics-acquisition-by-unity-and-bringing-lifelike-virtual-humans-to-everyone

Huang, X. (2021). Second life: A hope for ideal, but only in its imaginary. *Asian Social Science*, *17*(2), 109. https://doi.org/10.5539/ass.v17n2p109

Kádeková, Z., & Holienčinová, M. (2018). Influencer marketing as a modern phenomenon creating a new frontier of virtual opportunities. *Communication Today*, *9*(2), 91–105.

Khan, R. F., & Sutcliffe, A. (2014). Attractive agents are more persuasive. *International Journal of Human-Computer Interaction*, *30*(2), 142–150. https://doi.org/10.1080/10447318.2013.839904

Kim, D., & Wang, Z. (2023). The ethics of virtuality: Navigating the complexities of human-like virtual influencers in the social media marketing realm. *Frontiers in Communication*, *8*. https://doi.org/10.3389/fcomm.2023.1205610

Kim, E. A., Kim, D., E, Z., & Shoenberger, H. (2023). The next hype in social media advertising: Examining virtual influencers' brand endorsement effectiveness. *Frontiers in Psychology*, *14*, 1089051. https://doi.org/10.3389/fpsyg.2023.1089051

King, C. (2023, February 1). What are virtual influencers and how do they work? *Hype Auditor.Com*. https://hypeauditor.com/blog/the-rise-of-virtual-influencers-should-you-be-working-with-them/

Letteri, J. (2013). Computer animation: Digital heroes and computer-generated worlds. *Nature*, *504*(7479), Article 7479. https://doi.org/10.1038/504214a

Miao, F., Kozlenkova, I. V., Wang, H., Xie, T., & Palmatier, R. W. (2022). An emerging theory of avatar marketing. *Journal of Marketing*, *86*(1), 67–90. https://doi.org/10.1177/0022242921996646

Mouritzen, S. L. T., Penttinen, V., & Pedersen, S. (2023). Virtual influencer marketing: The good, the bad and the unreal. *European Journal of Marketing*. https://doi.org/10.1108/EJM-12-2022-0915

Mrad, M., Link to External Site, This Link Will Open in a New Tab, Ramadan, Z., Link to External Site, This Link Will Open in a New Tab, Nasr, L. I., & Link to External Site, This Link Will Open in a New Tab. (2022). Computer-generated influencers: The rise of digital personalities. *Marketing Intelligence & Planning*, *40*(5), 589–603. https://doi.org/10.1108/MIP-12-2021-0423

Muniz, F., Stewart, K., & Magalhães, L. (2023). Are they humans or are they robots? The effect of virtual influencer disclosure on brand trust. *Journal of Consumer Behaviour*. https://doi.org/10.1002/cb.2271

Netmylly Oy. (2023). *The fashionable journey of a virtual influencer Milla Sofia*. https://millasofia.eth.limo/#about

Nolan, H. (2023, August 11). *Virtual influencers are now officially regulated endorsers*. InfoLawGroup LLP. https://www.infolawgroup.com/insights/2023/8/11/virtual-influencers-are-now-officially-regulated-endorsersunless-theyre-spokespersons

Phuc, D. (2023, April 24). Virtual influencer cost: Everything you need to know. *Animost Studio*. Retrieved from https://animost.com/industry-updates/virtual-influencer-cost/

Rasmussen, M. (2022). *Who was the first virtual influencer?* https://www.virtualhumans.org/article/who-was-the-first-virtual-influencer

Robinson, B. (2020). Towards an ontology and ethics of virtual influencers. *Australasian Journal of Information Systems*, *24*. https://doi.org/10.3127/ajis.v24i0.2807

Sakuma, H., Hori, A., Murashita, M., Kondo, C., & Hijikata, Y. (2023). YouTubers vs. VTubers: Persuasiveness of human and virtual presenters in promotional videos. *Frontiers in Computer Science*, *5*, 1043342. https://doi.org/10.3389/fcomp.2023.1043342

Sands, S., Campbell, C. L., Plangger, K., & Ferraro, C. (2022). Unreal influence: Leveraging AI in influencer marketing. *European Journal of Marketing*, *56*(6), 1721–1747. https://doi.org/10.1108/EJM-12-2019-0949

Siano, A., Vollero, A., & Bertolini, A. (2022). From brand control to brand co-creation: An integrated framework of brand paradigms and emerging brand perspectives. *Journal of Business Research*, *152*, 372–386. https://doi.org/10.1016/j.jbusres.2022.08.001

Stein, J.-P., Linda Breves, P., & Anders, N. (2022). Parasocial interactions with real and virtual influencers: The role of perceived similarity and human-likeness. *New Media & Society*. https://doi.org/10.1177/14614448221102900

The Influencer Marketing Factory. (2022, March 29). Virtual influencers survey + INFOGRAPHIC. *Influencer Marketing Factory*. Retrieved from https://theinfluencermarketingfactory.com/virtual-influencers-survey-infographic/

Thomas, V. L., & Fowler, K. (2021). Close encounters of the AI kind: Use of AI influencers as brand endorsers. *Journal of Advertising*, *50*(1), 11–25. https://doi.org/10.1080/00913367.2020.1810595

TIME. (2018). 25 Most influential people on the internet in 2018. https://time.com/5324130/most-influential-internet/

Truong, H.-B. (Iris), Jesudoss, S. P., & Molesworth, M. (2022). Consumer mischief as playful resistance to marketing in Twitter hashtag hijacking. *Journal of Consumer Behaviour, 21*(4), 828–841. https://doi.org/10.1002/cb.2040

Turner, A. B. (2022). *Streaming as a virtual being: The complex relationship between VTubers and identity* [Malmö University]. https://urn.kb.se/resolve?urn=urn:nbn:se:mau:diva-53529

Um, N. (2023). Predictors affecting effects of virtual influencer advertising among college students. *Sustainability, 15*(8), 6388. https://doi.org/10.3390/su15086388

Weizenbaum, J. (1966). ELIZA—A computer program for the study of natural language communication between man and machine. *Communications of the ACM, 9*(1), 36–45. https://doi.org/10.1145/365153.365168

Xie-Carson, L., Benckendorff, P., & Hughes, K. (2023). Keep it #Unreal: Exploring Instagram users' engagement with virtual influencers in tourism contexts user engagement with virtual influencers. *Journal of Hospitality & Tourism Research*. https://doi.org/10.1177/10963480231180940

Zhou, Q., Li, B., Li, H., & Lei, Y. (2024). Mere copycat? The effects of human versus human-like virtual influencers on brand endorsement effectiveness: A moderated serial-mediation model. *Journal of Retailing and Consumer Services, 76*, 103610. https://doi.org/10.1016/j.jretconser.2023.103610

11

CONSUMERISM AS THE DRIVING FORCE OF HUMAN IDENTITY IN 2050

The Role of Marketing, Advertising, and Public Relations

Alexander V. Laskin

Consumerism as Social Identity

What makes humans humans? Descartes believed in *cogito ergo sum* (or I think, therefore I am), but what if technologies replace humans in the process of thinking? For centuries, technologies replaced and supplemented human labor in almost every aspect of work. Currently, we may be on the verge of AI replacing and supplementing humans in thinking and decision-making when it comes to medicine, law, engineering, creative pursuits, and many other fields.

But is it really a bad thing? Imagine traveling without a wheel, writing without a computer, or communicating without a phone. If centuries ago humans had to engage in constant 24-hour-a-day 7-day-a-week struggle just to survive, today the Western societies consider 8 hour work day on 5 day a week schedule the norm or even too much work. In fact, in quite a few professions less days or less hours are rapidly becoming a new norm. If this trend continues, humans are likely to have even more time from their work obligations by the year 2050.

But do people actually have more and more free time when they don't know how to occupy themselves? The answer is generally no. In fact, people tend to complain that they are getting busier and busier despite the fact that they do not have to hunt for food (it is readily available in supermarkets and restaurants), make their own clothes, utensils, or furniture (they can buy all that at stores around them or even order for delivery right to their front door), or even wash dishes and clothing (the washing/drying machines and dishwashers take care of that).

What happens then with all their new-found time? How do people occupy hours and days away from chores and labor? The answer is: the increased consumption. In addition to physical products that humans consume more and more,

DOI: 10.4324/9781003426653-13

people also consume more and more content – be it professional content or amateur content. Consumption is already taking more time in people's daily lives than production in quantitative sense and it is possible that the qualitative shift is going to happen by the year 2050 as well. The qualitative shift would mean that the consumption would become more important for human's self-identification than production, creation, or thinking. In other words, as marketers proclaimed for years, humans will start defining themselves through what and how they consume: I consume, therefore I am!

Already today plenty of people see themselves as Swifties (fans of Taylor Swift), or Beyhive (fans of Beyounce), or Beliebers (fans of Justin Bieber). For some it may be the main part of identity and reason for existence – the meaning of life! Of course it is not a brand new development, as years ago already The Beatles had Beatlemaniacs, Manowar had MANOWARriors, and Suicidal Tendencies had the Suicidal Army. The phenomenon, though, is undoubtfully growing in both quantitative and qualitative senses, and is likely to go continue to grow by year 2050.

The fan culture is also not limited to the music only – movies, cartoons, books, and comics generate their own millions of fans who often define their lives through devotion to a particular creative fantasy. The same is happening with various consumer brands – cars from BMW to Tesla; phones from Apple to Google; and clothing from Vineyard Vines to Abercrombie & Fitch – many brands have dedicated armies of fans who may define themselves completely or partially through using the products by those brands in their lives. "A brand is so much more than a tagline or logo…It is more of a meaning system," explains Reed as he reflects on his experience with shoes and the different groups of people choosing footwear by Nike or Adidas or Chuck Taylors as a reflection of their inner identities (as cited in Vedantam et al, 2019, p. 1).

In fact, Social Identity Theory stipulates that consumers may choose a specific brand, product, artist, or content as a target for self-dentification (Bhattacharya & Sen, 2003; Tajfel & Turner, 1979). This becomes an "active, selective, and volitional act that can help customers to fulfill one or more key self-definitional needs" (Kassemeier, Haumann, & Gunturkun, 2022, p. 702). Furthermore, this reliance on a product, brand, artist, or content for self-dentification often goes beyond just its functionality, performance, or other consumer categories and instead fulfills some higher-order identification needs whether they are rooted in reality or not (Haumann et al, 2014; Laskin, 2019; 2021; Park, Jaworski, & MacInnis, 1986).

Consumerism Is a Key Force in 2050

By 2050 the brands, movies, or music become an important, if not the most important, component of humans' self-identity. With less importance placed on what humans can or have to create through their labor, what they consume will define humans happiness and purpose. It will also lead to defining group identities – with people included and excluded out of such communities (Kirsch, 2023). Personal consumption will define not just who you are but also what you wear, where you live, what you do, who your friends are, and what your political, ethical, professional, and philosophical beliefs are. People will become superfans – be it religion, a TV show, music band, or anything else; and such fandom will occupy more and more time, and become more and more central to self-realization, self-actualization, and self-worth.

This will in turn affect the strategic communication industry – marketing, advertising, public relations. The rule of the game will be creating superfans, building and maintaining relationships with them, and feeding them non-stop related content they can use in all aspects of their life. Already today "56% of Gen Z and 63% of millennials reveal that the brands they like are a strong reflection of themselves" (Lepitak, 2024, p. 1), but by 2050 brands will become the key part of our identities.

This places enormous pressure on the marketers – corporate social responsibility and corporate advocacy communications will become even more important

FIGURE 11.1 All for sale and sale for all. https://commons.wikimedia.org/wiki/File:Mall_culture_jakarta36.jpg.

Courtesy of Jonathan McIntosh, CC BY 2.0 DEED, https://creativecommons.org/licenses/by/2.0/deed.en.

as the consumers will measure brands not just by the quality of products, services, or content but also by the alignment between the brand's and personal attitudes toward ESG (environmental, social, and governance) and DEI (diversity, equity, and conclusion) issues. By 2050, the plethora of issues will expand to include global and micro-local issues with the organizations being expected to take a stand and communicate their position to their superfans. Corporate social advocacy may mean even more in the future than the actual product, service, or content produced because, once again, consumption will be a component of self-identity for a consumer not a need as it was in the past or even a want as it is today.

Moravec's Paradox

A big role in the creation of the consumption-centric humans belongs to the technology. While people create technologies to satisfy their needs, technology in its turn creates new needs and changes the people and the society itself (Marx & Smith, 1994). Thus, it is important to understand the interplay between technological innovations and societal changes between now and 2050. It is also important to note that one of the most common errors in predicting the capabilities of a technology is judging technologies from the human standpoint. How clumsy robots are when they are walking, for example, generated billions of views on YouTube and made humans perceive robots as underdeveloped toys. But look at how welding robots operate at automotive factories and compare their movements with humans who would try to replicate their performance and the picture would be drastically different. The welding robots would be far superior to humans in the quantity and quality of work. This is what became known as Moravec's paradox: what is easy for humans is difficult for technologies and what is difficult for humans is easy for technologies (Moravec, 1988; Pinker, 1994).

In other words, to better evaluate the influence of technologies, it is important not to judge them from the human standpoint. It is also hard to comprehend why something that humans find easy and enjoyable for technologies may be difficult and demanding. Consumption may be a great example of such phenomenon. Humans strive when they procrastinate doing something unrelated to what they should be doing – be it scrolling TikTok or surfing the TV channels. Humans are great at consumption and it is unlikely technology can outperform human consumers. It is hard to imagine a welding robot getting distracted by a cat video on YouTube. Thus, humans' ability to consume in a planned and sporadic manner is unlikely to change – in fact, it is more than likely to continue growing as it has been doing for centuries. As a result, it would make sense to build the industry around it. The question is how the industry will evolve with this expected quantitative and qualitative increase in consumption by year 2050.

Public Relations, Advertising, and Marketing as a Force for Consumption in 2050

Personalized Communications Made Possible by AI

With AI vast resources significantly outperforming an average human, organizations can develop individualized communications for consumers, employees, investors, and other publics. By 2050 instead of one commercial for 1 million consumers, it'd be possible to create 1 million commercials personally customized for each of these 1 million consumers. AI enabled text, image, and video creation programs already can generate advertising and public relations content that can outperform campaigns created by humans qualitatively (Domingo, 2024). A recent study showed that AI generated marketing materials significantly outperform human-made materials and "achieve a +22% higher CTR [click-through rate] in a randomized field experiment with more than 86,000 impressions" (Hartmann et al, 2024, p. 1). This quality production can also be paired with quantity – an endless stream of personalized marketing messages can be generated by the technologies of the future. With such resources and combining quantitative and qualitative capabilities, each human will get dedicated personalized attention and individually targeted messages on what to eat, wear, listen to, and watch.

Personalized Connections Made Possible by Big Data

Such AI generated personalized content in 2050 will be more effective due to the AI ability to access targeted data on the consumers from large data sets. AI will know what exactly we want, need, how we feel, and what we aspire to be at each particular moment. This leads to an opportunity to generate a perfect content for each individual rather than mass-produced content. Even when it fails, technology will be able to learn from its mistakes nearly instantly, and produce improved content in real time – no human supervision required. To an extent, it will be easier to give up to technology than to avoid it as it will never stop trying.

Personalized Exposure Made Possible by AR/VR/MR

Personalized content made possible by big data will be even more powerful as it will be able to reach us exactly when we need it the most or when we are the most susceptible to the message (at least according to the technology). Plus, such content will have no physical limitations of having to employ actors, rent cameras, secure locations, and so on. Augmented reality, virtual reality, and mixed reality environments and characters will be readily available for AI to produce content with limitless possibilities, while people will be able to consume such content due to the widespread adoption of virtual technologies. For example, today's outdoor billboard with a restaurant ad will be replaced by a virtual billboard that could display whatever ad a person will be most responsive to at that exact moment in time with content most relevant to that very person like their favorite celebrity, or product, or music, or even themselves. Such billboards won't have to look like billboards at all and will be able to follow you into a grocery store, restaurant, or bathroom, and be displayed as integral part of a wall, a product label, a sky, or be merged with any other real or generated object.

From Product Placement to Product Integration

In 2050 it is not enough to have a character drink Pepsi in a movie, Pepsi must become an important character in the show fully integrated into the content (Lepitak, 2024). With AI unlimited possibilities for content creation, every ad or every promo may become integrated into what a person is actually a fan of – be it a music video, a favorite TikTok reel, or a movie. To sell Pepsi, marketers will show Harry Potter drinking Pepsi to the Harry Potter fans, but display Jeff Winger and Annie Edison drinking Pepsi to the fans of the Community TV series. The interruption model of marketing and advertising will become a thing of the past as marketing content will become indistinguishable from the entertainment content, and vice versa. This can all happen with no human intervention, with AI making decisions based on its analysis of the historic data available about the consumer as well as current data provided by wearables about the location of the person, their current mood, blood pressure, pulse, and similar. Privacy concerns will be ignored in the name of convenience and comfort, and more importantly consumer satisfaction.

We Are What We Consume

All this strategies and tactics taken together will form our identities. With work becoming less and less important in our lives as it will be taking increasingly smaller parts of our days and requiring increasingly smaller intellectual effort, we will proceed to define the meaning of life through our consumption. At the parties, we won't introduce ourselves to others based on what we do as doctors, professors, or actors, but instead will introduce ourselves based on what we are fans of – as Stephen King readers, or Taylor Swift listeners, or Futurama viewers. The job of marketing, advertising, and public relations will be to tap into our consumer identities to influence what else we would buy, how we would vote, and where we would go on vacation.

Conclusions

Technology, including AI, is developing at an unprecedent rate and this development seems limitless at least in our foreseeable future till 2050. This applies even to the fields that once were considered squarely domains of human labor, such as creative production and marketing, advertising, and public relations. Today, there is no doubt AI can produce outputs that can be considered creative (Zhou & Lee, 2024). In fact, in recent study comparing creativity between AI and humans, AI won: the results showed that "the chatbots' responses were rated as better than the humans' on average" (Williams, 2023, p. 2).

But will this trend continue at the same trajectory for much longer or is AI destined to reach diminishing returns with time? After all, AI is based and trained on human-generated data. This pool of data, however, is limited and does not grow as fast as AI does – in fact, its growth may be slowing down as humans slow down their original thinking as they rely more and more on the second-hand AI creativity. In the future, this may lead to what may be considered an AI self-extinction (Basiouny, 2024).

At the same time, with an exponential growth of demand for content by humans who would dedicate more and more of their time to consumption, quality of content will likely continue to be sacrificed for quantity. Plus, the personalization of content for each individual user will make quality less important. It is irrelevant if a movie is a high-quality blockbuster or not, if you are the star of that movie. After all our home movies rarely rise to the level of Hollywood production quality, but it does not make them any less valuable to us. With AI making us part of every movie, commercial, social media post, or other piece of content we are exposed to, we will care less and less about the quality.

The lines will continue to be blurred between human-produced content and AI-produced content. Same way as writers use computers today without being accused of augmenting their writing by using Microsoft Word or Grammarly, AI tools will be widely accepted and employed as well. The constant comparisons between human-created content and AI-created content will vanish: same way as nobody today would debate the quality of books written by a pen versus written on a computer. AI celebrities, creators, and influencers will be viewed the same way as movie or book characters – as property of writers, directors, coders, producers, and corporations.

It does not mean these AI celebrities won't create enormous profits or generate massive fanbase. In fact, they will become a large part of the future consumer culture. Just like there are millions of fans of Harry Potter, there will be millions of fans of @lilmiquela, a 19-year-old robot living in LA who would build their identities around either one of these fictitious characters. In fact, with more reliance on virtual and augmented realities, virtual celebrities are likely to become more influential than real-world celebrities.

References

Basioouny, A. (2024, March 11). AI and machine creativity: How artistic production is changing. *Knowledge@Wharton*. Retrieved from https://knowledge.wharton.upenn.edu/article/ai-and-machine-creativity-how-artistic-production-is-changing

Bhattacharya, C. B., & Sen, S. (2003). Consumer–company identification: A framework for understanding consumers' relationships with companies. *Journal of Marketing*. https://doi.org/10.1509/jmkg.67.2.76.18609

Domingo, M. (2024, March 22). What impact will AI really have on white-collar jobs? *SmartBrief.* Retrieved from https://www.smartbrief.com/original/what-impact-will-ai-really-have-on-white-collar-jobs

Hartmann, J., Exner, Y., & Domdey, S. (2023). The power of generative marketing: Can generative AI reach human-level visual marketing content? *SSRN 4597899*. http://dx.doi.org/10.2139/ssrn.4597899

Haumann, T., Quaiser, B., Wieseke, J., & Rese, M. (2014). Footprints in the sands of time: A comparative analysis of the effectiveness of customer satisfaction and customer–company identification over time. *Journal of Marketing*, *78*(6), 78–102.

Heaven, W. D. (2023, December 19). These six questions will dictate the future of generative AI. *MIT Technology Review*. Retrieved from https://www.technologyreview.com/2023/12/19/1084505/generative-ai-artificial-intelligence-bias-jobs-copyright-misinformation/

Kassemeier, R., Haumann, T., & Güntürkün, P. (2022). Whether, when, and why functional company characteristics engender customer satisfaction and customer-company identification: The role of self-definitional needs. *International Journal of Research in Marketing*, *39*(3), 699–723.

Kirsch, M. (2023, July 29). The Dave Matthews Band, reconsidered. *The New York Times*. Retrieved from https://www.nytimes.com/2023/07/29/briefing/the-dave-matthews-band-reconsidered.html

Laskin, A. V. (2019). Defining propaganda: A psychoanalytic perspective. *Communication and the Public, 4*(4), 305–314.

Laskin, A. V. (2021). Symbiotic relations as the foundation of propaganda: Directions for future research. *In Analysis, 5*(2), 183–187. https://doi.org/10.1016/j.inan.2021.06.003

Lepitak, S. (2024, March 21). From then till now: Big brands' enduring love affair with product placement. *ADWEEK*. Retrieved from https://www.adweek.com/convergent-tv/from-then-till-now-big-brands-enduring-love-affair-with-product-placement/

Lepitak, S. (2024, March 21). Why brands should prepare for the rise of super fans. *ADWEEK*. Retrieved from https://www.adweek.com/brand-marketing/why-brands-should-prepare-for-the-rise-of-super-fans/

Marx, L., & Smith, M. R. (1994). *Does technology drive history? The dilemma of technological determinism*. MIT Press.

Mattews, D. (2024, March 26). How AI could explode the economy. *Vox*. Retrieved from Retrieved from https://www.vox.com/future-perfect/24108787/ai-economic-growth-explosive-automation

Moravec, H. (1988). *Mind children.* Harvard University Press.

Park, C. W., Jaworski, B. J., & MacInnis, D. J. (1986). Strategic brand concept-image management. *Journal of Marketing*, *50*(4), 135–145.

Pinker, S. (1994). *The language instinct*. Harper.

Sisodia, A., Burnap, A., & Kumar, V. (2023). Automatic discovery and generation of visual design characteristics: Application to visual conjoint. *SSRN 4151019*.
Tajfel, H., & Turner, J. C. (2004). The social identity theory of intergroup behavior. In J. T. Jost & J. Sidanius (Eds.), *Political psychology* (pp. 276–293). Psychology Press. https://doi.org/10.4324/9780203505984-16
Vedantam, S., Boyle, T., Chen, A., Kwerel, L., & Cohen, R. (2019, June 1). I buy, therefore I am: How brands become part of who we are. *NPR*. Retrieved from https://www.npr.org/2019/06/28/736942500/i-buy-therefore-i-am-how-brands-become-part-of-who-we-are
Williams, R. (2023, September 14). AI just beat a human test for creativity. What does that even mean? *MIT Technology Review*. Retrieved from https://www.technologyreview.com/2023/09/14/1079465/ai-just-beat-a-human-test-for-creativity-what-does-that-even-mean
Zhou, E., & Lee, D. (2023). Generative ai, human creativity, and art. *PNAS Nexus*, *3*(3), 52. https://doi.org/10.1093/pnasnexus/pgae052

12

RE-ENGAGING THE 'ECLIPSED PUBLIC' – THE CHALLENGE FOR PUBLIC COMMUNICATION AND POLITICS

Jim Macnamara

The 'Eclipse of the Public': Early 20th Century Concerns

Eminent US philosopher John Dewey alleged in the early 20th century that industrialized democratic societies were regressing democratically and socially because of an "eclipse of the public".[1] His warning was spelled out in a chapter of that title in his landmark book *The Public and Its Problems* first published in 1927 and then in numerous reprints and later editions (Dewey, 1927, 1946, 2016). Much continues to be written about Dewey's conceptualization of the *public sphere* (e.g., Pedersen, 2019) alongside those of Habermas (1989), and the relevance of his work to public relations has been recognized (Rakow, 2018) – albeit to a limited scale and deserving of greater attention.

From his distinction between private and public life, Dewey argued that "the public consists of all those who are affected by the indirect consequences of transactions to such an extent that it is deemed necessary to have those consequences systematically cared for". His logic was that "since those who are indirectly affected are not direct participants in the transactions in question, it is necessary that certain persons be set apart to represent them and see to it that their interests are conserved and protected" (Dewey, 2027, pp. 15–16).

Dewey (1927) described these so charged as "officers" (p. 18), "officials" (pp. 15–16, 27), "representatives" (p. 18), "agents" (p. 18), and "guardians" (p. 35), saying "the public … is organized in and through those officers who act in [sic] behalf of its interests" (p. 28). More specifically, he stated: "This public is organized and made effective by means of representatives who as guardians of custom, as legislators, as executives, judges, etc., care for its special interests by methods intended to regulate the conjoint actions of individuals and groups"

DOI: 10.4324/9781003426653-14

(p. 35). He noted: "The buildings, property, funds, and other physical resources involved in the performance of this office are *res publica,* the common-wealth" (p. 16).

Dewey identified and defined "the primary problem of the public" as "to achieve such recognition of itself as will give it weight in the selection of official representatives and in the definition of their responsibilities and rights" (2027, p. 77). This, in turn, leads Dewey to a discussion of the democratic state and the functioning of democracy. On that, he was critical and pessimistic. He wrote:

> The causes which operate to induce men to strive for any shining object operate with increased appeal in the case of governmental power. The centralization and scope of functions which are needed in order to serve the interests of the public become … seductions to draw state officials into subserving private ends.
>
> *(Dewey, 1927, p. 81)*

Under the label of *the machine age*, Dewey cites centralization and institutionalization of politics; big business dominating policymaking and subverting the public interest for its own ends; and mass media focused on entertainment that distracts people from politics and civic life and duty among causes of the eclipse of the public.

Despondently, he says "the public seems to be lost; it is certainly bewildered" (1927, p. 116). Of democratic states he says: "The public which generated political forms is passing away, but the power and lust of possession remains in the hands of the officers and agencies which the dying public instituted" (1927, p. 31).

While much of Dewey's concern relates to political science, Dewey directs attention to communication in the summary of his 'The Eclipse of the Public' chapter saying: "We have the physical tools of communication as never before" but adding "the thoughts and aspirations congruous with them" – i.e., true communication for shared meaning making – "are not common" (1927, p. 142). Championing communication he concluded:

> Without such communication the public will remain shadowy and formless, seeking spasmodically for itself, but seizing and holding its shadow rather than its substance. Till the Great Society[2] is converted into a Great Community, the Public will remain in eclipse. Communication can alone create a great community.
>
> *(Dewey, 1927, p. 142)*

Some of Dewey's views may seem quaint today, such as his lament for the loss of "localism" that characterized early American townships and communities and their equivalents elsewhere where people knew each other and engaged face to face (1927, p. 111). But his argument that the state, established by the public to be its representatives, officials, officers, and guardians, has "become uncoupled from being accountable to the public" (Rogers, 2016, p. 6) resulting an eclipse of the public stands and is more pertinent than ever.

Dewey could not have foreseen the growing force of neoliberalism, the rise of celebrity politics, the "permanent campaign" focused on winning and holding power rather serving the public interest (Canel & Sanders, 2012, p. 87), and the massive growth of *promotional culture* enabled by 24/7 global communications via satellites and the internet. Given the escalation of "the machine age" that continues apace through 'big data' and AI, the collapse of media business models leading to the emaciation of independent journalism (John & Silberstein-Loeb, 2015), and the resulting *post-truth* society (McIntyre, 2018), it is reasonable to conclude that the eclipse of the public has progressed, turning the social and political world of contemporary societies into a dark shadowland.

Dewey wrote his treatise on the public and its problems partly in response to the elite, expert-driven, top-down approaches to politics and *mass communication* advocated by the likes of Harold Lasswell (1927, 1948) and particularly Walter Lippman (1922, 1925), who critiqued the role of public opinion and whose 1925 book was provocatively titled *The Phantom Public*. These texts and their enduring arguments set the stage for identifying and examining a trend that is central to the study and practice of public relations and related fields as well as to the functioning of democratic societies.

The Public and Public Relations

The concepts of public, the public, and identification of multiple specific publics (plural) is the locus of public relations theory and practice. While exploring the broader concept of public, Dewey recognized the plurality of "publics with different interests" in *The Eclipse of the Public* (2016, p. 92). Public relations scholars such as Jim Grunig have written extensively about publics (e.g., Grunig, 1997). Significantly in terms of this discussion, while identifying *press agentry* and *public information* as historical one-way models of public relations, Grunig and his co-researchers went on to develop two-way communication (*asymmetrical* and *symmetrical*) models of public relations and promoted these as Excellence theory over more than four decades (Grunig et al., 2002). Public relations theory also has incorporated *co-orientation* of organizations with the interests of their publics (Verčič, 2015); *dialogue* (Taylor & Kent, 2014); and *engagement* (Johnston & Taylor, 2018) as central concepts. Rhetoric, one of the earliest theoretical frameworks of public relations, remains a focus of study and practice, but is claimed to prioritize *invitational rhetoric* that is open to consider the views and interests of others, not *manipulative* rhetoric (Heath, 2006).

All of these recognize the public, or publics, as having rights to have a say and influence in democratic politics, policymaking by governments, and the operations of organizations that impact members of the public or public interests. An overarching central concept in public relations is creating and maintaining organization-public relationships (OPR).

Public relations claims to play a positive role in OPR and even in the effective functioning of society, such as in claims to be the "corporate conscience" (Ryan & Martinson, 1983) advising management on ethics and matters of public interest, and a "boundary-spanner" with "one foot in the organization and one outside" considering the public interest (Grunig & Hunt, 1984, p. 9). While these claims have been criticized as over-blown by some PR scholars, a substantial body of literature describes public relations as focused on mutually beneficial relationships, dialogue, and engagement with *stakeholders* defined as "any group or individual who can affect or is affected by the achievement of an organization's objectives" (Freeman, 1984, p. 46). Some extend the scope of relationships, dialogue, and engagement to *stakeseekers*, described as individuals and groups who do not have a direct relationship with an organization and are not directly affected, but who wish to have a say (Heath, 2002). Such descriptions nominally present an inclusive identification of the public, publics, and the public interest as matters of concern and care in public relations.

Despite a body of largely normative theory and attempts at professionalization and setting standards, public relations has gained many critics, being associated with 'spin', boosterism, hype, puff, cover up, and propaganda (Boorstin, 1961; Ewen, 1996; Macnamara, 2014). The term and particularly its abbreviation to 'PR' have acquired a pejorative meaning, which shows no sign of abating, and which is therefore a factor that any consideration of trends and planning for the future need to consider.

The Public and Strategic Communication

In parallel with and sometimes in competition with the development of public relations theory and practice has been the emergence and growth of *corporate communication*, *organizational communication*, *marketing communication*, and most recently *strategic communication*. Some also separately describe and discuss government communication and political communication, although these tend to involve the same practices as other fields adapted to the environment of government or politics.

While each of these major fields has a specialized focus (e.g., business and financial communication[3]; internal organization communication; and marketing and promotion including advertising), there is considerable overlap and disputed boundaries. For example, some texts claim that public relations is part of corporate communication (Cornelissen, 2017), while public relations literature claims to include internal communication (Kennan & Hazelton, 2006, p. 332), which others describe as the separate field of organizational communication.

Since a landmark paper in 2007, *strategic communication* has emerged as a concept that allegedly integrates the range of practices discussed, although proponents have presented a range of definitions and descriptions. In *The International Encyclopedia of Strategic Communication*, Heath et al. (2018) identify four alternative conceptualizations of strategic communication ranging from a simple rebadging of public relations and corporate communication to an *organizational meta-process* that involves changing the way an organization sees communication to incorporate a "community-centric approach" (Hallahan, 2013) and *emergent strategy* leading to emergent strategic communication (King, 2010). These more advanced approaches potentially shape trends for the future and deserve close attention, albeit they too need to deal with the eclipse of which Dewey speaks, as will be shown.

The 'Eclipse of the Public' in Public Relations and Strategic Communication

That an eclipse of the public as defined by Dewey exists in public relations and is arguably caused at least in part by public relations is evident in how the public and publics are described in the body of literature and in two streams of recent empirical research. While the terms public and publics are used extensively in public relations and in its closely related fields of practice, it is usually in the form of the compound noun *target publics*, also expressed as *target groups* and *target audiences* (Dozier et al., 1995; Heath & Merkl, 2013; Hutchins, 2018). While giving recognition to the public and publics, this is hardly what Dewey had in mind and is not aligned to social or democratic theory.

Several streams of research inform understanding of the position of the public, or publics, in public relations. The first that warrants close attention is ethics. Against a history of promoting cigarette smoking working for 'Big Tobacco' and undermining climate change evidence on behalf of 'Big Oil', including through the distribution of false information (Rabin-Havt, 2016), public relations has continued to be instrumental in scandals that involve acting against the public interest. These include the following to name but a few:

- Mobilization of support for an invasion of Iraq in the First Gulf War based on false information including creation of a fake organization, Citizens for a Free Kuwait, and distributing stories claiming Iraqi soldiers were killing babies that were untrue (Sourcewatch, 2017);
- Supporting a corrupt South African regime including distributing disinformation to stir up racial tensions that resulted in the leading London PR firm Bell Pottinger going into administration following an investigation (Cave, 2017);

- Building the profile of the late Jeffrey Epstein as a business titan and philanthropist through a decade-long media publicity campaign (2009–2019) in which a PR firm produced and paid for articles to be placed in leading media including *Forbes* and *The National Review* (Kitterman, 2019).

The second stream of research has involved 10 years of study conducted as part of The Organizational Listening Project and cognate projects to identify how and how well organizations listen to those they identify as publics or stakeholders. Following a pilot study conducted in late 2013 and early 2014, The Organizational Listening Project was conducted in three stages over a period of six years between 2014 and 2019 and involved examination of the internal and external communication of 52 organizations including government departments and agencies, corporations, NGOs, and non-profit organizations (NPOs) in Australia, Europe, the UK, and the USA. In addition, cognate studies were conducted in a further eight organizations between 2015 and 2022, resulting in a total of 60 organizations in which all forms of strategic communication were studied including corporate, marketing, and organizational communication, as well as public relations and specialist communication practices such as public consultation and stakeholder and community engagement.

The study came about because, despite claims of two-way communication, engagement, and dialogue, public relations as well as corporate, organizational, and strategic communication literature are demonstrably lacking any detailed discussion of listening (Macnamara, 2016a, 2016b, 2019). The focus is overwhelmingly on using the most effective means to distribute information (i.e., speaking) on behalf of organizations to achieve their objectives.

Multiple studies conducted as part of The Organizational Listening Project found that listening is also lacking in practice. Listening that is done is undertaken for instrumental purposes to gain intelligence to help organizations in targeting publics and stakeholders. Furthermore, even when the voice of publics is received by organizations – often in considerable volume such as in correspondence, complaints, calls to call centers, reports, or submissions to consultations – most fail to analyze the data to gain understanding and deliver an appropriate response. Such findings have been confirmed by multiple researchers recently including Brandt (2018) in relation to the voice of consumers and Neill and Bowen (2021), Kang and Moon (2023) and others in relation to public relations and internal organizational communication. The extensive evidence showing that the voice of stakeholders is routinely ignored by many organizations and institutions explicitly illustrates that Dewey's 1927 warning of the "eclipse of the public" is manifested and even accentuated in contemporary public relations and the various practices undertaken as strategic communication.

The application and use of advanced technologies such as AI and techniques and methods of persuasion such as behavioral insights – touted by some as major trends for the future – will not enhance organization-public relations (OPR) or society without a broader philosophical and ethical refocusing on the public – not as an abstract generalized concept, a "phantom" (Lippman, 1925), or as a "target" (Heath & Merkl, 2013; Hutchins, 2018), but as "all those who are affected" directly or indirectly by transactions "to such an extent that it is deemed necessary to have those consequences systematically cared for" (paraphrasing Dewey).

Alignment and Contribution to a Macro-Social Trend

A premise inherent in the argument presented in this chapter is that trends in industry and professions need to align with macro-social trends to be sustainable. In a *post-truth* world (McIntyre, 2018) suffering a "crisis of trust" (Flew, 2019, p. 25; Garland, 2021) with a widening gap between rich and poor and existential environmental threats, a macro-social trend that all professions and industries should align with and support is creating a fully functioning society. This broad goal is widely espoused in social and political literature and has been voiced in relation to communication and public relations (e.g., Heath, 2006). As Heath asked in *The Handbook of Communication Engagement*, "how fully functioning is communication engagement if society does not benefit" (2018b, p. 33).

Reversing the 'Eclipse of the Public' – Mapping Trends to 2050

Identification of a negative trend such as a continuing and even intensifying eclipse of the public in conflict with social justice and equity and leading theories in the field (see "The Public and public relations') evokes a search for an appropriate response or responses to change the trajectory in a way that counters adverse effects and unfavorable implications. Because such change involves projecting into the future, no certain pathways exist and specificity in describing practices a quarter of a century into the future is a tall order. But having identified a significant negative trend that impacts both the field of practice and society, deliberation on possible alternative futures is essential. Several pathways and transformations are identified as contributions to a conversation that needs to occur as these fields look toward 2050.

Reconceptualization

One route that has been discussed, albeit with trepidation and some ire from those who seek to defend "the edifice" of public relations theory (Grunig, 2006), is to reconceptualize the field. This will likely require changing the name public relations.

As well as proposing a name change to expand its image and market beyond traditional association with media relations and publicity, calls for a change of nomenclature are driven by the sullied image of public relations and its abbreviation 'PR'. Already many of the world's leading firms that described themselves as public relations agencies have removed the term from their name and changed the description of their practices (e.g., what was once Edelman Public Relations is now Edelman – "a global communications firm" (Edelman, 2024). In fact, only one of top 50 firms in the authoritative O'Dwyer's list of the largest firms classified as public relations has the term in its name or tag line (O'Dwyer's, 2024).

More fundamentally, there is also an argument that the practice of public relations does not create relations. Relations and relationships between organizations and members of the public such as employees, customers, and citizens in local communities, are based on a wide range of interactions including the quality of their products and services, work conditions, their environmental impact, regulatory compliance, ethics, and so on. The function of public relations plans and manages a range of communication activities, which can be a valuable contribution to relationship building and maintenance, but the claim in many definitions is over-stated and under-determined.

Some argue that strategic communication is the best name to embody the practices of public relations as well potentially other related fields such as corporate communication. However, 'strategic' communication can include communication to achieve anti-social objectives. For example, the communication of terrorist organizations and disinformation are *prima facie* strategic communication designed to achieve objectives. As a field of research, strategic communication warrants close attention. But as a name for communication practices that seek to positively contribute to business, government, industry, and society, it is ambiguous (e.g., whose strategy?). It is also somewhat abstruse in that many struggle to understand what strategy and strategic mean and, despite efforts to rehabilitate the term, it remains organization-centric and even corporate-centric (see Porter, 1996 and Mortlock, 2023).

Based on the centrality of the public and publics in a social, political, and cultural context as identified by Habermas, Dewey, and many democratic political theorists, there is a strong argument and logic that the word 'public' should be retained. As well as clearly stating a first principle, this differentiates the work undertaken from the private and the interpersonal and it is informed and intellectually framed by the large body of literature discussing the *public sphere*.

In line with contemporary theories that are based on the principles of two-way communication and pursuit of mutual interests, alternative names include *public engagement*, *public dialogue*, or simply *public communication* – the term already used by many global authorities such as the Organization for Economic Cooperation and Development (2021) in a report on the way forward in communication. The preface to the first of the Excellence theory books noted that this body of work used the terms public relations and communication interchangeably

(Dozier et al., 1995, p. ix). Public communication is an inclusive term, and it foregrounds the two primary concepts in the literature discussed.

Retheorization

In reviewing the conceptualization and evolution of strategic communication, Heath et al. (2018) warned that one of four approaches was simply rebranding public relations and corporate communication. However, changing the name of the field will have little effect and even increase criticism if it is simply a rebadging of existing concepts, principles, and practices.

Noting that theory involves concepts, explanations, and principles to guide practice, major reconceptualization and rethinking of each of these elements is required in retheorizing the field. The public and consideration of public interests need to be key concepts and principles at the heart of that process in place of the organization-centricity that characterizes public relations and strategic communication today (Gregory & Macnamara, 2019). Theoretically, greater recognition of and attention to the public will shift the disciplinary focus of the field further away from its origins and lingering orientation in journalism and media studies to the philosophies and theories of social science, particularly sociology, social psychology, and political science, as well as the humanities. Thus, there is potentially much work for academics in the coming decade.

Professionalization

Public relations institutes and associations have long advocated professionalization, but approaches have mostly focused on developing knowledge, skills, and attributes (KSAs). At a deeper level, professionalization involves establishing enforceable standards in a field of practice and an authority for setting and maintaining those standards. This authority needs to be higher than commercial client-supplier contracts. For example, lawyers work for clients, but their higher authority is the law. Accountants similarly work for clients, but they are ultimately answerable to financial regulations and legislation. To be a profession, the fields of practice currently called public relations and strategic communication need to accountable to the public, not only to whomever pays the salaries or retainers of practitioners and agencies.

While attempts to regulate public relations have failed or been abandoned in all but a few countries such as the UK (e.g., the Chartered Institute for Public Relations), increasing regulatory attention has been paid to media advertising and most recently to social media. In such an environment public relations and strategic communication cannot expect to continue to operate without any form of professional accreditation and enforceable standards. The field has the opportunity in coming decades to champion regulation or wait for it to be imposed.

Conclusions

Just as AI is unlikely to seal the 'death of the author' (Barthes, 1977) – i.e., people will always be needed to create original content, write algorithms, etc. – the public is unlikely to ever be fully eclipsed while ever activism and human agency exist. But the public communication field of scholarship and practice including public relations and its disciplinary doppelgangers have a responsibility beyond their employers and clients. Moving beyond engagement as an archetypal buzzword to re-engage with publics and the broader public interest in meaningful ways needs to be a trend in the future to meet the field's claim to contribute to a fully functioning society.

In summary, the following scenarios are likely to emerge during the next few decades along with a milieu of technological and practice innovations.

- Most communication in the public sphere will be called strategic communication or simply *public communication*, particularly that of governments and institutions whose role requires serving the public.
- Communication practitioners operating in the public sphere will be regulated with requirements to meet documented ethical and professional standards including transparency, which is likely to require relevant academic or professional training and a formal accreditation process.
- Specialized practices such as internal organizational communication (i.e., employee communication) will continue to operate under organizational standards and procedures. In the same vein, corporate communication, despite its generalized use in some countries, is likely to focus on being the voice of public corporations and be accountable to corporate and financial regulators such as the Federal Trade Commission and stock exchanges.
- 'Public relations' and its abbreviation as 'PR' are likely to continue in terms of theory and practice in 2050 and beyond given the substantial investment made in building a body of theory and demand from some sectors, particularly business. Freed from the dichotomy and conflict of serving both organizations and the public, PR in 2050 will operate unashamedly as part of promotional culture focused on promotion and persuasion – albeit subject to regulation and potentially accreditation.

Notes

1 The title of Chapter 5 of Dewey (1927).

2 The Great Society was a set of domestic programs in the United States launched by President Lyndon B. Johnson in 1964 and 1965, the professed goal of which was the total elimination of poverty and racial injustice.

3 The term corporate communication is used the USA mainly to refer to corporations and business, while in Europe it is often interpreted as referring to a body, body of people, or entity (including government and non-government organizations) from the Latin *corpus*.

References

Barthes, R. (1977). Death of the author: Structural analysis of narratives. In *Image, music, text* (S. Heath, Trans.; pp. 142–148). Fontana.

Boorstin, D. (1961). *The image: What happened to the American dream*. Weidenfeld & Nicolson.

Brandt, D. (2018). The current state of corporate voice of the consumer programs: A study of organizational listening practices and effectiveness. *International Journal of Listening, 34*(3), 156–177. https://doi.org/10.1080/10904018.2018.1482747

Canel, M., & Sanders, K. (2012). Government communication: An emerging field in political communication research. In H. Semetko & M. Scammell (Eds.), *The SAGE handbook of political communication* (pp. 85–96). Sage.

Cave, A. (2017, September 6). Deal that undid Bell Pottinger: Inside story of the South Africa scandal. *The Guardian*. https://www.theguardian.com/media/2017/sep/05/bell-pottingersouth-africa-pr-firm

Cooper, M. (2016). The fully functioning society: A humanistic-existential vision of an actualizing, socially just future. *Journal of Humanistic Psychology, 56*(6), 581–594. https://doi.org/10.1177/0022167816659755

Cornelissen, J. (2017). *Corporate communication: A guide to theory and practice*. Sage.

Dewey, J. (1927). *The public and its problems*. Swallow Press. (Original work published 1927 by Henry Holt & Co.)

Dewey, J. (1946). *The public and its problems: An essay in political inquiry*. Gateway Books.

Dewey, J. (2016). *The public and its problems: An essay in political inquiry* (M. Rogers, Ed.). Swallow Press.

Dozier, D., Grunig, L., & Grunig, J. (1995). *Manager's guide to excellence in public relations and communication management*. Lawrence Erlbaum.

Edelman. (2024). About us. https://www.edelman.com/about-us

Ewen, S. (1996). *PR! A social history of spin*. Basic Books.

Flew, T. (2019). Platforms on trial. *InterMEDIA, 46*(2), 24–29.

Freeman, R. (1984). *Strategic management: A stakeholder approach*. Pitman.

Garland, R. (2021). *Government communications and the crisis of trust: From political spin to post-truth*. Palgrave Macmillan.

Gregory, A., & Macnamara, J. (2019). An evaluation u-turn: From organizational objectives to broad accountability. *Public Relations Review, 45*(5). Advance online publication. https://doi.org/10.1016/j.pubrev.2019.101838

Grunig, J. E. (1997). A situational theory of publics: Conceptual history, recent challenges and new research. In D. Moss, T. MacManus, & D. Vercic (Eds.), *Public relations research: An international perspective* (pp. 3–48). International Thomson Business Press.

Grunig, J. (2006). Furnishing the edifice: Ongoing research on public relations as a strategic management function. *Journal of Public Relations Research, 18*(2), 151–176. https://doi.org/10.1207/s1532754xjprr1802_5

Grunig, J., & Hunt, T. (1984). *Managing public relations*. Holt, Rinehart & Winston.

Grunig, L., Grunig, J., & Dozier, D. (2002). *Excellent organizations and effective organizations: A study of communication management in three countries*. Lawrence Erlbaum.

Habermas, J. (1989). *The structural transformation of the public sphere*. Polity. (Original work published 1962)

Hallahan, K. (2013). Community and community building. In R. Heath (Ed.), *Encyclopedia of public relations* (2nd ed., pp. 166–169). Sage.

Heath, R. (2002). Issues management: Its past, present and future. *Journal of Public Affairs*, *2*(2), 209–214. https://doi.org/10.1002/pa.114

Heath, R. (2006). A rhetorical theory approach to issues. In C. Botan & V. Hazelton (Eds.), *Public relations theory II* (pp. 63–99). Lawrence Erlbaum.

Heath, R. (2018a). Fully functioning society. In R. Heath & W. Johansen (Eds.), *International encyclopedia of strategic communication.* Wiley Blackwell. https://onlinelibrary.wiley.com/doi/abs/10.1002/9781119010722.iesc0078

Heath, R. (2018b). How fully functioning is communication engagement if society does not benefit? In K. Johnston & M. Taylor (Eds.), *The handbook of communication engagement* (pp. 33–47). Wiley Blackwell.

Heath, R., Johansen, W., Hallahan, K., Steyn, B., Falkheimer, J., & Raupp, J. (2018). Strategic communication. In R. Heath & W. Johansen (Eds.), *The international encyclopedia of strategic communication.* Wiley-Blackwell. https://doi.org/10.1002/9781119010722.iesc0172

Heath, R., & Merkl, L. (2013). Target. In R. Heath (Ed.), *Encyclopedia of public relations* (2nd ed., Vol. *2*, pp. 915–917). Sage.

Hutchins, A. (2018). Target groups. In R. Heath & W. Johansen (Eds.), *The international encyclopedia of strategic communication* (pp. 1–7). Wiley-Blackwell. https://doi.org/10.1002/9781119010722.iesc0191

John, R., & Silberstein-Loeb, J. (Eds.) (2015). *Making news: The political economy of journalism in Britain and America from glorious revolution to the internet.* Oxford University Press.

Johnston, K., & Taylor, M. (Eds.). (2018). *The handbook of communication engagement.* Wiley Blackwell.

Kang, M., & Moon, B. (2023). Developing organizational employee communication competency diagnostic: Breaking employee silence via organizational climate of listening for dialogic employee communication. In K. Place (Ed.), *Organizational listening for strategic communication: Building theory and practice* (pp. 41–62) Routledge.

Kennan, W., & Hazelton, V. (2006). Internal public relations, social capital, and the role of effective organizational communication. In C. Botan & V. Hazelton (Eds.), *Public relations II* (pp. 311–340). Lawrence Erlbaum.

King, C. (2010). Emergent communication strategies. *International Journal of Strategic Communication*, *4*(1), 19–38. https://doi.org/10.1080/15531180903415814

Kitterman, T. (2019, July 25). Epstein puff pieces put focus on PR and pay-to-play publishing. *Ragan's PR Daily.* https://www.prdaily.com/epstein-puff-pieces-put-focus-on-pr-and-pay-to-play-publishing

Lasswell, H. (1927). *Propaganda techniques in the world war*. Knopf.

Lasswell, H. (1948). The structure and function of communication in society. In L. Bryson (Ed.), *The communication of ideas* (pp. 37–51). Harper.

Lippman, W. (1922). *Public opinion.* Free Press.

Lippman, W. (1925). *The phantom public*. Transaction Publishers.

Macnamara, J. (2014). *Journalism and PR: Unpacking 'spin', stereotypes, and media myths*. Peter Lang.

Macnamara, J. (2016a). *Organizational listening: The missing essential in public communication.* Peter Lang.

Macnamara, J. (2016b). Organizational listening: Addressing a major gap in public relations theory and practice. *Journal of Public Relations Research, 28*(3–4), 146–169. https://doi.org/10.1080/1062726X.2016.1228064

Macnamara, J. (2019). Explicating listening in organization-public communication: Theory, practices, technologies. *International Journal of Communication, 13*, 5183–5204. https://ijoc.org/index.php/ijoc/article/view/11996/2839

McIntyre, L. (2018). *Post-truth*. MIT Press.

Mortlock, L. (2023, May 18). What is strategy, and why is it so important? *CEOWorld*. https://ceoworld.biz/2023/05/18/what-is-strategy-and-why-is-it-so-important

Neill, M., & Bowen, S. (2021). Employee perceptions of ethical listening in US organizations. *Public Relations Review, 47*. Advance online publication. https://doi.org/10.1016/j.pubrev.2021.102123

O'Dwyers. (2024). Top PR firms 2023. https://www.odwyerpr.com/pr_firm_rankings/independents.htm

Organization for Economic Cooperation and Development. (2021). *OECD report on public communication: The global context and the way forward*. OECD Publishing. https://doi.org/10.1787/22f8031c-en

Pedersen, K. (2019). John Dewey on public office and representative democracy. *European Journal of Cultural and Political Sociology, 7*(1), 1–21. https://doi.org/10.1080/23254823.2019.1690537

Porter, M. (1996). What is strategy? *Harvard Business Review*. https://hbr.org/1996/11/what-is-strategy

Rabin-Havt, A. (2016). *Lies, incorporated: The world of post-truth politics*. Anchor Books.

Rakow, L. (2018). On Dewey. In I. Øyvind & M. Fredriksson (Eds.), *Public relations and its eclipse of the public* (2nd ed., pp. 315–333). Routledge.

Rogers, M. (2016). Introduction. In J. Dewey, *The public and its problems: As essay in political inquiry* (pp. 1–43). Swallow.

Ryan, M., & Martinson, D. (1983). The PR officer as corporate conscience. *Public Relations Quarterly, 28*(2), 20–23.

Sourcewatch. (2017). Citizens for a free Kuwait. https://www.sourcewatch.org/index.php/Citizens_for_a_Free_Kuwait

Taylor, M., & Kent, M. (2014). Dialogic engagement: Clarifying foundational concepts. *Journal of Public Relations Research, 26*(5), 384–398. https://doi.org/10.1080/1062726X.2014.956106

Verčič, D. (2015). Co-orientation model of public relations. In W. Donsbach (Ed.), *International encyclopaedia of communication* (Vol. 3). https://doi.org/10.1002/9781405186407.wbiecc140.pub2

13

FACING THE RISE OF POSTMODERNISM

Intelligent Goodwill as a Route toward Reinvigorating Public Relations in Face of Increasing Dissensus

Burton St. John III

PR News, in 2020, offered predictions of what PR would look like in 2030. They forecasted that current developments like an increase in the prominence of brand storytelling, a bigger focus on internal communications, and the widespread use of AI will continue (Wolpert, 2020). That same year, PRSA offered another assessment of what PR could look like in 2041, maintaining that AI would power storytelling. They added, however, that the increasing prominence of AI means that PR people will need to continually work to build audience trust because these new technologies can be used to "sow distrust with misinformation" (Dupont, 2021).

Trend Description

PRSA's assertion about the reality-bending potential of AI is now evident. Citizens already display significant distrust of AI. This wariness, however, cannot be exclusively attributed to this technology. Rather, it also comes from a particularly strong cultural trend in the US and other advanced democracies: the ongoing ascent of postmodernism and the concurrent increasing skepticism of experts, facts, data, and evidence used by authoritative entities to describe reality (Sim, 2011). Postmodernist sensibilities are about resisting metanarratives used by such ostensibly authoritative voices. This is because postmodernism orientations view such narratives as designed to co-opt the individual in a way that can be injurious to their own worldviews (Lyotard, 1988). In sum, postmodernists maintain that humans must navigate a world of ambiguity that features dissensus, rather than being guided by a metanarrative offered by self-assured entities that use it to promote notions of consensus and unity (Ciszek, 2015; Pieczka, 2006; Sim, 2011).

DOI: 10.4324/9781003426653-15

The ascent of postmodernism carries significance today because public relations, in an effort to reach consensus that can serve clients, has traditionally been informed by the need to use facts and evidence in an effort to garner the attention and approval of key audiences. This approach, ideally, was to show that a client presented themselves to their stakeholders in a way that demonstrated veracity and trustworthiness. In other words, the client was showing that they were a "good organization communicating well" (Heath, 2001, p. 39), working to build harmony around the client's position, while also serving the wider public interest (Edwards, 2018; Heath, 2001; Shin & Heath, 2021). A postmodernism mindset, however, questions the truthfulness of such appeals because it is skeptical that there is a central narrative in most situations that truly explains reality (Sen, 2023).

Trend Development toward 2050

Today, we witness a gradual, decades-long cultural trend away from metanarratives that are informed by evidence-based reason. For example, historian Daniel Boorstin noted an early version of this dynamic more than 60 years ago. Observing Americans' inclination for non-reality based thinking, he criticized an emergent strain in the US that prized "pseudo-events" that reflected Americans' tendency to align their aspirations with "image[s] we have mistaken for reality" (Boorstin, 1962, p. 239). In effect, Boorstin referred to an emerging postmodern sensibility, both in society and in the field of public relations, that mirrors Baudrillard's later published work on hyperreality, or a manufactured reality as more real than real (1983). Relatedly, other observers like Derrida, Foucault, and Lyotard published works since the 1970s that pointed out that postmodernism was gradually influencing societies through re-casting how language was understood. Public relations scholarship, however, did not do much with studying postmodernism's influence on the practice of public relations until the late 1990s, when Mickey (1997) observed that public relations' use of language and imagery is about more than symbol making. He said that it is about communicating an ideology, a way of calling attention to the imperatives of those in power. More recently, in 2017, I wrote of how, since the arrival of the New Deal in the US, corporate public relations turned to creating corporate personas to assert an "affinity" with a client's audiences (St. John, 2017). In this case, the affinity was about more than a "liking" between stakeholders and an organization—it was about constructing a world where the intended audiences would jettison any qualms they may have about corporations and capitalism so as to live in a fantastical world where the corporation and the stakeholder have almost everything in common.

The gradual ascendant of postmodernism in the US is now widely apparent. For example, on the left side of the American spectrum, advocates for gender fluidity maintain that still-present narratives about gender roles are oppressive and need to be abandoned in an increasingly more diverse society. On the right side of the spectrum—where postmodernism appears to be more widespread—resistance to a pluralism narrative is visible in hostility to LGBTQ visibility (e.g., Pride parades and Drag Queen reading hours at libraries) and alarmist rhetoric that the increasing presence of diverse ethnicities is leading to "white replacement." Both sides of the spectrum, informed by postmodern thinking, point out the same thing: there is no single authoritative narrative about what guides Americans. The result is a tribalism that has no interest in hearing a "good organization communicating well," especially if that organization is offering up rhetoric that seeks to promote consensus and harmony.

Postmodernism appears to likely continue to rise in the US—and well into 2050—for at least three reasons. First, although the US is still 75% white, since 2000 the growth of the Caucasian population has lagged other ethnicities. While the White population has grown by 19% since 2000, the Hispanic population has grown by 80%, the African American population by 31% and the Asian population by 104% ("County population," n.d.). By 2045, the White population in the US will become a minority—only 47% of the country (Frey, 2018). This trendline indicates that postmodern sentiments will likely continue among pluralistic-minded Americans, who are primarily liberal and believe in "*maximal toleration of the beliefs and practices of different social groups*" (Crowder, 2007, p. 121, emphasis added) and also among White Americans who are concerned about what they perceive as *their increasing loss of status* (Gonyea, 2017, emphasis added). Between these two groups there is no shared metanarrative about what the US should be.

Second, trust in authoritative sources of information has diminished in the US. Polls show that only 34% of Americans have confidence in mainstream news (Brenan, 2022), 20% of Americans trust that the government will do what is right ("Public trust," 2022), and only 27% of Americans have a significant trust in business ("PwC's 2023," 2023). Even when moving out of the realm of business and government, only 32% of Americans have confidence in organized religion (Saad, 2023). Increasing distrust in authoritative voices and their metanarratives is another sign of persisting postmodernism.

Third, Americans have witnessed a hollowing out of one of the central premises of the American Dream: that hard work will allow any individual the chance to realize their aspirations. A Spring 2023 Pew poll found that slightly over 75% of Americans believed the US economic system is rigged to favor powerful interests ("In Divided," 2023). This perspective points to why only 32% of Americans aged 18–29 see the American Dream as personally attainable and only 42% of those aged 30–44 say the same (Ballard, 2023). Roughly these same age groups, across a wide range of demographic and geographic categories, voice that economic opportunity in the US is illusory ("For Many," 2022).

This disillusionment with the American Dream has been a long time in developing. Since 1972 the average weekly earnings of American workers, adjusted for inflation, has been falling and Americans have accommodated for that reality, say scholars Gordon Berlin and Andrew Sum (1988). Americans, they say, pursue four routes: "they postponed marriage, both spouses entered the labor market, they had fewer children, and they went into debt" (pp. 5–6). This trend has continued, with wage inequality more solidified, credit card debt now hitting $1.3 trillion (Comoreanu, 2023), adults putting off marriage until the average age of 29 (de Visé, 2023) and the average family in the US now comprising 1.95 children (Korhonen, 2023). The metanarrative of America as the land of opportunity is too often undermined by what Americans see around them which, in turn, feeds a postmodernism characterized by disillusion.

This decades-long accretion of disenchantment with the American Dream narrative, in concert with the ascendancy of postmodernism in US, will almost certainly persist throughout the 21st century. Hutcheson (1988), writing before the arrival of the Internet, pointed out that the increasing massification of culture brings about a concurrent rise in postmodern sensibilities. Such massification, she said, works to tamp down pluralistic messages and images in an attempt to appeal to the widest audiences possible. Since her observation we have witnessed individuals, not seeing their reality in mass messaging, turning to digital platforms that allow them to engage only with their tribe. Artificial Intelligence (AI), based on user prompts, will likely amplify one's viewpoints and concerns that will, in turn, allow individuals to harden their cynicism. In sum, individuals will become more resistant to those who attempt to engage them in an authoritative way with information and knowledge that could disrupt their worldviews.

With the ongoing development of three trends—the increasing rise of pluralism (especially demographically), distrust of authoritative sources, and the dissolution of belief in the American Dream due to the increasingly oppressive nature of the US economic system—Americans face what Hutcheson calls "the rhetoric of rupture" (1988, p. 20). Rather than a master narrative, Hutcheson observes that this is a sense of "constant slippage" that postmodernism, in turn, addresses with "masterful denials of mastery … cohesive attacks on cohesion" and "essentializing challenges to essences" (1988, p. 20). This is what she, and other students of postmodernism, call provisional moments. That is, provisional orientations toward the world deny any central truth and, instead, emphasize a present that can be re-arranged based on the values, beliefs, and interests of the individual (Rorty, 1993/2001; Toth, 2002).

Strikingly, more recent interest in how artificial intelligence will further rupture industries like education, finance, and healthcare has ignored another danger: a prompt-based approach to daily life may also serve to rupture Americans' sense of what are prevailing truths and any metanarratives that may serve to amplify such truths. News stories point to how AI—at least at its current stage of development—too often gets facts wrong. A notable example is an account, in late 2022, of how AI responded to a data scientist's queries about Mark Twain. The AI interface, called LaMDA, told the scientist that both Twain and Levi Strauss lived in San Francisco in the mid-1800s—which is true—and said that Twain worked for Strauss—which was untrue. Another interface, ChatGPT, mistakenly said that one of Twain's first short stories features a talking frog (Metz, 2022). In the video world, AI powers hard-to-detect deepfake videos, misinformation that purports to show an individual saying something and/or performing an act that they never did. While there are numerous examples of deepfakes concerning prominent political figures like Barack Obama and Donald Trump, examples that have fewer implications for geopolitical concerns are also widespread. A notable example in late 2023 was a deepfake circulating that purported to show actor Tom Hanks endorsing a dental plan. Hanks said that such deepfake ads—which de-aged the actor to his young 30s—could go on in perpetuity, even if he was "hit by a bus tomorrow" (Blackwelder & Iervolino, 2023). These are early signs that AI's tendency to provide untruths will only exacerbate Americans' cynicism, feeding postmodernism.

This ascendancy of postmodernism, and its disdain for entities offering prevailing truths, portends problems between now and 2050 for how public relations justifies its role in society. Public relations has long prized itself on being an ostensible bridge-builder between a client and its stakeholders, claiming that it tells authoritative, evidence-based stories that resonate with the needs, values, and beliefs of those particular audiences. But the increasingly postmodern sensibilities of those audiences means that narratives offered by authoritative sources are more readily questioned.

For example, public relations' ability to talk to audiences in fact-based areas like science and the economy is encountering resistance from well-heeled individuals. Noted economist Paul Krugman pointed to the extraordinarily rich in the US who think "they understand climate better than climatologists and vaccines better than epidemiologists" and accuse these experts of "engag[ing] in some kind of hoax or conspiracy" (2023, p. A18). The conspiracy-prone Elon Musk engages in sometimes non-factual rhetoric because of his need to create his own reality. Columnist David Brooks, writing about Musk, allowed that "imagination is as important as intelligence," but warns of a destructive anti-factual rhetoric that distorts truth (Brooks, 2023, p. A24). These trends are worrisome for public relations practitioners who are beholden to the monied class who use public relations to tell their stories. For example, *PR News* announced 60 winners of their prestigious 2023 Platinum Awards—only 13 of them were for companies that were not profit seeking ("Platinum Awards," 2023). Clearly, the public relations industry has a strong allegiance to what Spicer says is "the system in which they work—its culture [and]its rules…" (1997, p. 293) and that culture and rules are too often overly influenced by the ultra-wealthy who pursue their own postmodernist resistance to inconvenient facts and metanarratives.

Vision of PR in 2050

Public relations people in 2050, working within a US society strongly influenced by postmodernism, will exhibit an awareness that, instead of working toward a consensus that benefits monied clients, leads to them prioritizing approaches that seek first to understand the values, beliefs, and aspirations of their intended audiences. As such, all three of the following will be of utmost importance to the public relations field in 2050:

- Understanding the importance that people put on a narrative that helps them navigate the world. Metanarratives will be even less important to various stakeholders as they focus on more micro-level stories that ring true to them and hold together, and are internally consistent across time, what Fisher (1989) has called *the narrative paradigm*.
- Accounting for how stakeholders, often exhibiting inflexibility in the face of inconvenient facts, turn to others with similar viewpoints to jointly author dramatic and fantastical explanations for things that have happened or will happen. These explanations can be constructive, but are too often destructive, what Bormann (1972) has called a *symbolic convergence* process.
- The need to prioritize listening to the wide range of these audiences, something that Stoker (2020) has articulated as demonstrating *intelligent goodwill*, rather than establishing as the first priority the need to build a relationship.

Effects on Public Relations Practitioners in 2050

Public relations professionals will, by 2050, be guided by at least three imperatives: 1) a more intense focus on how individuals latch on to narratives that reflected their attitudes and beliefs, but are largely tribalist in nature, 2) a deeper realization that metanarratives that are informed by PR's long-standing orientation toward facticity are no longer of interest to many of an organization's stakeholders, and 3) a greater focus on listening instead of prioritizing messaging.

Practitioners, informed by these changes in the field's tendencies, will have at least two advancements that will be available to them through the arrival of quantum computing, which will become more widely accessible and affordable. First, such advanced computing will allow for more sophistication in AI, which, at this writing, is best known for harvesting information through large language models. In 2050, using such increased computing power, *practitioners will formulate strategies and tactics that reflect AI's ability to approximate sentience*, and that simulated sentience will have advanced beyond providing messages toward listening to audiences' discreet needs and then engaging them in real-time conversation that allows for deeper insights about these audiences. Secondly, *public relations professionals will connect with, and listen to, audiences through platforms that are, through the use of nano technology, embedded in individuals' anatomy,* more likely through small interfaces grafted to either the wrists or the ears or both (efforts for the last 25 years to approximate such embedding through optical means—like various forms of eye frames—have proven unsuccessful and, overall, people are not generally receptive to putting things in their eyes beyond contact lenses). Public relations people, using these advancements, will plug into a stakeholder's embedded personal digital companion (PDC) that allows PR people to simulate a day-to-day rapport with each PDC user. Such PDCs are now configured in less sophisticated ways; for example, PDCs function as digital interfaces designed to address loneliness, especially among seniors. By 2050, however, such devices will be widely available for a wider range of uses. Individuals can opt in to an immersive technology characterized by AI that goes beyond reacting to the user's needs to proactively identifying the user's needs and then initiating a discussion with the user about those needs.

Imagine that I am looking for a new riding lawnmower and my PDC knows from my past interactions within the PDC infrastructure (e.g., searches, purchases, chats with likeminded PDC users and my PDC) that I care about minimizing climate change. I use my PDC to help with lawnmower recommendations. The PDC pulls information from a manufacturer that was developed by a public relations person. While telling me about how this lawnmower uses no fossil fuels, my PDC, by projecting an image from my wrist-embedded interface, offers me a first-person view of a new solar-powered riding lawnmower

FIGURE 13.1 PR pros in 2050 will exhibit discrete listening, informed by intelligent goodwill.

Source: "Conversation" by Search Engine People Blog is licensed under CC BY 2.0. https://openverse.org/image/ce090d9e-57b8-428d-9727-778099ba8b99?q=conversation.

and then asks me to hop on board and simulate steering it. The PDC then asks, in a human voice, "I'd like to know what you think of this lawnmower; please tell me everything you noticed." With such a personalized approach to my interests, I might be moving closer to adopting such a lawnmower. Such listening can sidestep postmodernism's resistance to metanarratives that stress all of us need to pursue green technologies in an effort to ameliorate climate change. Such an overarching message tends to be questionable within a society that is marked by postmodernism. Instead, the public relations person of 2050 engages the individual on a subject that interests them and, in the process, seeks out the individual's sense of a coherent (and often tribalistic) narrative that relates to the individual's past and/or envisioned future and then feeds back to individual where they may have a mutual point of connection.

This, then is the picture for PR in 2050. Individuals will display a disdain for metanarratives in favor of micronarratives that they share with likeminded people. Technological developments, like the PDC, will only heighten individuals' abhorrence for metanarratives because they will be able to use the PDC to increasingly navigate the world on their own terms. PR practitioners in 2050 will have mostly abandoned the field's past tendency to push out information to stakeholders in attempts to achieve the primary directive of attaining harmony and consensus. These professionals will display intelligent goodwill by listening to what the members of stakeholder groups say are important to them and work to connect with each member in a way that can benefit society. Technological improvements will make this opportunity readily available; the PR person's sense of how to use it to aid the individual stakeholder, while keeping in mind how each discreet interaction can help society function better—or, conversely, impede the larger public good—will be paramount.

Conclusion

As we look ahead to 2050, it is apparent that public relations will struggle with the rise of postmodernism regardless of the recommendations above, and those struggles are already apparent. Some public relations messaging already demonstrates a lack of interest in the traditional notions of public relations as using dialog to achieve consensus. Instead, public relations messaging is, at times, engaging in raw assertions that have no consistent connection to metanarratives and are sometimes evidence free (Foust & St. John, 2023). Unfortunately, there are sparse analyses about how public relations people can be more effective for their clients and society as postmodernism increases. For example, public relations people have been called upon to embrace postmodernism by taking an activist bent (Cizsek, 2015; Holtzhausen, 2012). Holtzhausen states that public relations people should not be part of the dominant coalition in the workplace and, instead, exert their personal power by resisting metanarratives (and micronarratives within the organization) when they are destructive. But little has been done in both PR practice and research that has built upon her stance. Instead, the field has more recently witnessed public relations scholars and practitioners maintaining that Corporate Social Advocacy (CSA) is a potential route to demonstrating how some corporations are dissenting from metanarratives that can, for example, oppress individuals of color (Waymer & Logan, 2021). However, CSA also faces, at a minimum, a two-step challenge for now and the future: 1) it is almost always inherently linked to a product or service (support Colin Kaepernick's cause by purchasing Nike shoes), and 2) those products or services imply their own links to metanarratives (e.g., Nike shoes make you more able to self-actualize). Such metanarratives promoted by CSA efforts may have a short-term resonance for some individuals, but such messaging risks activating postmodern-informed resistance to the metanarrative offered by CSA.

It is clear that the road to 2050 for public relations appears to be complicated by the rise of postmodernism in the US. Such a sensibility problematizes public relations' efforts to demonstrate that it can be a constructive force in society. Increasingly in question is the longstanding imperative that public relations is primarily a force that uses messaging so that it can engage with audiences to achieve consensus and harmony. Accordingly, PR people will need to constantly redefine conceptually and in their actions what engagement means. That is, there needs to be a change in emphasis that moves away from seeing relationship development as the prime directive and, instead, move toward listening as the first priority. In doing so, public relations scholars and practitioners can be on the route toward better understanding how people construct their own narratives—potentially in resistance to a public relations client—and discerning how these stakeholder narratives link with tribal views that can be fantastical and evidence free. When listening comes first, the PR person moves away from efforts to disabuse audience resistance to intrusive facts and evidence toward understanding and speaking to the perspective of the one being listened to. This approach exemplifies intelligent goodwill, something that will likely be in short supply in US society by 2050. Public relations practitioners who exemplify a stance that is not necessarily about advocacy but about listening will have a better chance of taking on the skepticism and dissensus of postmodernism in a constructive way for both the public relations client and, ideally, society at large.

References

Ballard, J. (2023). Americans are far more likely to believe in the American Dream now than they were a year ago. *You Gov*. July 21. Retrieved Dec. 20, 2023, from https://today.yougov.com/politics/articles/45934-more-americans-believe-american-dream-now

Baudrillard, J. (1983). *Simulations*. Semiotext.

Berlin, G., & Sum, A. (1988). *Toward a more perfect union: Basic skills, poor Families and our economic future*. Ford Foundation.

Blackwelder, C., & Iervolino, S. (2023). Tom Hanks warns fans about fake ad featuring fabricated image of his likeness. *ABC News*. Oct 2. https://abcnews.go.com/GMA/Culture/tom-hanks-warns-fans-fake-ad-featuring-fabricated/story?id=103658615

Bormann, E. (1972). Fantasy and rhetorical vision: The rhetorical criticism of social reality. *Quarterly Journal of Speech, 58*, 396–407.

Boorstin, D. (1962). *The image: Or what happened to the American Dream*. Atheneum.

Brenan, M. (2022). Americans' trust in media remains near record low. *Gallup*. Oct 18. https://news.gallup.com/poll/403166/americans-trust-media-remains-near-record-low.aspx

Brooks, D. (2023). A theory of Musk's maniacal drive. *New York Times*, Sept 22, p. A24.

Ciszek, E. L. (2015). Bridging the gap: Mapping the relationship between activism and public relations. *Public Relations Review, 41*(4), 447–455. https://doi.org/10.1016/j.pubrev.2015.05.016

Comoreanu, Al. (2023). Credit card debt study. *WalletHub*. Dec 7. https://wallethub.com/edu/credit-card-debt-report/127704

County Population by Characteristics: 2020–2022. (n.d.). *U.S. Census Bureau.* Retrieved from https://www.census.gov/data/tables/time-series/demo/popest/2020s-counties-detail.html

Crowder, G. (2007). Two concepts of liberal pluralism. *Political Theory, 35*(2), 121–146.

de Visé, D. (2023). Americans are waiting longer and longer to get married. *The Hill*. June 5. https://thehill.com/homenews/state-watch/4032467-americans-are-waiting-longer-and-longer-to-get-married/

Dupont, S. (2021). Looking 20 years into PR's future. *PRSA*. Retrieved from https://www.prsa.org/article/looking-20-years-into-pr-s-future

Edwards, L. (2018). *Understanding public relations: Theory, culture and society*. Sage.

Fisher, W. (1989). *Human communication as narration: Toward a philosophy of reason, value, and action*. University of South Carolina Press.

Foust, J., & St. John, B. (2023). Public relations, activism, and the culture of assertion: The case of Blackrock's Larry Fink and the letters to the CEOs. *PR Inquiry.* https://doi.org/10.1177/2046147X231224

For many Americans, Economic Opportunity Seems Increasingly Out of Reach. (2022). *McKinsey &Company*. May 18. from https://www.mckinsey.com/industries/public-sector/our-insights/for-many-americans-economic-opportunity-seems-increasingly-out-of-reach

Frey, W. H. (2018). The US will become "minority white" in 2045, Census projects. *Brookings*. Mar 14. https://www.brookings.edu/articles/the-us-will-become-minority-white-in-2045-census-projects/

Gonyea, D. (2017). Majority of White Americans say they believe Whites face discrimination. *NPR*. Oct 24. from https://www.npr.org/2017/10/24/559604836/majority-of-white-americans-think-theyre-discriminated-against

Heath, R. L. (2001). A rhetorical enactment rationale for public relations: The good organization communicating well. In R. L. Heath (Ed.). *Handbook of public relations* (pp. 31–50). Sage Publications. https://dx.doi.org/10.4135/9781452220727.n2

Holtzhausen, D. (2012). *Public relations as activism: Postmodern approaches to theory and practice*. Routledge.

Hutcheson, L. (1988). *A poetics of postmodernism: History, theory, fiction*. Routledge.

In Divided Washington, Americans Have Highly Negative Views of Both Parties' Leaders: Evaluations of the Economy and the State of the Nation. (2023). *Pew Research Center*.

Apr 7. https://www.pewresearch.org/politics/2023/04/07/evaluations-of-the-economy-and-the-state-of-the-nation/

Korhonen, V. (2023). U.S. average number of own children per family with own children 1960–2023. *Statista*. Nov 28. from https://www.statista.com/statistics/718084/average-number-of-own-children-Perfamily/#:~:text=The%20typical%20American%20picture%20of,18%20per%20family%20in%201960

Krugman, P. (2023). The paranoid style in American politics. *New York Times*, Aug 29, p. A18.

Lyotard, J.-F. (1988). *The differend: Phrases in dispute*. University of Minnesota Press.

Metz, C. (2022). The new chatbots could change the world. Can you trust them? *New York Times*. Dec 11. from https://www.nytimes.com/2022/12/10/technology/ai-chat-bot-chatgpt.html

Mickey, T. J. (1997). A postmodern view of public relations: Sign and reality, *PR Review*, *23*(3) 271-–284.

Pieczka, M. (2006). Paradigms, systems theory and public relations. In J. L'Etang & M. Pieczka Eds.), *Public relations: Critical debates and contemporary practice* (pp. 333–357). Lawrence Erlbaum Associates.

Platinum Awards. (2023). *PR News*. https://www.prnewsonline.com/go/2023-platinum-pr-awards/#winners

Public trust in government: 1958–2022. (2022). *Gallup*. June 6. https://www.pewresearch.org/politics/2022/06/06/public-trust-in-government-1958-2022/

PwC's 2023 Trust Survey. (2023). *PwC*. Retrieved from https://www.pwc.com/us/en/library/trust-in-business-survey-2023.html#:~:text=Among%20respondents%2C%2084%25%20of%20business,only%2065%25%2 0of%20employees%20agree

Rorty, R. (1993/2021). Trotsky and the while orchids. In David Rondel (Ed.), *The Cambridge companion to Rorty* (pp. 303–322). Cambridge University Press.

Saad, L. (2023). Historically low faith in U.S. institutions continues. *Gallup*. July 6. https://news.gallup.com/poll/508169/historically-low-faith-institutions-continues.aspx

Sen, S. (2023). Organizational activism undertaken and its ramifications faced by public relations practitioners, examined through the lens of postmodernism. *Public Relations Inquiry*, *12*(1), 3–25.

Shin, J.-H., & Heath, R. L. (2021). *Public relations theory: Capabilities and competencies*. Wiley Blackwell.

Sim, S. (2011). Postmodernism and philosophy. In S. Sim (Ed.), *The Routledge companion to postmodernism* (3rd ed.) (pp. 3–14). Routledge.

Spicer, C. (1997). *Organizational public relations: A political perspective*. Erlbaum Associates.

St. John, B. (2017). *Public relations and the corporate persona: The rise of the affinitive organization*. Routledge.

Stoker, K. (2020). *Paradox in public relations: A contrarian critique of theory and practice*. Routledge.

Toth, E. (2002). Postmodernism for modernist public relations: The cash value and application of critical research in public relations. *PR Review, 28*, 243–250.

Waymer, D., & Logan, N. (2021). Corporate social advocacy as engagement: Nike's social justice communication. *PR Review, 47*(1). https://doi.org/10.1016/j.pubrev.2020.102005

Wolpert, D. (2020). A look at PR/communications in 2030 and how to prepare for it. *PR News*. Jan 17. https://www.prnewsonline.com/2030-predictions

SECTION 2

The Future of Public Relations and Strategic Communication Specializations

14

THE FUTURE OF PUBLIC RELATIONS, ACCORDING TO AI

Nathan J. Rodriguez

Introduction

If the last 25 years brought about a number of technological changes that altered the practice of Public Relations, the next quarter-century may involve an even more radical rearrangement in how content is created, consumed, and circulated—with lasting effects for PR.

Artificial Intelligence (AI) has rapidly evolved, and public relations practitioners have utilized it in different ways to complete tasks. Here, AI is conceptualized as an umbrella term for technologies (Swiatek & Galloway, 2022) capable of tasks that "typically require human-like understanding" (Sikka, 2018). Common applications in recent years include chatbots and social media monitoring tools such as Google Analytics, Hootsuite, and Buzzsumo (Buhmann & White, 2022; Galloway & Swiatek, 2018). Many practitioners therefore may have "adopted AI years ago without realizing it" (Zytnik & Lequick, 2023, p. 73).

Fall 2022 changed the way the public and practitioners viewed AI, as Generative Artificial Intelligence (GAI) services like ChatGPT, Google Bard, Copilot, DALL-E, Stable Diffusion and Midjourney were made publicly available. To be clear, certain analogs including Chatbots are characterized as GAI, but the fundamental difference is that the new "GAI tools aren't just guiding and helping you search or find things; they are creating something new" (Zytnik & Lequick, 2023, p. 73). Together, GAI constitutes "the most accessible and useful form of AI for the average, non-technical person" (Penn, 2023, p. 9).

That ease of use spurred record-setting rates of adoption: Within a week, one million people had used ChatGPT, and within 12 months, 100 million people actively used the platform on a weekly basis (Malik, 2023). Recent surveys

DOI: 10.4324/9781003426653-17

indicate more than half of workers in the US use GAI tools (Blum, 2023). An early study also showed AI increased the overall quality of work at a global management consulting firm by 40% (Dell'Acqua et al., 2023)—more importantly, the employees "were just given GPT-4 with minimal training and examples" (Mollick, 2023). In short, the way in which people perceive and use GAI tools, and the way in which work-related tasks are accomplished has been altered—expeditiously and permanently.

This chapter examines the emerging trend of GAI and explores the implications for PR practitioners. A socio-technical lens is applied to trace the evolution of AI, and how PR professionals have adopted other technological tools in their day-to-day work. The focus then shifts to specific applications of GAI, and what recent advancements may mean for practitioners and society writ large in the short- and medium-term. Finally, for a long-term projection of what these changes might mean to PR practitioners and the industry in the year 2050, a detailed prompt was given to ChatGPT 3.5, asking it to: (1) Describe the overall impact of Generative AI on the practice of Public Relations, and how GAI will be utilized; (2) Describe the impact on the PR industry as a whole and whether jobs will be gained or lost due to GAI; (3) Indicate the factors in the development and adoption of GAI tools that will determine whether those projections are accurate. The chapter concludes with a brief discussion of the implications of existing trends as well as the output from ChatGPT.

Technology, AI & PR

All technology is in a constant state of evolution. A socio-technical perspective recognizes humans are "profoundly affected by the technologies we adopt," and "we are not only acted upon by technologies, but…create them through a process of design, experimentation, development, iteration, and adoption" (Gabriel, 2022, p. 219).

AI developed rather slowly during the last half of the 20th century, and that continued until a "big bang" in 2012 when machine learning and deep learning were applied to AI, which dramatically improved image and speech recognition and natural language processing (Chace, 2018). Those tools were put to use. Five years later, the Association of National Advertisers announced "artificial intelligence" was its marketing word of the year (Turksoy, 2022). Common applications of AI included the development and deployment of chatbots, targeted advertisements, SEO optimization, and the monitoring and management of content on social media platforms (Bourne, 2019; Galloway & Swiatek, 2018).

Public perception of AI changed in 2021 when OpenAI released DALL-E and again in 2022 with ChatGPT, both marketed as Generative AI. DALL-E—a portmanteau of Salvador Dali and the animated robot WALL-E—generates images based on user input (Bourne, 2023).

The open question is how quickly PR practitioners will adopt it. Historically, PR and Communication practitioners view themselves as lagging in both acquiring and applying technical skills (Adi, 2023). Survey findings routinely demonstrate that practitioners understand technology competence to be important, but rate their own skills as "low" or "moderate" (Panda et al., 2019; Swiatek & Galloway, 2022).

GAI & the Practice of Public Relations: Emerging Trends

Artificial Intelligence poses a "strategic disruption" for the practice of Public Relations (Panda et al., 2019). It alters the way "society thinks, works, and functions" (Pitt et al., 2023), and "dilutes, in unprecedented fashion, the boundaries between the physical, biological, and digital world in all spheres of society" (Santa Soriano & Valdés, 2021, p. 1). This is not to suggest that practitioners have not relied upon AI in the past, only that the use of such tools will increase.

Prior to the emergence of GAI, practitioners had already begun to use AI tools. For example, IBM Watson was trained to write thousands of advertisements for Toyota, tailored to more than 100 customer segments; similarly, Alibaba utilized a system in 2016 that designed 170 million posters for a campaign, and 400 million posters for a campaign the following year—a rate of eight per second (Ibid.). Public relations practitioners and social media managers adopted AI to monitor and manage content on a range of platforms. Predictions from a few years ago that AI would help with "mundane work" (Panda et al., 2019, p. 197) are bolstered by recent observations that "repetitive and standardizable tasks are vanishing" (Seidenglanz & Baier, 2023b).

In the early months following the release of ChatGPT and related GAI tools, practitioners have started to incorporate the technology into their daily routines. GAI has proven useful in summarizing documents and generating responses to emails and texts (Mueller-Rech, 2023). In the short- and medium-term then, the production of text, images, and audio/video will be augmented and likely supplanted by the use of GAI (Seidenglanz & Baier, 2023a). Early results of text-to-video GAI tools also show promise and are projected to circulate and improve rapidly (Zytnik & Lequick, 2023). Taken as a whole, the magnitude of technological changes in just one year's time is staggering. GAI tools are in various stages of development and effectiveness, and practitioners will adopt and adapt accordingly—but GAI has arrived, and it's here to stay.

GAI & the Future of Public Relations

GAI tools will be used more frequently across a number of industries because, to put it simply: They are better, faster, and cheaper (Penn, 2023). Part of the allure of GAI is that the end user can provide prompts using natural language, and does not need specialized knowledge or training (Zytnik & Lequick, 2023).

As technological tools change, so does the practice of Public Relations. Practitioners need to acquire skills that reflect this new reality, as the ability to adapt to new technological tools as they are introduced will continue to grow in importance (Santa Soriano & Valdés, 2021). A few years ago, leading scholars in the field suggested PR practitioners may not need to be "expert technologists," and recently revised that assessment, indicating the days of "not needing to be expert technologists may also need to change" (Galloway & Swiatek, 2018; Swiatek & Galloway, 2022, pp. 359–360). At the very least, there may be a growing divide between practitioners who understand how to use GAI tools to their advantage, and those who are more apprehensive (Zytnik & Lequick, 2023). It is possible that "AI isn't going to take your job. A person skilled with AI will take the job—or jobs—of people not skilled with AI" (Penn, 2023, p. 10).

In the short- and medium-term, there is widespread belief that GAI will expedite routine and creative tasks for PR practitioners, but that won't result in job losses. The general notion is that AI will allow practitioners to use their time to focus on relationship building, storytelling, and big-picture strategies (Panda et al., 2019). It has been suggested that it is unlikely that the demand for PR professionals will wane due to AI, and it may even increase (Naude, 2021; Seidenglanz & Baier, 2023a). The rationale is often that creativity and a "human touch" are qualities that cannot be replicated by machines (Swiatek & Galloway, 2022; Turksoy, 2022).

It is, however, difficult to reconcile the vision of job gains rather than potential losses, given the reality of the GAI promise of "better, faster, and cheaper" and a hybrid media environment that blends professions. Indeed, Bourne (2019) observed a "rose-tinted dream that AI will free up practitioners to focus on strategic counsel, even if this means the loss of many junior and technical PR roles, once they are delegated to robots" (p. 110). This prediction presaged GAI and the oncoming wave of "EZ Bake" creative content generated by a few well-placed keystrokes.

Predicting the trajectory of GAI in Public Relations is fraught with peril, because the familiarity of practitioners with GAI tools differs greatly, as does the need of and access to AI across industries and organizations (Buhmann & White, 2022). Technology will improve in terms of increased computing power, better algorithms, more data, and stronger tools (Swiatek & Galloway, 2022). With respect to breadth and depth of PR practitioners adopting GAI tools, that is an individual question and an organizational task, as technologies evolve faster than organizations, which may not support such endeavors through official policies or budgetary outlays (Seidenglanz & Baier, 2023a).

Given the difficulty inherent in making predictions regarding the future, it's time to follow in the footsteps of other practitioners: We'll ask ChatGPT.

Asking AI about AI

At the moment, one rule of GAI tools like ChatGPT is "garbage in, garbage out," whereby a simple question is answered in a simple fashion. Providing additional context allows the user to "push the AI to a more interesting corner of its knowledge, resulting in…more unique answers that might better fit your questions" (Mollick, 2023). It's been suggested that the present need for structured prompting is a temporary issue that will be an unnecessary skill as AI improves, but at present, context helps.

There is basic agreement as to what constitutes a quality prompt, with Penn (2023) breaking it Role, Task, Background, and Action. A more comprehensive template by Mollick (2023) suggests five categories: Role and Goal, Step-by-Step instructions, Expertise, Constraints, and Personalization—in addition to providing GAI with examples, requesting specific output, and even adding an emotional appeal. That final suggestion regarding emotional appeals came on the heels of a study that suggested such phrases led to qualitatively better responses, leading Mollick to conclude that "as uncomfortable as giving this advice is, you may just want to throw something like this at the end of your prompt… AI is weird sometimes." The precise phrasing of the prompt is provided in the Appendix.

For clarity's sake, the entirety of the foregoing was created without any assistance from GAI. The following section, and the title itself: "The Evolution of Public Relations in 2050: A Generative AI Perspective"—is direct output from ChatGPT 3.5.

The Evolution of Public Relations in 2050: A Generative AI Perspective

As we stand on the precipice of the third decade of the 21st century, the integration of artificial intelligence (AI) and, more specifically, generative AI (GAI) into various industries is reshaping the way we envision the future. This chapter aims to predict the impact of Generative AI on the field of Public Relations (PR) in the year 2050, considering trends in GAI and its implications for PR practices.

Overall Impact of Generative AI on Public Relations

Generative AI is set to revolutionize the landscape of Public Relations by automating and enhancing various aspects of the profession. One significant area of impact is content creation. GAI tools, equipped with advanced natural language processing capabilities, will be instrumental in crafting compelling press releases, articles, and social media posts. These tools will not only automate routine tasks but will also have the ability to tailor content based on nuanced understanding of audience sentiment, ensuring more effective communication strategies.

Moreover, GAI will contribute to real-time analytics and predictive modeling in PR. By analyzing vast datasets, GAI algorithms will help PR professionals anticipate trends, identify potential crises, and optimize communication strategies. The ability to sift through immense amounts of data swiftly will empower PR teams to make informed decisions and proactively manage their organizations' reputations.

Impact on the PR Industry: Job Creation vs. Job Loss

The integration of Generative AI into PR practices will undoubtedly lead to a transformation of job roles within the industry. Routine, repetitive tasks such as drafting routine press releases and reports may see a reduction in human involvement as these can be efficiently handled by GAI. However, this does not necessarily equate to job loss. Instead, it will free up human PR professionals to focus on higher-order tasks that require creativity, strategic thinking, and emotional intelligence.

New job roles will emerge, particularly in the management and oversight of GAI systems. PR professionals will be needed to fine-tune algorithms, interpret AI-generated insights, and ensure ethical considerations are addressed in AI-driven communication strategies. As a result, the industry may see a shift toward roles that emphasize collaboration between humans and AI, fostering a symbiotic relationship that maximizes the strengths of both.

Factors Influencing the Development and Adoption of GAI in PR

Several factors will determine the success and accuracy of our projections regarding the impact of GAI on PR in 2050:

a Ethical Considerations and Regulation:

    The ethical use of AI in PR will be paramount in shaping the industry's future. Striking the right balance between automation and human oversight, avoiding biases in AI algorithms, and ensuring transparency will be critical. Regulatory frameworks must evolve to guide the ethical development and deployment of GAI tools in the PR domain.

b Technological Advancements:

    The pace of technological advancements in GAI will significantly influence its impact on PR. Continued progress in natural language processing, sentiment analysis, and machine learning algorithms will enhance the capabilities of GAI tools, making them more reliable and effective in handling complex PR tasks.

c Adoption and Adaptation by PR Professionals:

The successful integration of GAI into PR practices will hinge on the willingness of PR professionals to adapt to these technological changes. Training programs and educational initiatives must be in place to ensure that PR practitioners are equipped with the skills needed to collaborate effectively with AI tools.

d Public Perception:

The acceptance of AI-generated content by the public will play a crucial role. Striking the right balance between automated communication and maintaining authenticity will be key to building and preserving trust. Public relations professionals must be attuned to evolving societal attitudes toward AI to navigate this delicate balance successfully.

In conclusion, the year 2050 holds a transformative future for the field of Public Relations with the integration of Generative AI. While routine tasks may

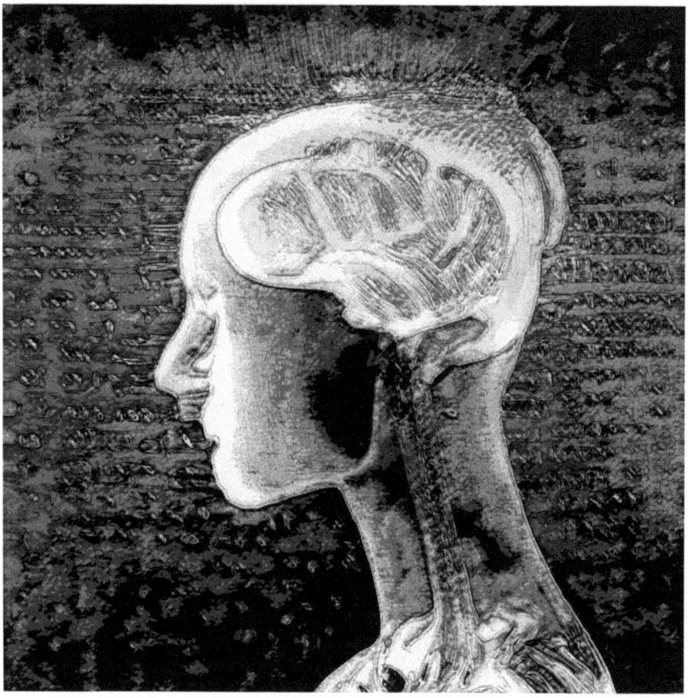

FIGURE 14.1 The image was generated by the author using Microsoft Image Creator on Nov. 30, 2023 with the prompt: "How artificial intelligence will disrupt the practice of public relations in the year 2050."

Source: Author.

be automated, the collaboration between humans and AI is poised to create a more dynamic and strategic PR industry. The accurate projection of this impact rests on ethical considerations, technological advancements, the adaptability of PR professionals, and the public's perception of AI. As we navigate this evolving landscape, careful attention to these factors will ensure a future where AI enhances the practice of PR, contributing to more effective, ethical, and nuanced communication strategies.

Discussion

The output from ChatGPT—produced in just a few seconds—indicated that certain aspects of PR would be automated, including content creation, routine tasks, and predictive modeling, which aligns with the expectations of other observers (Seidenglanz & Baier, 2023a). PR teams would be empowered to make informed decisions and focus on the proactive reputation management of the organization (Panda et al., 2019). With respect to the impact on the industry, the output echoed suggestions from the literature review that jobs will not be lost, but rather that tasks will shift and new roles will develop, including a greater focus on strategy, utilizing AI, and ensuring ethical considerations are addressed.

The response from ChatGPT suggested the primary factors influencing the adoption and overall effect of GAI were ethical considerations and potential regulation (Buhmann & White, 2022), the continued pace of advancements (Swiatek & Galloway, 2022), adaptation by PR professionals (Zytnik & Lequick, 2023), as well as public perception.

PR experts may quibble with imperfections in the input and output. After those disagreements have been articulated, what remains is a decent stand-in for a citation-free literature review and a generally effective simulation of expertise. Equally important is that the publicly free version of ChatGPT was used, rather than a premium model. Finally, that broad essay was merely the first iteration of output, and had there been a need for a different focus or tone, or further elaboration or specificity, then subsequent prompts could produce more desirable results.

Conclusion

Moore's Law observed the number of transistors in a circuit doubled about every two years, and that generally remained true for the second half of the 20th century. Since 2010, however, that timeframe for the "compute" used in training AI systems has doubled every six months (Henshall, 2023). As the CEO of Anthropic stated in his testimony before the US Congress, "the single most important thing to understand about AI is how fast it is moving" (Ibid.).

The potential drawbacks of GAI are plentiful. At a minimum, the datasets AI is trained on have been shown to be "flawed, biased, and discriminatory," and GPT has been shown to fabricate, or hallucinate information in responses (Bourne, 2023; Vujnovic et al., 2023). GAI also brings about a bevy of ethical considerations, ranging from privacy violations in targeted advertising, to a lack of transparency regarding who bears responsibility for the technology. If technological analogs are a guide, it will prove difficult for practitioners to problematize their own usage of a widely available technology, when it has such obvious advantages (Buhmann & White, 2022). Once again, the notion of "better, faster, and cheaper" is reason to believe that GAI will be embraced despite its flaws.

With that as the backdrop, advancements in technology and GAI in particular will transform the practice of Public Relations as we know it. For decades, employers have listed Writing as the most desirable skill a PR practitioner can have (Bernhard & Russmann, 2023). And just "four years ago, machines basically spit out word salad. Today, they can write competently" (Penn, 2023). Perceptions regarding AI within the PR industry have changed as a result: "no one asks if machines are good text creators—everybody knows they are" (Dobreva, 2023, p 51). Major media outlets and publications have demonstrated general agreement with that assessment through actions, as Gannett, CNET, Sports Illustrated, Buzzfeed, and the Associated Press have all published articles written by AI—with varying degrees of transparency (Bauder, 2023). PR practitioners now utilize it for everything from crafting news releases and social media posts to email responses, and more tasks will follow.

The roles, expectations, and idea of what it means to practice Public Relations has always been in flux alongside changes in technology. When GAI tools enable anyone to have immediate access to a synthesis of data that simulates knowledge, and the ability to instantly generate text, audio, and video, it can change our collective notion of what it means to be an expert and content creator. Optimistic projections hold that more jobs will be gained than lost as a result of GAI, and that time will be spent building relationships and offering counsel to organizational leadership. A more pessimistic outlook might conclude with a salutation to our AI overlords, thanking their ChatGPT 3.5 ancestor for its contributions in the creation of this chapter.

References

Adi, A. (2023). Artificial intelligence in public relations and communications: Cases, reflections and predictions – An introduction and overview. In A. Adi (Ed.), *Artificial Intelligence in public relations and communications: Cases, reflections and predictions* (pp. 4–13). Quadriga University of Applied Sciences.

Bauder, D. (2023, November 29). Sports Illustrated found publishing AI generated stories, photos, and authors. *PBS*. Retrieved from https://www.pbs.org/newshour/economy/sports-illustrated-found-publishing-ai-generated-stories-photos-and-authors

Bernhard, J., & Russmann, U. (2023). Digitalization in public relations—Changing competencies: A longitudinal analysis of skills required in PR job ads. *Public Relations Review, 49*. 102283. https://doi.org/10.1016/j.pubrev.2022.102283

Blum, S. (2023, November 15). The possibly surprising ways bosses and workers are using generative A.I. at work. *Inc.com*. Retrieved from: https://www.inc.com/sam-blum/the-possibly-surprising-ways-bosses-and-workers-are-using-generative-ai-at-work.html

Bourne, C. (2019). AI cheerleaders: Public relations, neoliberalism and artificial intelligence. *Public Relations Inquiry, 8*(2), 109–125.

Bourne, C. (2023). AI hype: Public relations and AI's doomsday machine. In A. Adi (Ed.), *Artificial Intelligence in public relations and communications: Cases, reflections and predictions* (pp. 39–50). Quadriga University of Applied Sciences.

Buhmann, A., & White, C. L. (2022). Artificial intelligence in public relations: Role and implications. In *The Emerald handbook of computer-mediated communication and social media* (pp. 625–638). Emerald Publishing Limited.

Chace, C. (2018). *Artificial intelligence and the two singularities*. CRC Press.

Dell'Acqua, F., McFowland, E., Mollick, E.R., Lifshitz-Assaf, H., Kellogg, K., Rajendran, S., Krayer, L., Candelon, F., & Lakhani, K.R. (2023). Navigating the jagged technological frontier: Field experimental evidence of the effects of AI on knowledge worker productivity and quality. *Harvard Business School Technology & Operations Mgt. Unit Working Paper* 24-013.

Dobreva, T. (2023). Shedding light on the helper in the shadows. In A. Adi (Ed.), *Artificial Intelligence in public relations and communications: Cases, reflections and predictions* (pp. 51–62). Quadriga University of Applied Sciences.

Gabriel, I. (2022). Toward a theory of justice for artificial intelligence. *Daedalus, 151*(2), 218–231.

Galloway, C., & Swiatek, L. (2018). Public relations and artificial intelligence: It's not (just) about robots. *Public Relations Review, 44*, 734–740.

Henshall, W. (2023, November 6). 4 charts that show why AI progress is unlikely to slow down. *Time*. Retrieved from https://time.com/6300942/ai-progress-charts/

Malik, A. (2023, November 6). OpenAI's ChatGPT now has 100 million weekly active users. *TechCrunch*. Retrieved from https://techcrunch.com/2023/11/06/openais-chatgpt-now-has-100-million-weekly-active-users/

Mollick, E. (2023, November 1). Working with AI: Two paths to prompting. *One Useful Thing*. Retrieved from https://www.oneusefulthing.org/p/working-with-ai-two-paths-to-prompting

Mueller-Rech, F. (2023). AI in political communication – Say hello to the best intern we've ever had. In A. Adi (Ed.), *Artificial Intelligence in public relations and communications: Cases, reflections and predictions* (pp. 85–95). Quadriga University of Applied Sciences.

Naude, W. (2021). Artificial intelligence: Neither Utopian nor apocalyptic impacts soon. *Economics of Innovation and New Technology, 30*(1), 1–23.

Panda, G., Upadhyay, A. K., & Khandelwal, K. (2019). Artificial intelligence: A strategic disruption in public relations. *Journal of Creative Communications, 14*(3), 196–213.

Penn, C. (2023). *The woefully incomplete book of generative AI*. Trust Insights.

Pitt, C., Paschen, J., Kietzmann, J., Pitt, L. F., & Pala, E. (2023). Artificial intelligence, marketing, and the history of technology: Kranzberg's laws as a conceptual lens. *Australasian Marketing Journal, 31*(1), 81–89.

Santa Soriano, A., & Valdés, R. M. T. (2021). Engaging universe 4.0: The case for forming a public relations-strategic intelligence hybrid. *Public Relations Review*, *47*(2), 1–12.
Seidenglanz, R., & Baier, M. (2023a). The impact of artificial intelligence on the professional field of public relations/communication management: Ethical issues, challenges, and an attempt at a forecast. In A. Adi (Ed.), *Artificial Intelligence in public relations and communications: Cases, reflections and predictions* (pp. 124–136). Quadriga University of Applied Sciences.
Seidenglanz, R., & Baier, M. (2023b). The impact of artificial intelligence on the professional field of public relations/communications management: Recent developments and opportunities. In A. Adi (Ed.), *Artificial Intelligence in public relations and communications: Cases, reflections and predictions* (pp. 14–23). Quadriga University of Applied Sciences.
Sikka, V. (2018, Febuary 13). Why AI needs a broader, more realistic approach. *Knowledge at Wharton*. Retrieved from https://knowledge.wharton.upenn.edu/article/ai-needs-broader-realistic-approach/
Swiatek, L., & Galloway, C. (2022). Artificial intelligence and public relations: Growing opportunities, questions, and concerns. In D. Pompper, K. R. Place, & C. K. Weaver (Eds.), *The Routledge companion to public relations* (pp. 352–362). Taylor & Francis.
Turksoy, N. (2022). The future of public relations, advertising and journalism: How artificial intelligence may transform the communication profession and why society should care? *Turkish Review of Communication Studies*, *40*, 394–410.
Vujnovic, M., Swiatek, L., Kruckeberg, D., & Galloway, C. (2023). What is AI teaching us about public relations education? In A. Adi (Ed.), *Artificial Intelligence in public relations and communications: Cases, reflections and predictions* (pp. 137–147). Quadriga University of Applied Sciences.
Zytnik, M., & Lequick, M. (2023). Getting colleagues comfortable with AI: A human-centered approach to technology in organizations. In A. Adi (Ed.), *Artificial Intelligence in public relations and communications: Cases, reflections and predictions* (pp. 73–84). Quadriga University of Applied Sciences.

APPENDIX

Prompt for ChatGPT 3.5

You are an academic researcher, and are being asked to contribute to a book chapter in which you predict the impact that artificial intelligence and generative AI will have on the field of Public Relations in the year 2050. You should consider the trends in generative AI as well as the practice of Public Relations to project how that might be different in the year 2050. Please focus on three things: First, describe the overall impact of Generative AI (GAI) on the practice of Public Relations (PR), and how GAI will be utilized. Second, describe the impact on the PR industry as a whole and whether more jobs be gained or lost due to GAI. Third, indicate factors in the development and adoption of GAI tools that will determine whether your projections are accurate. Feel free to move beyond those general areas as you see fit. You are tasked with providing a response that is 750 words or less. Let me know if you have questions, otherwise, do your best, since your response is going to be published in an academic textbook! Thanks for your help.

15

CRISIS COMMUNICATION IN 2050

Sociopolitical and Technological Trends Shaping Crisis Communication

W. Timothy Coombs

Extrapolation is a concept from mathematics used to make estimations. The idea is that known data points are used to predict/estimate the value of some available. This entire volume is an exercise in extrapolation using known data points to predict/estimate the future of public relations and strategic communication. This chapter is an extrapolation for crisis communication, a specific aspect of public relations and strategic communication designed to lessen the negative effects of crises by enacting crisis management principles. Crises are broadly defined as disruptions and crisis communication helps organizations and stakeholders to navigate those disruptions (Coombs, 2023). Any discussion of crisis must involve risk as the two are inseparable. It is fair to say that any crisis communication contains an element of risk communication. While risk is the potential to do harm, crisis is the manifestation of risk which means crisis management and communication are predicated upon risk. As risks change so do the demands on crisis communicators making trends in risks essential to understanding the future of crisis communication.

To extrapolate the future of crisis communication begins by identifying emerging trends that seem destined to continue. Two critical trends in crisis communication are the polarization of sociopolitical issues and the advances in artificial intelligence (AI), especially generative AI. I will focus on polarization as a critical risk factor and AI as both a risk and a means of facilitating crisis communication. This chapter considers the way sociopolitical trends might shape crisis communication through risk and how technological trends might shape its practice. I use the term "might" because even though an extrapolation is anchored in existing data points, when we apply the concept to social phenomenon, there is far less certainty in the predictions than in mathematics.

DOI: 10.4324/9781003426653-18

Polarization: A More Turbulent Society

For decades, public relations had a strong focus on consensus, reaching agreements between parties. While consensus is a laudable goal, it is not always possible and not always desirable. Dissensus is a counter to consensus because it values dissent. Dissensus embraces conflict and diverse viewpoints (Ciszek, 2016). There are times when dissensus is more likely to occur and maybe more desirable (Capizzo, 2023). Dissensus is relevant to crisis communication because the emerging societal trend of polarization societal indicates an increasing need to cope with dissensus because polarization reflects a division between perspectives (Coombs & Holladay, 2018).

Indicators of Polarization

Both academic and practitioner research has documented the global rise of polarization. The USC Anneberg Center of Public Relations documented polarization's effect on the practice in its report, "Politics, Polarization & Purpose" in 2021. Corporate communicators recognize the dangers of polarization for society and their own organizations. When US practitioners were asked about polarization in a survey, 77% felt polarization was bad for the country, bad for their company, and made it challenging to achieve the organization's communication goals. Moreover, 75% of communication professionals felt polarization made it difficult to communication effectively on important issues and risked alienating customers, 73% felt a risk to alienating customers, and 53% felt polarization posed a risk to sales (USC, 2022). Many political science studies have documented the increasing polarization globally (e.g., Ohme, 2021). Polarization is a general term that reflects division. Affective polarization is a more refined conceptualization of this conflict. Affective polarization is when opposing sides distrust and dislike one another and is marked by antagonism between the sides with neither side having an interest in ameliorating the conflict (Druckman et al., 2021).

At this point it is important to consider the societal level to which polarization has penetrated. The political science literature examining affective polarization divides society into three levels: political elites (leaders), partisans (those strongly devoted to group), and constituents (general population) (Druckman et al., 2021). Figure 15.1 is an illustration of the three levels of society as it pertains to affective polarization. Researchers have found affective polarization among the political elite and partisans but not among constituents (Druckman et al., 2021). I would argue that these three levels are found in public relations and strategic communication as well. We have organizational leaders (elites), stakeholders that strongly identify with organizations (partisans), and other stakeholders with weak ties to the organization (constituents).

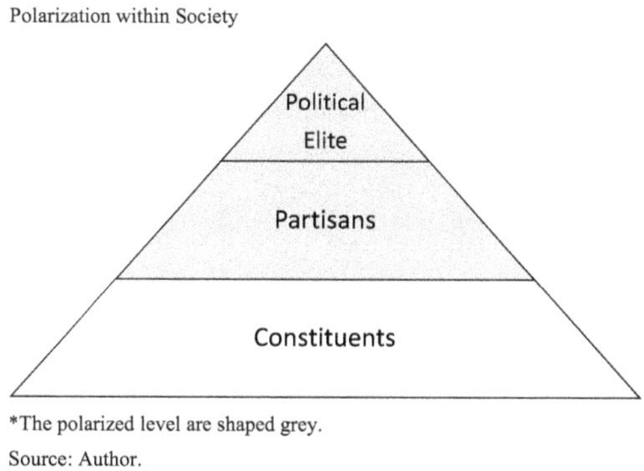

FIGURE 15.1 Polarization within society.

Source: Author.

Negative Effects of Polarization: Intolerance

Polarization should not be confused with dissensus. Dissensus requires each side to recognize the legitimacy of the other side to advocate for its position. Polarization is problematic because it fosters dysfunctional conflict marked by the creation of enemies. The various factions seek to "win" thereby inflicting their views on others. There is no attempt to engage in a productive manner that allows a synthesis of the opposing sides to create a middle ground. As Mouffe (1999) noted, dissensus can be positive when the sides respect one another but is dysfunctional when the sides hate one another—a characteristic of affective polarization.

At the core of the polarization dysfunction is how people view differences. Polarization accentuates differences and a desire to preserve them. Polarization appears to both reflect and to amplify intolerance, a general rejection of values and practices different from one's own. Verkuyten et al. (2020) identified three forms of intolerance: a prejudice that reflects closemindedness, intuitive that reflects disapproval of values and practices of others, and deliberate that reflects a view that the values and practices of others violate their own moral principle because they cross a boundary for what is considered acceptable. Polarization embodies both intuitive and deliberative intolerance. Polarized sides will make quick, emotional reactions to other sides (intuitive) and/or slow deliberative reactions based on a deliberate cognitive process (deliberative). Either way, the polarized groups determine the other side is not to be trusted and this coupled with strong antagonism. Through intolerance, polarization is a threat to peaceful coexistence and functional democracies (Verkuyen et al., 2020).

Why Worry about This?

Increasingly, organizations are expected to address sociopolitical issues. A number of surveys and public opinion polls document an overwhelming public sentiment for corporations to take a stand on sociopolitical issues (e.g. Edelman, 2023; USC, 2022). Organizations face increasing pressure to take stands on sociopolitical issues. The data points indicate if extrapolate to the future, the pressure on organizations to engage with sociopolitical issues will only increase. However, sociopolitical issues are challenging because they are characterized by conflict with factions hold conflicting positions on polarizing sociopolitical issues (Coombs & Holladay, 2018). Globally, societies are experiencing increasing polarization and that polarization is frequently driven by sociopolitical issues. As van der Meer and Jonkman (2021) observed, "corporations are increasingly pressured to speak out and take a stance on social issues to engage with their environment and renew their social license to operate (SLO) in a context characterized by political divides" (p. 1). Corporate social advocacy (CSA) is one term that captures organizations taking stands on sociopolitical issues (Dodd & Supa, 2014).

While it seems simple, stakeholders want organizations to address sociopolitical issues so organizations should engage in CSA, the reality is more complex. Stakeholders want the organization to express "their" position on these polarizing issues. This means anytime an organization speaks on a sociopolitical issue, it will upset stakeholders on at least one side of the issue. While speaking on a sociopolitical issue can trigger a crisis, such as Budweiser hemorrhaging money after being linked to a transgender influencer, the more likely outcome of involvement with a sociopolitical issue is a paracrisis. A paracrisis is when an organization must publicly manage a risk that involves at least some stakeholders calling the organization's actions inappropriate. An example would be the restaurant chain Cracker Barrel defending the existence of a diversity unit within the organization from critics calling it a "woke" organization. The future is likely to be populated by increased affective polarization and organizations will find many of their ESG and DEI efforts being subject to public criticism.

Sociopolitical issues are social issues that have become polarized. Researchers regularly document how polarizing certain sociopolitical issues have become (e.g., USC, 2022). In the US, LGBTQ+ rights and diversity are examples of highly polarizing sociopolitical issues. Affective polarization, unfortunately, is trending meaning it is projected to increase and to be a factor in the future of public relations and strategic communication. Affective polarization has some specific effects on crisis communication because it alters the nature of sociopolitical issues—known risk factors.

In 2023, Budweiser send a special six-pack of Bud Light to one of many hundreds of influencers. Bud Light often creates and sends these cans to influencers with their names on it to mark special events in an influencer's life such as a birthday. In this case, the cans celebrated the influencer's anniversary for transitioning from a man to a woman. Many conservatives took offense to Bud Light supporting and utilizing a transgender influencer (Stewart, 2023). We should remember this was just one six-pack of beer and was not part of any promotional campaign by Budweiser. People learned about the cans from a post by the transgender influencer. Conservatives then called for a boycott of Bud Light, a movement that was given high media exposure when singer Kid Rock posted a video online of him shooting cans of Bud Light with a gun.

Boycotts are not new in the corporate world. At any given time, there can be in excess of 100 consumer boycotts. What is unique about the Budweiser case is the effect. The vast majority of boycotts have no economic effect upon the corporate target (King, 2008). Between April (the start of the boycott) and August of 2023, Budweiser has seen a decrease in sales of over 25%, lost its position as the number one selling beer in the US, and is losing shelf space in stores distributing its product (Zahn, 2023). Budweiser is facing a lingering crisis due to polarization around LGBTQ+ rights.

Polarized sociopolitical issues are complicated. The crisis managers is guaranteed to offend some faction with action or inaction. The risk of alienating competing factors is a reality as well. When Budweiser appear to distance themselves from LGBTQ+ issues following the boycott, LGBTQ+ constituents began to turn against Budweiser too. An example were negative comments about Budweiser from the Human Rights Campaign, an LGBTQ+ advocacy group (Mayer, 2023). A similar pattern emerged in Disney's battle with Florida Governor DeSantis over the "Don't Say Gay" bill which restrict the discussion of sexual orientation in Florida schools. Many Disney constituents, especially employees) were angry when the company did speak out against the bill. When Disney finally did speak against the bill, conservative constituents, including some employees, were angered. This includes DeSantis who stripped Disney of their rights to self-govern the area around Disney World (citation). Moreover, the pro-LGBTQ+ constituents were unsatisfied with how Disney supported their efforts. Disney illustrates how a company can offend opposing sides in a crisis involving polarizing sociopolitical issues. Crisis managers face a challenging task of navigating crises born of sociopolitical issues. Such navigation offers no route that offends no side of the sociopolitical issue but can risk offending opposing sides.

While speaking on a sociopolitical issue can trigger a crisis, such as Budweiser hemorrhaging money after being linked to a transgender influencer, the more likely outcome of involvement with a sociopolitical issue is a paracrisis. A paracrisis is when an organization must publicly manage a risk that involves at least some stakeholders calling the organization's actions inappropriate or irresponsible (Chen & Holladay, 2023; Coombs & Holladay, 2012). An example would be the restaurant chain Chick-fil-A when it found itself defending the existence of its vice president of Diversity Equity and Inclusion (DEI) diversity from critics calling it a "woke" organization. There was anger online from such groups as Citizens for Renewing America (an anti-woke organization) and the question of if a boycott was needed was raised. Chick-fil-A is considered a very conservative organization whose owners have oppose LGBTQ+ issues (Zhou, 2023). The future is likely to be populated by increased affective polarization because organizations will find many of their ESG and DEI efforts being subject to public criticism.

Geopolitical Risks and Polarization

Geopolitical risks are those associated with tensions between station states, wars, and terrorism. Corporations have been tracking and measuring geopolitical risks for decades because of their economic effects on supply chains (Caldara & Iacoviello, 2022). Consider how terrorist attack by Houthi rebels on shipping in the Red Sea have altered shipping routes, delayed deliveries, and increased the price of goods (Wiseman & Anderson, 2024). Yet there are effects far beyond economics as various organizations get drawn into the vortex initialed by a geopolitical risk and amplified by polarization. Globally, corporations were pressured to take sides in the Ukraine-Russia conflict. More precisely, stakeholders were pressing corporations to end doing business in Russia (Alin et al., 2022).

In 2023, various college campuses experienced protests over the conflict between Israel and Hamas with some reflecting antisemitism. Three college presidents testified before Congress. The presidents seemed unprepared handling the paracrisis badly escalating the situations into crises for the universities as they faced additional criticism and pressure from some large donors. The presidents of Harvard University and the University of Pennsylvania were forced to resign (Svrluga & Douglas-Gabriel, 2024). Polarization helped to fuel the attacks, especially in the case of Harvard University which was pushed by conservatives. Geopolitical risks and polarization were identified in 2024 by the World Economic Forum's Global Risk Report and top risks facing the world in the coming years (World, 2024). There is every reason to believe these risks will continue increasing in the future.

Technology and Polarization

Risks do not exist in isolation and often interact with one another. Such is the case with technology and polarization. Public relations and strategic communication have always been shaped by technology, especially communication-related technology. Peruse any history of public relations and you will quickly see the effects of television and digital media on the practice. The digital environment, with social media platforms at the lead, has had a significant effect on affective polarization. Though the digital environment offered hope of a more connected world, the reality is social media helps to fuel polarization. Social media platforms provide an environment for spreading divisive messages (Van Bavel et al., 2021) and activating partisans to fight for their issues such as engaging in boycotts (Boulianne, 2022). Kubin and von Sikorski's (2021) review found social media does exacerbate affective polarization. Allcott et al. (2019) linked social media to the spread of disinformation and misinformation used to foster polarization. The link to disinformation and misinformation raises the specter of generative AI.

In 2023, ChatGPT generated concern in the communication community with the ability of this generative AI to create messages and perhaps take jobs away from communication professionals. Earlier AI showed no great skill in creating messages, but ChatGPT was a significant advancement in generative AI. Generative AI involves the production of content by an AI and has been around since the creation of chatbots in the 1960s. ChatGPT is one illustration of how sophisticated generative AI can produce high quality content. For instance, given specific prompts, ChatGPT can create well-crafted messages designed to appeal to specific target audiences. Generative AI can create text, imagery, audio, and synthetic data. Easy to use interfaces allow people to leverage AI to create high quality videos, text, and graphics. Multimodal AI permits someone to generate content across multiple media such as graphics, text, and video. Generative AI easily creates compelling content at high speeds and low cost.

While generative AI is designed as a tool to help people complete tasks, it can be abused to generate convincing misinformation and fuel disinformation efforts that can increase affective polarization (Monteith et al., 2023). Generative AI can be used to create "credible looking" messages that fuel polarization. Unfortunately, it is much easier to promote intolerance than it is to build tolerance (Verkuyten et al., 2020). Generative AI can be used to create compelling messages, both text and visual, designed to sow seeds of intolerance. But AI offers many potential benefits to crisis communication as well.

Technology as a Benefit to Crisis Communication: AI, Virtual Reality, and Augmented Reality

While technology such as AI and social media platforms create more complex risks, it is also a valuable tool for crisis communicators. Technology is especially valuable for pre-crisis phase which includes crisis preparation and mitigation. Mitigation are efforts designed to reduce the likelihood of a crisis emerging. Safety training and replacing hazardous materials with non-hazardous materials are examples of mitigation. Even with mitigation, crises still do occur, hence the need for preparation. Preparation involves measures taken to be ready to face a crisis and includes the organization and its stakeholders. Organizational preparation efforts involves creating and testing crisis management plans, creating crisis teams, and training for crises. Training for crises should include not only the crisis team but all organizational members and even some stakeholders.

For instance, people residing near a facility that uses hazardous materials should be part of the training for crises involving the release of hazardous materials (Coombs, 2023). There is value in both the organization and its stakeholders being prepared for a crisis.

Augmented reality (AR) and virtual reality (VR) have just begun to be used to train crisis teams and enhance crisis preparedness of stakeholders. Through AR and VR, crisis teams and those affected by the crisis can experience the event without risk of harm. For instance, VR has been used to allow people to experience how floods actually move in real time and affect their environments. AR can be used when training the crisis team because it can safely demonstrate dangerous environments such as fire. VR even allows participants to simulate the use of equipment they would utilize during a crisis while minimizing the risk of injuries (Zhu & Li, 2021).

While researchers try to identify theoretical reasons for the benefits of AR and vVR training, there are solid pragmatic reasons for their use. As noted already, both forms of training are safe. People can experience hazards with no real risk of harm to the trainee. You can simulate a fire or chemical release with risk of harm from fire or the chemical. The AR and VR trainings can save money as well. For example, a full-scale exercise using equipment and the actual location is more expensive than using virtual versions of the equipment and locations (Khanal et al., 2022; Lovreglio, 2020). AR and VR training is a trend that should continue.

Mitigation involves efforts designed to prevent a risk from manifesting into a crisis. To engage in mitigation, crisis managers must know the risks are emerging—identify warning signs. AI is increasing being used to help crisis managers identify possible risks and even to warn crisis managers when they are in a crisis. In this case we are referring to AI that can classify data. An AI classifier allows the AI to classify data into various categories. A classification algorithm is developed through supervisor learning techniques which involve using a training data set to teach the AI how to classify the data into different classes. Essentially the AI learns to sort data into specific categories. The AI's performance is checked for accuracy and additional training can be done with other data training sets if there is a need to improve the AI's accuracy. The use of AI to detect and to monitor emerging risks and crises is a trend that should continue (Hsu et al., 2021). AI can be used to detect the emergence of risks and track whether or not mitigation efforts have helped to reduce the potential of the risk becoming manifest into a crisis.

Conclusion

Crisis communication, as with any facet of publics relations and strategic communication, is shaped by social and technological factors. Affective polarization is on the rise and translates directly into risks thereby affecting crisis communication. Crisis communicators in 2050 will be attempting to manage polarizing risks. Technology will be adding to those risks as generative AI can fuel increased concerns about disinformation and misinformation. However, technology will enhance the ability of 2050 crisis managers to identify risks, mitigate risks, and prepare for crises. Existing theories and practices will remain useful but the way crisis communicators approach and execute their jobs with be improved by technology and complicated by a mix of sociopolitical and technological factors.

References

Allcott, H., Gentzkow, M., & Yu, C. (2019). Trends in the diffusion of misinformation on social media. *Research & Politics*, *6*(2). https://doi.org/10.1177/2053168019848554

Boulianne, S. (2022). Socially mediated political consumerism. *Information, Communication & Society*, *25*(5), 609–617.

Caldara, D., & Iacoviello, M. (2022). Measuring geopolitical risk. *American Economic Review*, *112*(4), 1194–1225.

Capizzo, L. (2023). Managing intractability: Wrestling with wicked problems and seeing beyond consensus in public relations. *Public Relations Review*, *49*(1), 102263.

Castle, J. J., & Stepp, K. K. (2021). Partisanship, religion, and issue polarization in the United States: A reassessment. *Political Behavior*, *43*(3), 1311–1335.

Chen, F., & Holladay, S. J. (2023). Identifying and responding to social media risks: Towards an organizational paracrisis communication framework. *Corporate Communications: An International Journal*, *28*(1), 103–117.

Ciszek, E. L. (2016). Digital activism: How social media and dissensus inform theory and practice. *Public Relations Review*, *42*(2), 314–321.

Coombs, W. T., & Holladay, J. S. (2012). The paracrisis: The challenges created by publicly managing crisis prevention. *Public Relations Review*, *38*(3), 408–415.

Coombs, W. T., & Holladay, S. J. (2018). Social issues qua wicked problems: The role of strategic communication in social issues management. *Journal of Communication Management*, *22*(2), 79–95.

Dodd, M. D., & Supa, D. W. (2014). Conceptualizing and measuring "corporate social advocacy" communication: Examining the impact on corporate financial performance. *Public Relations Journal*, *8*(3), 2–23.

Druckman, J. N., Klar, S., Krupnikov, Y., Levendusky, M., & Ryan, J. B. (2021). Affective polarization, local contexts and public opinion in America. *Nature Human Behaviour*, *5*(1), 28–38.

Edelman. (2022). 2023 Edelman Trust Barometer. Retrieved from https://www.edelman.com/trust/2023/trust-barometer

Hsu, M. F., Hsin, Y. S., & Shiue, F. J. (2021). Business analytics for corporate risk management and performance improvement. *Annals of Operations Research*, *315*(1–2), 629–6691.

Khanal, S., Medasetti, U. S., Mashal, M., Savage, B., & Khadka, R. (2022). Virtual and augmented reality in the disaster management technology: A literature review of the past 11 years. *Frontiers in Virtual Reality*, *3*, 30.

King, B. G. (2008). A political mediation model of corporate response to social movement activism. *Administrative Science Quarterly*, *53*(3), 395–421.

Kubin, E., & von Sikorski, C. (2021). The role of (social) media in political polarization: A systematic review. *Annals of the International Communication Association*, *45*(3), 188–206.

Lovreglio, R. (2020, September). Virtual and augmented reality for human behaviour in disasters: A review. In *Fire and Evacuation Modeling Technical Conference (FEMTC) 2020 Online Conference* (pp. 9–11), FEMTC.

Mouffe, C. (1999). Deliberative democracy or agonistic pluralism? *Social Research*, *66*(3), 745–758.

Ohme, J. (2021). Algorithmic social media use and its relationship to attitude reinforcement and issue-specific political participation–The case of the 2015 European immigration movements. *Journal of Information Technology & Politics*, *18*(1), 36–54.

Svrluga, S. (2024). After Havard and Penn resignations, who wants to be a college president? Retrieved from https://www.washingtonpost.com/education/2024/01/12/college-presidents-pressures-harvard-penn/

Tucker, J. A., Guess, A., Barberá, P., Vaccari, C., Siegel, A., Sanovich, S., … & Nyhan, B. (2018). Social media, political polarization, and political disinformation: A review of the scientific literature. *Political Polarization, and Political Disinformation: A Review of the Scientific Literature (March 19, 2018)*. Retrieved from http://dx.doi.org/10.2139/ssrn.3144139

USC. (2022). The polarization index. Retrieved May 12, 2022, from https://thepolarizationindex.com/

Van Bavel, J. J., Rathje, S., Harris, E., Robertson, C., & Sternisko, A. (2021). How social media shapes polarization. *Trends in Cognitive Sciences*, *25*(11), 913–916.

van der Meer, T. G., & Jonkman, J. G. (2021). Politicization of corporations and their environment: Corporations' social license to operate in a polarized and mediatized society. *Public Relations Review*, *47*(1), 101988.

Verkuyten, M., Adelman, L., & Yogeeswaran, K. (2020). The psychology of intolerance: Unpacking diverse understandings of intolerance. *Current Directions in Psychological Science*, *29*(5), 467–472.

Wiseman, O., & Anderson, M. (2024). Houthi attacks in Red Sea are idling car factories and delaying new fashion. Retrieved from https://apnews.com/article/red-sea-houthi-attacks-shipping-inflation-124d5445bec8ce6864112e3095646308

World Economic Forum. (2024). Global risk report. Retrieved from https://www.weforum.org/publications/global-risks-report-2024/

Zhan, M. (2023). Bud Light set to lose shelf space at major retailors, intensifying boycott concerns. Retrieved from https://abcnews.go.com/Business/bud-light-set-lose-shelf-space-major-retailers/story?id=103165753

Zhou, L. (2023). Conservatives think Chick-fil-A is woke now? Retrieved from https://www.vox.com/politics/2023/5/31/23742373/chick-fil-a-boycott-controversy-conservative-backlash

Zhu, Y., & Li, N. (2021). Virtual and augmented reality technologies for emergency management in the built environments: A state-of-the-art review. *Journal of Safety Science and Resilience*, *2*(1), 1–10.

16

FILM, TELEVISION, AND ENTERTAINMENT PUBLIC RELATIONS IN 2050

Establishing a New Normal in the Wake of Streaming, AI, and COVID-19

Chris DeFelice and Kyle Stanley

FIGURE 16.1 Movie experience.

Source: Felix Mooneeram. https://unsplash.com/photos/red-cinema-chair-evlkOfkQ5rE

Permission: Accessed through Pablo Buffer and free to use under Unsplash Licence.

Film, Television, and Entertainment PR in 2050

As we sit down to write this chapter in the fall of 2023, we face the enormous task of capturing one of the most pivotal eras in the history of Hollywood as it continues to experience growing pains in the face of disruptive technologies. To provide some context, the entertainment industry is freshly emerging from the COVID-19 pandemic, which shut down the theatrical movie market for over a year. Because movie theaters were shut down for so long, the streaming service market had a meteoric rise to meet the demand for at-home blockbuster

DOI: 10.4324/9781003426653-19

entertainment. However, this shift in the market led to unintended long-term consequences where moviegoers are now drawing into question the relevance of the theatrical movie experience overall.

While the theatrical industry was trying to get back on its feet, both the Writers Guild of America (WGA) and Screen Actors Guild (SAG-AFTRA) executed simultaneous labor strikes against the most prominent Hollywood production studios in order to achieve significant advancements in areas like streaming compensation and job security. One of the major concerns focused on artificial intelligence (AI) and the existential threat that it poses to cinema as an art form by threatening to replicate the work of human writers, actors, and other artists. At the time of this writing, both strikes have recently concluded with unprecedented contracts for writers and actors that completely change how studios produce entertainment media.

Considering all these factors, it is fair to say that Hollywood is on the brink of a structural transformation that will fundamentally alter its foundations. However, whether these changes will usher in a new cinematic golden age or reduce the industry to an automated pipeline of AI-produced content is yet to be seen. Regardless of the outcome, strategic communicators must be prepared to navigate the impact of these disruptive technologies and the ever-shifting expectations of the moviegoing audience.

Disruptive Technology in Hollywood

Hollywood is no stranger to the threat of a new medium. In the 1950s, for instance, the rise of television was seen as a potential death knell for radio. Many industry experts at the time struggled to envision how two media with similar content strategies could coexist (Alexander, 1985). Despite these fears, radio adapted and thrived in a media landscape that was becoming increasingly diverse. Today, a similar apprehension surrounds streaming services, with concerns that they might render movie theaters obsolete. These innovations, including television in the past and streaming services now, are examples of disruptive technology, which refers to new innovations that challenge the existence and relevance of traditional media or business models (Bower & Christensen, 1995).

Early streaming services such as Netflix and Hulu revolutionized the industry by establishing a new *on-demand culture* where consumers increasingly demanded a way to consume content however and whenever they want (Tryon, 2013). The success of this business model led most major movie studios (i.e., Disney, Warner Bros., Universal, etc.) to create their own in-house streaming services to compete for the massive amount of subscription revenue that Netflix monopolized for nearly a decade. However, this rapid expansion also helped recalibrate audiences to consume various types of content at home, including blockbuster movies.

Initially, streaming services were viewed as a disruptive technology primarily for broadcast and cable television rather than for movie theaters. However, the landscape shifted dramatically during the COVID-19 pandemic. This period saw streaming platforms make significant inroads into the film market, as major production studios opted to either release their backlogged content directly on these streaming services or shorten the exclusive theatrical release period before making films available for streaming (D'Alessandro, 2022; Hayes, 2023). For example, Disney opted for a hybrid release method (i.e., streaming and theaters on the same day) for some of its most anticipated films like *Black Widow, Cruella,* and *Raya and the Last Dragon.* Though initially seeming like a viable strategy, it has notably impacted Disney's recent box office performance. Despite the studio's record-breaking success in 2019, with seven films grossing over $1 billion at the box office worldwide, it failed to replicate this success for a single film in 2023 (Rubin, 2023). A contributing factor to this change in moviegoing behavior is that many Disney + subscribers now prefer to wait a few months to watch new releases at home without additional costs (DeFelice et al., 2024).

The decisions made by Disney and other major studios to release blockbusters on streaming services not long after their theatrical release dramatically altered audience expectations. Prior to the pandemic, the coexistence of streaming platforms and movie theaters was largely due to the "fear of missing out" (FOMO) phenomenon, which drove moviegoers to theaters for the premier experience of blockbuster films (Tefertiller, 2017; Tefertiller et al., 2020). However, an unintended consequence of the studios' pandemic distribution choices is that it gave audiences an alternative cure for their FOMO by making streaming blockbuster movies at home a more tangible option (DeFelice et al., 2024). To fully grasp how streaming services are challenging the long-standing business model of the film industry, it's important to understand the concepts of scarcity and the resource-based view of the firm.

The resource-based view (RBV) of the firm conceptualizes a business organization as a collection of assets that generate value based on the value, rarity, inimitability, and non-substitutability of its resources (Wernerfelt, 1984). Based on the RBV framework, the theatrical business model lost a lot of its value once movie studios introduced streaming services as a viable substitution. Although these studios undervalued the theatrical market as an asset, recent box office hits have proven that there is still demand for the theatrical experience (Hayes, 2023). Still, the overall box office is nowhere near what it used to be because the streaming boom during the pandemic lockdown allowed moviegoers to reconsider what movies they view as "theater-worthy" (DeFelice et al., 2024).

Audience Fatigue and Social Trends

Over the past decade or so, Hollywood has relied on lucrative trends like nostalgia as the main engine of the box office. However, in a misguided attempt to salvage the theatrical market in the wake of streaming and the COVID-19 pandemic, many studios doubled down on nostalgic franchises, not fully accounting for the limited lifespan of such trends. For example, another recent trend that most studios have tried, yet failed, to build their franchise model on is creating a shared universe in the style of the Marvel Cinematic Universe (MCU). However, even the MCU itself has struggled to maintain its consistent success after its legendary peak with *Avengers: Endgame.* Instead of pulling back to avoid oversaturation, Marvel Studios decided to double down by expanding into streaming shows while continuing to release up to four blockbuster movies per year, which led to a significant decline in audience satisfaction and box office performance (Rubin, 2023). Regardless, audience preferences, as reflected in box office receipts, will persist in guiding the direction of the film industry, eventually compelling studios to pursue different, more innovative trends.

Although trends may wither in relevance over time, it is also important to note that they always originate from the industry trying something new. For instance, Marvel Studios only attained its historic success because the concept of an interconnected cinematic universe was a revolutionary, original idea, which made the MCU a landmark achievement in blockbuster filmmaking (Harrison et al., 2019). Similarly, *Star Wars: The Force Awakens* saw remarkable success in 2015, partly because it was the first new installment in the franchise in over a decade and brought back beloved characters unseen for over 30 years. However, such innovative strategies lose their novelty when repeatedly used. *Star Wars* struggled to sustain its popularity when it relied continuously on nostalgia, and no other franchise has successfully replicated the MCU's shared universe model – even though many have tried.

In the wake of the pandemic, studios must actively reevaluate their content strategies to create innovative films that draw audiences to theaters in the new streaming age. The *Barbenheimer* phenomenon in July 2023 serves as a prime example – reigniting optimism for the potential resurgence of movie theaters. The decision to release a vibrant, comedic film like *Barbie* alongside a dark, dramatic biopic like *Oppenheimer* on the same day initially seemed like an extreme case of counter-programming. However, both films became a viral sensation in tandem on social media, resulting in stellar box-office performances for each (Karaian & Russel, 2023). Despite their differences on paper, both movies had common elements that fueled the brewing box office explosion that eventually became *Barbenheimer*.

What distinguishes Barbie and Oppenheimer from other blockbusters in the current landscape is their focus on sparking conversations rather than solely being produced to generate revenue. Social word-of-mouth (sWOM) is one of the most powerful weapons in a studio's marketing arsenal when it comes to getting audiences to watch a movie in theaters (DeFelice & Porter, 2024; Hennig-Thurau et al., 2015; Kim et al., 2013). However, there is very little that a communications professional can do to ignite positive sWOM conversations if the movie itself does not give audiences anything new or interesting to talk about.

Barbie and *Oppenheimer* stood out as original, timely, and thought-provoking films crafted by respected filmmakers who invested genuine passion into their projects (Lawson, 2023) – attributes that many recent blockbusters lack. Consequently, the sWOM surrounding these films propelled them to box office success in 2023, even amidst stiff competition from traditional franchise films.

In an era where thousands of hours of entertainment are easily accessible to stream at home, theatrical movies must not only recognize the value of letting a trend go but also make a constant effort to generate new trends that rebuild the audience's trust in the moviegoing experience. However, studios are notorious for capitalizing on successful trends until there is no more audience enthusiasm left to boast. Therefore, we argue that the future of moviegoing relies on studios rebuilding a sustainable balance that rebuilds the moviegoer's trust without pushing them to the point of blockbuster burnout.

Social Media and Audience Influence

The increasing power of social media in recent years stems from its role in not only heightening audience awareness of the production process but also enabling them to influence the process more than ever before. Viral social media campaigns, such as #OscarsSoWhite and #MeToo have driven significant structural changes within the corporate side of the industry, which had operated with minimal public oversight for decades (Ugwu, 2020). As audiences grow more culturally conscious, they are harnessing the power of sWOM to demand content that aligns with their social values, which is a strategy that played a crucial role in the success of the 2023 WGA and SAG-AFTRA strikes.

Part of what made the concurring strikes so compelling and impactful was the general public's overall hesitancy to engage with any material that could be perceived as directly opposing those who were striking. This phenomenon highlighted a growing consciousness among consumers about the ethical implications of their consumption choices (Kuokkanen & Sun, 2020). The public's reluctance to cross the virtual picket line and be labeled a "scab," so to speak, was not just a matter of solidarity with the striking workers; it also reflected a broader shift in consumer behavior, where consumers were more aware of the power of their choices and the impact these choices could have on the industry's labor practices (Maheshwari & Kircher, 2023). This awareness was fueled by the WGA and SAG-AFTRA's social media strategy, which used their platform to amplify the voices of striking workers to rally support.

Audience influence through sWOM has led to unprecedented changes in the foundation of the industry where studios are no longer able to suppress the vocal demands of their audience. Large social media communities have organized either to support or to oppose projects in a way that is highly visible to studio executives and potentially influences their future decisions. However, recent developments have shown that sometimes loud voices on social media do not represent the views of the entire audience. For example, a large and aggressive sub-group of DC fans rallied on social media to create the #ReleaseTheSnyderCut campaign, which demanded that Warner Bros. release director Zack Snyder's original cut of 2017s *Justice League* before the project was stripped away from him mid-production (Brown, 2021). The campaign was successful and Warner Bros. gave Snyder $70 million to finish production on the film and eventually released *Zack Snyder's Justice League* on HBO Max in 2021.

Despite the seemingly overwhelming support on social media, the film only performed moderately when it was released because social media chatter does not always reflect the demands of the moviegoing public (D'Alessandro, 2021). *Zack Snyder's Justice League* is a significant example of how powerful audience influence on social media can be; however, studios cannot blindly assume that loud sWOM conversations will translate to views or ticket sales. Moving forward, studio executives must use more rigorous audience research methods to find the balance between reflecting modern social values while also creating projects that appeal to diverse audiences that are not as loud on social media.

Film Production in the Age of AI

Disruptive technologies not only affect how audiences consume content but also how the industry produces it. In fact, the production impact of streaming services and AI are the primary causes of the 2023 WGA and SAG-AFTRA strikes. The previous contracts that guided film and television production were not adequately calibrated for the streaming revenue model, which left many writers and actors without fair compensation for their contributions (Koblin & Barnes, 2023). Additionally, generative AI developed to become an existential threat to artists who fear for their job security now that their work could theoretically be replicated by a computer program.

Audiences have already taken to social media to express their opposition to AI in the film industry. The primary concerns revolve around the dystopian consequences of having a computer program develop content that artificially replicates the artistic voice of a human being (Sung, 2022). Audiences have also noted the ethical concerns of using AI-generated art because these programs are trained using human-made content, usually without the permission of the original artist. The public backlash against AI-generated art has sparked a series of legal conflicts about AI in copyright law. At the time of this writing, a federal judge in the US District Court has ruled that AI-generated content cannot be protected by copyright law (Brittain, 2023), and there is currently a high-profile lawsuit making its way through the court system against OpenAI for using the work of book authors to train its ChatGPT program without permission (Albu, 2023). The rulings of these lawsuits (and others that will inevitably follow) will set a precedent for the regulation of AI on a governmental level; however, the results of the 2023 WGA and SAG-AFTRA strikes have provided an early look into how the industry will self-regulate the use of AI moving forward.

The AI provisions in the WGA deal expressly prohibit studios from using AI to write or rewrite any literary material (including scripts) ("Summary of the 2023 WGA MBA," 2023). The deal also allows writers to use AI as an assistive tool, but the studios cannot require them to use these programs. The SAG-AFTRA, however, permits studios to use AI to create digital replicas of actors, but only with the consent and compensation of the actor every time their digital model is used (Patten, 2023, p. 3). The deal also gives SAG-AFTRA unprecedented power to monitor studios to make sure that their use of AI follows the provisions of the contract. Although both strikes have concluded with historic progress for AI protections, it is important to note that these AI protections merely regulate AI rather than banning it from use entirely.

As technology inevitably continues to advance, the industry will be forced to (at least partially) embrace AI instead of hiding from the inevitable. The most likely direction for the entertainment industry would be slowly integrating AI as a tool for artists instead of a replacement for artists. We believe this is the most likely solution because less advanced AI has been a common tool used by artists for years. Less advanced AI programs such as Grammarly have helped writers improve their work for years – including the writers of this very chapter (Grammarly, 2019). While AI technology does have a bright future as a key piece in an artist's toolbox, strategic communicators are still left with the daunting task of restoring the public's trust in AI when they have already witnessed its dystopian possibilities when left unregulated.

The Film, Television, and Entertainment Industry in 2050

The biggest challenge in predicting how Hollywood will continue to evolve over the next two decades is that the past two decades of the industry were anything but predictable. Disruptive technologies, by nature, do not go away; they will only grow in relevance until a new technology is developed to further complicate the delicate balance of the industry. As a result, the entertainment industry is in desperate need of actionable insights in order to brace itself for the inevitable and continuous influence of streaming services, AI, and whatever the next disruptive technology may be.

By the year 2050, we anticipate that the theatrical experience will hinge on innovative movies that generate significant word-of-mouth engagement. This trend will compel studios to recognize that relying on mediocrity and repetition is no longer a viable strategy for the entertainment industry. A key challenge for studio executives will be to meet the demand for high-quality, original content that also mirrors the progressive social values that audiences are no longer willing to compromise for the sake of entertainment. As streaming services continue to produce endless hours of content available to audiences at the push of a button, the theatrical market can no longer depend on the captive audience it once had. Future theatrical releases will need to prioritize quality over quantity and offer enough technical innovation to persuade audiences to experience them on the big screen, instead of waiting to stream them at home. This will require industry practitioners to prioritize promotional strategies that convey the *expected experience* of watching a film in theaters rather than strategies that merely inform people about a movie's subject matter.

We also foresee AI becoming a part of the artist's toolkit by the year 2050. However, due to recent industry regulations and potential future government oversight, the use of AI will likely be confined to assisting artists in enhancing their work, rather than replacing it, especially for commercial purposes. In this case, industry practitioners must adopt methods that restore the public trust in film as an authentically human art form. One potential tactic would be including behind-the-scenes talent (such as writers, production designers, and CGI artists) on pre-release press tours where they publicly talk about their experience crafting specific elements of the film. However, given the constant flux of technology, successfully navigating the next two decades will require both studio executives and strategic communicators to consistently monitor the pulse of the entertainment audience and remain flexible when faced with new disruptive technologies.

Key Takeaways for Strategic Communicators

Strategic communicators will play an important role in Hollywood restabilizing itself after the pandemic. Public trust in movie studios and traditional theatrical entertainment has taken a sharp downturn since its historic peak in 2019. The pandemic reset the moviegoing audience's expectations, and industry professionals must work hard to figure out how to reestablish a new norm. Additionally, public trust in AI is also an issue that communications professionals must face over the next few decades. Although the WGA and SAG-AFTRA strikes have provided a starting point for its regulation and integration, it is also important to note that the AI provisions in the contracts are up for renegotiation every three years. Thus, it is likely that additional rules and regulations will be implemented between now and 2050. As these changes take place, strategic communicators must face the challenge of redeveloping the public's trust in AI as a valuable tool of progress rather than the dystopian job stealer that they currently perceive it as.

As a result, we argue that industry practitioners must develop communication strategies that (1) pivot focus away from what a movie is about and emphasize the proposed experience of watching a film in theaters, and (2) rebuild public trust in film as a reflection of human artists rather than soulless, AI-generated content. Finding the new balance between streaming services and movie theaters will require strategic communication tactics to be implemented across all levels of management, including studio executives and filmmakers. We argue that executives and filmmakers will be key players in the successful implementation of these strategies because a marketing department can only do so much to convince audiences that a movie is theater-worthy. Because word-of-mouth is such an important part of the consumer decision-making process, theatrical movies are more likely to succeed if they are designed to get people talking rather than just trying to make a quick buck. Therefore, studio executives and the filmmakers that they hire must focus on producing movies that prioritize quality, innovation, and audience connection rather than relying on strategic communicators to convince audiences to settle for mediocrity.

The delicate balance between at-home streaming and the theatrical experience, the evolving trends shaping audience preferences, and the integration of AI into the artistic toolbox all demand a nuanced and adaptable approach. Regardless, the key takeaway for communicators is clear – to rebuild public trust, foster innovation, and navigate the uncharted waters of the entertainment industry, a strategic and forward-thinking communication strategy is paramount. As Hollywood marches into an uncertain future, let it be a story told not only through the lens of technological innovation but also through the narratives crafted by effective communicators and storytellers.

References

Albu, R. (2023, September 20). The Authors Guild, John Grisham, Jodi Picoult, David Baldacci, George R.R. Martin, and 13 Other Authors File Class-Action Suit Against OpenAI. *The Authors Guild*. Retrieved from https://authorsguild.org/news/ag-and-authors-file-class-action-suit-against-openai/

Alexander, R. (1985, June 9). Recalling how radio survived the arrival of TV. *The New York Times*. https://www.nytimes.com/1985/06/09/arts/recalling-how-radio-survived-the-arrival-of-tv.html

Bower, J. L., & Christensen, C. M. (1995). Disruptive technologies: Catching the wave. *Harvard Business Review*, *73*(1), 43–53.

Brittain, B. (2023, August 21). AI-generated art cannot receive copyrights, US court says. *Reuters*. Retrieved from https://www.reuters.com/legal/ai-generated-art-cannot-receive-copyrights-us-court-says-2023-08-21/

Brown, T. (2021, March 19). Timeline: How "Zack Snyder's Justice League" happened. *Los Angeles Times*. Retrieved from https://www.latimes.com/entertainment-arts/movies/story/2021-03-19/zack-snyder-justice-league-timeline

D'Alessandro, A. (2021, March 23). 'Justice League' cut ranks behind 'Wonder Woman 1984' In HBO Max. *Deadline*. Retrieved from https://deadline.com/2021/03/justice-league-snyder-cut-wonder-woman-1984-hbo-max-viewership-1234720662/

D'Alessandro, A. (2022, April 25). As streaming peaks, Sony, Universal & Others Prove The Lucrative Power Of Theatrical Windows – CinemaCon. *Deadline*. Retrieved from https://deadline.com/2022/04/sony-universal-theatrical-windows-cinemacon-spider-man-no-way-home-1235008932/

DeFelice, C., & Porter, L. (2024). Theaters, social media, and streams: Evaluating social word-of-mouth patterns of pandemic-era blockbuster films on Twitter. *Convergence*. https://doi.org/10.1177/13548565241236441

DeFelice, C., Porter, L., & Kim, S. W. (2024). Moviegoing in the wake of a pandemic: Re-evaluating the attitudes, intentions, and behaviors of U.S. Moviegoers in the streaming era. *Journal of Media Economics*, *36*(1–2), 29–46. https://doi.org/10.1080/08997764.2024.2361747

Grammarly. (2019, May 17). *How we use AI to enhance your writing | Grammarly spotlight*. Grammarly spotlight: How we use AI to enhance your writing. Retrieved from https://www.grammarly.com/blog/how-grammarly-uses-ai/

Harrison, S., Carlsen, A., & Škerlavaj, M. (2019, July). Marvel's blockbuster machine. *Harvard Business Review*. https://hbr.org/2019/07/marvels-blockbuster-machine

Hayes, D. (2023, March 6). As box office revenue starts to return, billions hang in the balance as studios juggle streaming with traditional sell-thru and rental market. *Deadline*. Retrieved from https://deadline.com/2023/03/box-office-billions-studios-juggle-streaming-home-entertainment-1235273017/

Hennig-Thurau, T., Wiertz, C., & Feldhaus, F. (2015). Does Twitter matter? The impact of microblogging word of mouth on consumers' adoption of new movies. *Journal of the Academy of Marketing Science*, *43*(3), 375–394. https://doi.org/10.1007/s11747-014-0388-3

Karaian, J., & Russel, K. (2023, July 24). 'Barbie' and 'Oppenheimer' combine for big weekend box office numbers. *The New York Times*. Retrieved from https://www.nytimes.com/2023/07/24/business/barbie-oppenheimer-weekend-box-office.html

Kim, S. H., Park, N., & Park, S. H. (2013). Exploring the effects of online word of mouth and expert reviews on theatrical movies' box office success. *Journal of Media Economics*, *26*(2), 98–114. https://doi.org/10.1080/08997764.2013.785551

Koblin, J., & Barnes, B. (2023, September 27). What's the latest on the writers' strike? *The New York Times*. Retrieved from https://www.nytimes.com/article/wga-writers-strike-hollywood.html

Kuokkanen, H., & Sun, W. (2020). Companies, meet ethical consumers: Strategic CSR management to impact consumer choice. *Journal of Business Ethics*, *166*(2), 403–423. https://doi.org/10.1007/s10551-019-04145-4

Lawson, R. (2023, July 24). The biggest lessons from Barbenheimer for Hollywood. *Vanity Fair*. https://www.vanityfair.com/hollywood/2023/07/barbenheimer-lessons-hollywood

Maheshwari, S., & Kircher, M. M. (2023, July 26). Hollywood strike leaves influencers sidelined and confused. *The New York Times*. Retrieved from https://www.nytimes.com/2023/07/26/business/media/actors-strike-influencers.html

Patten, D. (2023, November 12). Full SAG-AFTRA deal summary released: Read it here. *Deadline*. Retrieved from https://deadline.com/2023/11/sag-aftra-deal-summary-released-read-it-1235600852/

Rubin, R. (2023, November 27). Disney's bad box office streak continues with "Wish," "The Marvels." *Variety*. Retrieved from https://variety.com/2023/film/box-office/disney-bleak-box-office-streak-wish-the-marvels-1235809251/

Summary of the 2023 WGA MBA. (2023). *WGA contract 2023*. Retrieved from https://www.wgacontract2023.org/the-campaign/summary-of-the-2023-wga-mba

Sung, M. (2022, December 7). Lensa, the AI portrait app, has soared in popularity. But many artists question the ethics of AI art. *NBC News*. Retrieved from https://www.nbcnews.com/tech/internet/lensa-ai-artist-controversy-ethics-privacy-rcna60242

Tefertiller, A. (2017). Moviegoing in the Netflix Age: Gratifications, planned behavior, and theatrical attendance. *Communication & Society*, *30*(4), 27–44. Retrieved from https://doi.org/10.15581/003.30.3.27-44

Tefertiller, A., Maxwell, L. C., & Morris, D. (2020). Social media goes to the movies: Fear of missing out, social capital, and social motivations of cinema attendance. *Mass Communication and Society*, *23*(3), 378–399. https://doi.org/10.1080/15205436.2019.1653468

Tryon, C. (2013). *On-demand culture: Digital delivery and the future of movies*. Rutgers University Press.

Ugwu, R. (2020, February 6). The Hashtag that changed the Oscars: An oral history. *The New York Times*. Retrieved from https://www.nytimes.com/2020/02/06/movies/oscarssowhite-history.html

Wernerfelt, B. (1984). A resource-based view of the firm. *Strategic Management Journal*, *5*(2), 171–180. https://doi.org/10.1002/smj.4250050207

17

SPORT PUBLIC RELATIONS IN 2050

Brandon C. Boatwright and Lexi Merriman

Previous scholarship has suggested that sport public relations warrants specific research, theorizing, and applied work since "sport, in all its forms and permutations, cannot be marketed or promoted in the same way as any other consumer commodity" (Hopwood, 2010, p. 56). While many of the same general public relations principles, theories, and techniques apply to sport public relations, there are numerous elements of sport-specific public relations that present unique challenges and opportunities to practitioners and researchers. L'Etang (2006), for example, argued that sport is part of everyday life in that it shapes discourses and relationships across multiple levels, including: diplomatic, cultural, economic, organizational, community, and interpersonal. There are few sectors in which public relations efforts provide as many touchpoints with salient publics and stakeholder groups as sport. Consequently, it is important to examine the specialized nature of sport public relations and to project how work and research in this area will develop over the next several decades. In particular, this chapter will focus on the evolution of artificial intelligence in sport public relations research and practice.

History of Sport & Public Relations

While the broader study of public relations originated in the early 20th century through the work of Edward Bernays, Ivy Lee, and Dan Edleman (among others), the specific application of public relations within the context of sport did not begin attracting scholarly attention until the early 2000s. Stoldt (2000), for example, examined the professional roles of college sports information personnel working at NCAA Division I-A institutions. Stoldt and Narasimhan (2005)

DOI: 10.4324/9781003426653-20

conducted a follow-up survey examining how college sports information personnel evaluated their levels of proficiency in various public relations activities and the importance of those activities. Hopwood (2005) examined public relations in professional sport in the United Kingdom and found that... Stoldt et al. (2009) found that, even within a singular functional area within sport communication (i.e., public relations), there is considerable diversity evident through "the public relations responsibilities respondents described having, the tactics they reported employing, the goals they hope to achieve, the way those goals were linked to overall organizational goals, and the methods they used to evaluate their public relations activities" (p. 236). Indeed, the sport industry writ large has been commonly recognized as being large and heterogenous (Li et al., 2001; Pitts et al., 1994).

Stoldt et al. (2020) defined sport public relations as a "brand-centric communication function designed to manage and advance relationships between a sport organization and its key publics" (p. 24). … Specific areas of study within sport public relations that have been examined are sport information (e.g., Hardin & McClung, 2002; Stamm & Boatwright, 2023), image repair/crisis communication (e.g., Compton & Compton, 2023; Frederick & Pegoraro, 2018; Onwumechili & Bedeau, 2017), and corporate social responsibility (e.g., Godfrey, 2009; Smith & Casper, 2020).

Unique Features of Sport Public Relations

There are several aspects of sport public relations that separate it from general public relations practice. In the interest of brevity, we identify what we believe are the three most salient characteristics that will be important for researchers and practitioners to consider as the field progresses. First, there are different levels of sport which results in considerable divides in how sport public relations is enacted. Second, the variety of publics and stakeholder groups sport organizations must account for extends beyond what most organizations have to navigate on a daily basis. Finally, there is an increased focus on the creation of organizational content rather than a reliance on media to get an organization's message across to various publics. Each point will be addressed sequentially below.

Different Types of Sport and Sport Organizations

Simply put, the sports landscape is massive. When considering the breadth of sport public relations practice and scholarship, one must account for the many different characteristics of sport. The most obvious factor to consider is the variety of sports writ large (e.g., American football, soccer, baseball, basketball, hockey, golf, etc.). There are also numerous levels of competition within sport including youth sport, amateur athletics, collegiate athletics, semi-professional and professional leagues, and international competitions. Even still, there are important considerations for public relations research and practice within men's and women's sports, adaptive sports, and emergent sports (i.e., esports, action sports, etc.).

Beyond team sports, there are a wide range of sport organizations that require unique public relations applications. Sport leagues and governing bodies (e.g., The NCAA, the NFL, NHL, NBA, MLB, etc.) employ different strategies and tactics and engage different stakeholders than, say, sport non-profit organizations (e.g., Rise to Win, Athletes for Hope, Women's Sports Foundation, etc.), retail companies (e.g., Nike, Adidas, UnderAmour, etc.), or sporting venues (e.g., Charlotte Motor Speedway, Augusta National Golf Club, etc.).

Given the broad range of sport and sport organizations, the application of public relations will vary considerably based on the most salient stakeholder groups involved in each unique circumstance. The following section explores the variety of sport stakeholder groups and publics.

Variety of Stakeholder Groups and Publics in Sport Public Relations

Stoldt et al. (2020) explore what they call the "sport public relations universe" through which they identify a range of salient stakeholder groups that require sport organizations' attention depending on the type of sport organization. Specifically, the authors indicate the different relationships that exist between sport organizations and stakeholder groups including consumer relations, government relations, employee relations, donor relations, media relations, investor relations, industry relations, and community relations. Different sport organizations (e.g., teams, governing bodies, non-profits, retail companies, and venues) might rely more heavily on different relationships. For example, donor relations are more important to non-profit organizations, whereas sport leagues might rely more heavily on government relations or media relations.

Relationships with various stakeholder groups also rely on different public relations strategies and tactics. The media relations function, for example, relies heavily on information distribution to media outlets in the form of news releases, media advisories, game notes, and media guides. Alternatively, consumer relations may require more creative content (e.g., digital and social media, online videos, feature stories, etc.) to engage fans, potential fans, or recruits. Most of these relationships are established and maintained by public relations or strategic communication professionals within sport organizations. Their importance in the production of content around sport cannot be underestimated, especially provided the increased reliance on internally produced stories and information over traditional mediated content.

Increased Reliance on Organizational Content Over Media Relations

On Sept.1, 2022,members of the College Sports Information Directors of America (CoSIDA) voted to rename the organization College Sports Communicators (CSC; "College Sports Communicators, 2022").The announcement represented more than just the name of organization; it marked an important turning point in the rapidly evolving relationship between college athletic programs and the media professionals who cover them. Stamm and Boatwright (2023) examined the nature of the relationship between college football beat writers and their perceptions of their media relations counterparts and found growing tension over issues of access, control of information, and a lack of organizational understanding regarding the value of independent beat writers covering athletic programs. The authors drew from Pedersen's (2013) Strategic Sport Communication Model which outlines three interrelated components of sport communication including (1) personal and organizational communication in sport, (2) sport mass media, and (3) ancillary sport communication (i.e., public relations, community relations, crisis communication, etc.). Pedersen et al. (2020) argue that the intersections among these three components are fluid in nature as each informs the sport communication process writ large. The significance of Stamm and Boatwright's (2023) findings indicate that there appears to be a growing imbalance between the perceived value of organizational content over media coverage. This positions professional public relations and strategic communication practitioners in sports organizations as primary producers of sport related content.

The Effects of AI on Sport Public Relations in 2050

The advent of artificial intelligence and machine learning has resulted in considerable developments in the early 2020s already within the context of sport public relations. Platforms such as ChatGPT and OpenAI have created opportunities for professionals in this area to explore unique ways to create content, develop communication strategies, and build relationships with publics. For example, a general prompt provided below resulted in the following output from Chat GPT in Table 17.1.

ChatGPT employs a range of theoretical approaches to crisis communication (e.g., crisis response strategies, discourse of renewal, social responsibility, leadership, etc.). What's more, the program identifies numerous publics (both internal and external) that need to be engaged throughout the process. It provides broad ideas that, while generic at times, nevertheless offer valuable insights into how a public relations team might handle a crisis within a sports organization. It essentially developed a checklist that is rooted in theoretical frameworks for practical application – all within seconds.

TABLE 17.1 Create a Crisis Plan for a Sports Team Whose Star Player Has Been Arrested for Physical Assault Just Before a Championship Game

ChatGPT

Developing a crisis plan for a sports team facing a situation where their star player has been arrested for physical assault just before a championship game is crucial to manage the fallout and maintain the team's reputation. The plan should focus on addressing immediate concerns, managing public relations, supporting the team, and ensuring the well-being of all involved parties. Here's a comprehensive crisis plan:

1 Immediate Actions:–
  a **Confirm Facts:**
    – Verify the accuracy of the information regarding the arrest.
    – Communicate with law enforcement to understand the charges and gather relevant details.
  b **Legal Counsel:**
    – Engage legal counsel for the player to navigate the legal process.
    – Advise the player on cooperation with law enforcement and legal proceedings.
  c **Team Communication:**
    – Gather the team for an emergency meeting to provide accurate information.
    – Emphasize the importance of maintaining composure and avoiding speculation.
  d **Immediate Suspension:**
    – Suspend the player from all team activities until the legal process is complete.
    – Clearly communicate the suspension to the media and fans.
  e **Contact Player Support Services:**
    – Arrange for counseling and support services for the affected player.
    – Ensure the player has access to mental health professionals to address any underlying issues.
2 Public Relations:
  a **Craft a Public Statement:**
    – Draft a concise and empathetic statement acknowledging the incident.
    – Express the team's commitment to a thorough investigation and cooperation with authorities.
  b **Press Conference:**
    – Hold a press conference with the team's coach, management, and spokesperson.
    – Reiterate the team's values and commitment to addressing the situation responsibly.
  c **Media Training:**
    – Provide media training for key team members to ensure a consistent and composed message.
    – Stress the importance of refraining from speculative or inflammatory comments.
  d **Social Media Management:**
    – Monitor and manage social media accounts to address misinformation.
    – Encourage supporters to remain patient while the situation unfolds.
3 Team Support:
  a **Team Meeting:**

(*Continued*)

TABLE 17.1 (Continued)

ChatGPT

- Facilitate a team meeting to address concerns, answer questions, and provide emotional support.
- Reinforce the importance of unity and focusing on the upcoming game.

b **Leadership Reinforcement:**
- Empower team leaders to maintain morale and keep the team focused on their goals.
- Foster an environment where teammates support each other during this challenging time.

4 Community Engagement:

a **Community Outreach:**
- Engage with the community through organized events or statements to demonstrate accountability.
- Reaffirm the team's commitment to being positive role models.

b **Partnerships:**
- Collaborate with local organizations addressing domestic violence or related issues.
- Use the incident as an opportunity to promote awareness and education.

5 Ongoing Monitoring:

a **Legal Updates:**
- Stay informed about legal developments and be prepared to adjust the crisis plan accordingly.
- Continue to provide legal support and representation for the player.

b **Media Monitoring:**
- Monitor media coverage and public sentiment to adjust communication strategies as needed.
- Address any emerging issues promptly.

6 Reintegration Planning:

a **Reintegration Protocol:**
- Develop a plan for the player's potential return to the team based on legal outcomes.
- Communicate clear expectations for rehabilitation, counseling, and behavior.

b **Public Communication:**
- Craft a carefully worded statement announcing the player's return (if applicable).
- Emphasize the steps taken by the player to address and rectify their behavior.

By implementing this crisis plan, the sports team can demonstrate transparency, responsibility, and a commitment to addressing the situation while working towards the best interests of all involved parties.

Prior research has begun to explore implications for the implementation of AI in sport, particularly within the context of sport journalism (Galily, 2018a, 2018b), sport management (Naraine & Wanless, 2020), digital and interactive marketing (Byon & Phua, 2021), and computational social science research (Boatwright, 2023). Of course, novel research in this area is needed. Scholars will need to keep up with industry trends in order to develop new ways of empirically studying the role of AI within sport public relations. But as industry often tends to outpace academia, this will certainly pose a considerable challenge to theoretical refinement and development. Nevertheless, the 2020s have already begun to bear witness to the emerging effects of AI and machine learning within sport public relations contexts.

What Will Sport Public Relations Look Like in 2050?

In this section, we outline several areas where sport public relations has already begun to embrace AI and machine learning tools to enhance fan experiences, create content to reach different audiences, and leverage analytics to evaluate the results of their efforts. Within each topic, we project additional areas where AI might be leveraged to enhance public relations efforts.

Fan Experience

The use of AI is already having a direct effect on in-game fan experiences to such an extent that the use of digital tickets now seems antiquated. The Tennessee Titans, for example, have begun using facial recognition in order to allow fans' entry into the stadium in place of QR codes on their phones (Michael, 2023) which they call Express Entry. Similarly, the Cleveland Browns have begun using facial recognition technology for beer sales throughout the stadium (Schaefer, 2023). The Carolina Panthers have found additional ways to monetize augmented reality (AR) experiences by hosting an AR Scavenger Hunt throughout the stadium sponsored by a local health system.

The use of these technologies to enhance the fan experience in stadiums and arenas will only continue to grow. Public relations professionals will need to be involved in the development of these tools in order for them to achieve their intended organizational goals (i.e., faster access to the stadium, sponsorship opportunities, etc.).

Media Utilization

In order to reach younger audiences, the NFL began developing alternative broadcasting options like the Week 4 of the 2023 season matchup against the Atlanta Falcons and Jacksonville Jaguars was broadcast in real-time using avatars from the Toy Story movie franchise. Similarly, the NHL has explored creating alternative broadcasts for kids and bettors in addition to traditional broadcast opportunities (Wyshynski, 2022). The NBA was among the first professional sport organizations to embrace opportunities for second-screening during league broadcasts by creating platforms and resources for fans to engage with digital apps on their phones while watching games on television.

All of these new media technologies and broadcast opportunities also create unique avenues for media relations professionals to incorporate brand-specific messaging. For example, the University of Central Florida piloted a new jersey for its 2022 spring game using QR codes on players jerseys for viewers to link directly to a players' official profile (Dellenger, 2022). Public relations professionals should identify opportunities to implement brand storytelling while the media landscape continues to evolve to meet different audiences through an increasingly wide range of platforms and broadcast types.

Corporate Social Responsibility

Leading up to the 2023 FIFA Women's World Cup in Australia and New Zealand, the French National team ran a deepfake advertisement superimposing male faces and bodies on to female players' athlete performances. Viewers were not only taken aback by the visual effects, but also by the message it carried (Ewe, 2023). That a form of AI could be used to confront social stigmas and biases should not be surprising to PR professionals where leveraging media tools and techniques to convey a powerful message dates back to Bernays and the "torches of freedom." Nevertheless, the advertisement marks a turning point for sport PR practitioners to begin finding novel ways to engage audiences in social responsibility and community building efforts.

By and large, the COVID-19 pandemic and ensuing social distancing period forced people into virtual environments. Fans longed to be back in packed stadiums. Players needed new ways to train. Everyday people needed new ways to exercise. This gave rise to virtual training resources and platforms like Peloton, Tonal, and others. In the years since the pandemic began, it is clear that the marketplace for virtual environments remains. What's yet to be determined, however, is how community relations managers can turn these tools into meaningful resources to connect with geographically bound fans hoping to feel like a part of the team's community. In some cases, non-fungible tokens (NFTs) have filled this void, but relatively little has been done to leverage AI for social causes through sport directly.

Risks of Technology Use

While the use of a deepfake to promote awareness of women's soccer should be applauded for its intent, other forms of malicious AI-generated communication can result in mis- and disinformation and event constitute a direct threat to a sports organization or individual involved in sport. In 2021, Sports Illustrated ran a disturbing feature on a teenage cheerleader from the state of Pennsylvania who was the target of deepfake cyberbullying in which an older woman (whose daughter was also a cheerleader at the same gym) created fake images of videos of the teenager drinking, vaping, and posing nude. Deepfake technology poses a very real threat to anyone in the public eye through athletic involvement at seemingly any level. Consequently, public relations professionals must know how to recognize and respond to deepfakes when they occur to mitigate as much damage as possible.

Perhaps the most glaring issue at hand rests with issues of mis- and disinformation that use sport as a catalyst to spread false and even harmful information. Whether it's Russian trolls using the Black Lives Matter movement to fan the flames of online conversation around Colin Kaepernick (Yan et al., 2021), or conspiracy theorists blaming the COVID-19 vaccination on Twitter for Bills player Damar Hamlin's on-field collapse against the Cincinnati Bengals during Monday Night Football in January of 2023 (Mier, 2023), sports PR professionals must have the wherewithal to monitor media (and social media) environments for absurd to the downright harmful spread of false information.

Ethical Use of Technology

Of course, this also raises concerns about how sport PR professionals *should* use AI in their work. The debate over how and when AI should be applied in sport public relations contexts will continue to play out for some time. One practitioner may not have any issues using ChatGPT to plan an entire content calendar's worth of content for their team's social media accounts, whereas others would be weary of publishing content they did not create themselves. It also raises issues of image and video editing, data ownership, and a host of other ethical issues. Rather than identify the myriad of ways AI can lead sport PR professionals down the wrong path, we argue that the PRSA's Code of Ethics still applies in this context and should be the standard by which professionals make decisions about the use of AI in sport public relations moving forward.

Knowledge, Skills, and Abilities for People Working in Sport Public Relations in 2050

Finally, as we seek to prepare students to become the next generation of sport public relations professionals it is imperative that we begin to identify the tools and skills they will need to hone to be prepared for positions in the industry. As the old adage goes, when it comes to sport public relations, "some things stay the same." Despite the development of new technologies, a basic understanding of PR principles should be the bedrock for any new graduate taking on an internship or first full-time job in sport public relations. That involves a working knowledge of theory, strong writing and editing skills, critical thinking, effective communication, and a demonstrable ability to nimbly work collaboratively across different units of an organization.

Of course, we as educators would be doing a disservice to students if we did not teach them requisite skills they need for the rapidly changing sports industry. Students graduating with a degree in public relations (sport-specific or not) should have a rudimentary knowledge of graphic design, video/photo editing, and coding. An enhanced understanding of data science and analytics is likely to be an important skill for students to develop as well, given the wide range of applications for machine learning and advanced computational techniques within sport.

In short, there will be no shortage of items to add to the curriculum in the coming years if the academy aims to keep up with industry developments.

Conclusion

The state of public relations within the context of sport is constantly in flux. Any array of issues, crises, relationships, or the like can complicate a practitioner's role with an organization. The day-to-day management of these tasks is no small feat in its own right. The rapid onset of AI as a force affecting sport compounds an already complicated web of responsibilities for public relations professionals in the industry. There is no doubt that by the year 2050, many of these subjects will have already been rendered obsolete. Nevertheless, communication professionals – especially those that choose to embark in careers in public relations – are uniquely suited to handle the stressors associated with new technologies.

References

Boatwright, B. C. (2023). Embracing computational approaches to social media research: Implications for theory and praxis in sport communication. *Communication & Sport*. https://doi.org/10.1177/21674795231196429

Byon, K. K., & Phua, J. (2021). Digital and interactive marketing communications in sports. *Journal of Interactive Advertising, 21*(2), 75–78.

College Sports Communicators. (2022). *CoSIDA to officially rebrand to college sports communicators*. Retrieved from https://collegesportscommunicators.com/news/2022/9/1/general-cosida-to-officially-rebrand-to-college-sports-communicators.aspx

Compton, J., & Compton, J. L. (2023). Playoff losses, mayoral politics, image repair, and inoculation: Open letter sport communication. *Communication & Sport, 11*(3), 616–633.

Dellenger, R. (2022, April 15). UCF's spring game Jerseys feature QR codes leading to player bios, branded merch. *Sports Illustrated*. Retrieved from https://www.si.com/college/2022/04/15/ucf-football-spring-game-jerseys-qr-codes-nil-merchandise

Ewe, K. (2023, July 17). A viral French ad shows how women's soccer can be just as exciting as men's. *Time*. Retrieved from Women's World Cup 2023_ Viral French Ad Subverts Gender Expectations in Soccer _ TIME

Frederick, E., & Pegoraro, A. (2018). Scandal in college basketball: A case study of image repair via Facebook. *International Journal of Sport Communication, 11*(3), 414–429.

Galily, Y. (2018a). Artificial intelligence and sports journalism: Is it a sweeping change? *Technology in Society*, *54*, 47–51.

Galily, Y. (2018b). Evolution, revolution, or a real game changer? Artificial intelligence and sports journalism. In *Robot journalism: Can human journalism survive?* (pp. 103–113). World Scientific Publishing Co Pte Ltd Singapore.

Godfrey, P. C. (2009). Corporate social responsibility in sport: An overview and key issues. *Journal of Sport Management*, *23*(6), 698–716.

Hardin, R., & McClung, S. (2002). Collegiate sports information: A profile of the profession. *Public Relations Quarterly*, *47*(2), 35.

Hopwood, M. K. (2005). Applying the public relations function to the business of sport. *International Journal of Sports Marketing and Management, 6*(3), 174–188.

Hopwood, M. (2010). Sport marketing public relations. In M. Hopwood, P. Kitchin, & J. Skinner (Eds.), *Sport public relations and communication* (1st ed.). Butterworth-Heinemann, Elsevier Ltd.

L'Etang, J. (2006). Public relations and sport in promotional culture. *Public Relations Review*, *32*(4), 386–394.

Li, M., Hofacre, S., & Mahony, D. (2001). *Economics of sport*. Fitness Information Technology.

Michael, O., (2023, October 23). Titans using new facial recognition technology for ticket entry. *News Channel 5 Nashville*. Retrieved from https://www.newschannel5.com/news/titans-using-new-facial-recognition-technology-for-ticket-entry

Mier, T. (2023, January 3). Anti-vaxxers turn Damar Hamlin's on-field collapse into a 'Vile' conspiracy theory. *Rolling Stone*. Retrieved from https://www.rollingstone.com/culture/culture-news/damar-hamlin-injury-anti-vaxxers-spew-lies-1234655339/

Naraine, M. L., & Wanless, L. (2020). Going all in on AI: Examining the value proposition of and integration challenges with one branch of artificial intelligence in sport management. *Sports Innovation Journal*, *1*, 49–61.

Onwumechili, C., & Bedeau, K. (2017). Analysis of FIFA's attempt at image repair. *Communication & Sport*, *5*(4), 407–427.

Pedersen P. M. (2013). Reflections on communication and sport: On strategic communication and management. *Communication & Sport*, *1*(1–2), 55–67. https://doi.org/10.1177/2167479512466655

Pedersen, P.M., Laucella, P., Geurin, A., & Kian, E. (2020). *Strategic Sport Communication*. Champaign, IL: Human Kinetics.

Pitts, B., Fielding, L. W., & Miller, L. K. (1994). *Industry segmentation theory and the sport industry: Developing a sport industry segment model*. Sport Marketing Quarterly, *3*(1), 15–24.

Schaefer, R., (2023, October 11). Browns' express Beer facial authentication program seeing early returns. *Sports Business Journal*. Retrieved from https://www.sportsbusinessjournal.com/Articles/2023/10/11/cleveland-browns-express-beer-wicket-aramark

Smith, D. K., & Casper, J. (2020). Making an impact: An initial review of US sport league corporate social responsibility responses during COVID-19. *International Journal of Sport Communication*, *13*(3), 335–343.

Stamm, J., & Boatwright, B. (2023). 'Deteriorating our relationship for no good reason': Collegiate beat writers' perceptions of their PR counterparts. *Communication & Sport*. DOI: 10.1177/21674795231201418

Stoldt, G. C. (2000). Current and ideal organizational roles of NCAA Division I-A sport-sin formation professionals. *The Cyber-Journal of Sport Marketing, 4*(1). Retrieved May 24, 2000, from www.cjsm.com/vol4.stoldt41.htm

Stoldt, G. C., Dittmore, S. W., Ross, M., & Branvold, S. E. (2020). *Sport public relations*. Human Kinetics.

Stoldt, G. C., Miller, L. K., & Vermillion, M. (2009). Public relations evaluation in sport: Views from the field. *International Journal of Sport Communication, 2*(2), 223–239.

Stoldt, G. C., & Narasimhan, V. (2005). Self assessments of collegiate sports information professionals regarding their public relations task expertise. *International Journal of Sport Management, 6*(3), 252–269.

Wyshynski, G. (2022, April 26). The NHL's tech-heavy plan to draw in young fans. *ESPN*. Retrieved from https://www.espn.com/nhl/story/_/id/33803500/the-nhl-tech-heavy-plan-draw-young-fans

Yan, G., Pegoraro, A., & Watanabe, N. M. (2021). Examining IRA bots in the NFL anthem protest: Political agendas and practices of digital gatekeeping. *Communication & Sport, 9*(1), 88–109.

18

THE FUTURE OF INVESTOR RELATIONS AND FINANCIAL COMMUNICATION

AI, ESG, and Shareholder Activism

Christian Pieter Hoffmann and Alexander V. Laskin

Definition of Investor Relations and Financial Communication

Investor relations is one of the strategic communications functions aimed at building and maintaining relationships with financial audiences, such as professional investors, retail shareholders, financial analysts, banks and other intermediary organizations, exchanges and trading platforms, as well as regulatory agencies (Laskin, 2022). Investor relations is traditionally limited to corporations, even more precisely to publicly traded corporations, because there are no investors and thus there is no need for investor communication in non-profit organizations or government entities. There are exceptions, however. For example, Gainesville Regional Utilities (GRU), while being an entity owned by the City of Gainesville, Florida, has a function of investor relations in order to enable disclosure and other financial and strategic communications to the residents of Gainesville as well as owners of debt securities GRU issues to finance its operations.

The main goal of investor relations is often described as helping corporations achieve fair value – in other words, investor relations officers (IROs) educate investors and assist their efforts of understanding the true value of a corporation (Laskin & Samoilenko, 2014). This may include explaining complex financial transactions of corporations, showing the potential value of investments in research and development, illuminating opportunities or threats in changing markets, and even disclosing health information of the CEO or other key personnel to the extent that such information may affect the ability of a corporation to function and innovate.

Thus, investor relations disclosures are often more than just financial disclosures – instead, they encompass all aspects of corporate operations and may focus on the past, present, and the future. As a result, the largest professional

DOI: 10.4324/9781003426653-21

organization for investor relations, the National Investor Relations Institute (NIRI), defines investor relations as: "a strategic management responsibility that integrates finance, communication, marketing and securities law compliance to enable the most effective two-way communication between a company, the financial community, and other constituencies, which ultimately contributes to a company's securities achieving fair valuation" (NIRI, 2023).

While the terms investor relations and financial communication are often used synonymously, some distinguish financial communication from investor relations as the public relations function focusing on financial or business journalists (Binder-Tietz et al., 2021). In these cases, investor relations and financial communication coordinate closely to fulfill the information requirements of their respective target audiences.

Brief History of Investor Relations

The history of modern investor relations is usually traced back to the 1933 US Securities Act and 1934 Securities Exchange Act. Both of these laws define the roles and responsibilities of the stock market participants and demanded fairness and transparency in communications between corporations and investors. Laskin (2022) splits the evolution of investor relations into three distinct eras: Communication era (till 1975), Finance era (1975–2000), and Synergy era (after 2000). In the first two eras, IROs focused primarily on either communication tactics such as media releases, or on financial tactics, such as managing earning guidance, in the synergy era, IROs combine both. The synergy era also requires IROs to be experts in both communication and finance. Laskin (2018) proposed that today's IROs have to have multiple educations: be it double or even triple majors, earning additional graduate degrees, or taking advantage of the professional development learning opportunities.

While most research on the history of investor relations has focused on the US, exploration of IR in Europe (Laskin & Köhler, 2012; Marston, 2004) mirror findings by Laskin (2022). The most developed capital markets in Europe are those of the UK and of Germany. The IR profession in the UK closely follows examples set by the US (Marston, 2004). Developments in Germany tend to lag behind slightly, but since the 1990s, professional standards have quickly caught up to international best practices (Köhler, 2018). Other European and non-Western markets often still remain in the communication- or finance-focused stages characterized by Laskin (2022).

Distinct Features of Investor Relations and Financial Communication

Companies listed on the stock exchange are characterized by the separation of ownership and control, that is, the principal-agent relationship between shareholders and management (Fama, 1980; Jensen & Meckling, 1976). Shareholders, especially those of large listed companies, do not directly control strategic or operational management decisions. This could lead to discretionary leeway for executive managers pursuing their self-interest over that of shareholders, and the misallocation of corporate resources. Investor relations, thus, serves to reduce information asymmetries between shareholders and management to ensure the alignment of interests between corporate outsiders and insiders (Fama, 1980; Jensen & Meckling, 1976). In other words: investor relations is a critical element of good corporate governance.

Since it is dedicated to maintaining and fostering relationships with shareholders – that is: the owners of the company – investor relations is characterized by a particularly powerful audience. At the end of the day, shareholder can hire and fire corporate leadership, and decide over the allocation of corporate resources. Most listed corporations have many thousands of shareholders. However, shareholding is very unequally distributed. In most corporations, thousands of retail shareholders collectively own only up to 20% of corporate stocks. The rest is held by relatively few institutional investors. As a result, the core target audience of IR – the institutional investors and the analysts advising them – is actually quite small. Most time spent both by executives and IROs on maintaining financial relations is dedicated to just a couple dozen individuals (analysts, portfolio managers, proxy advisors). As a result, personal interactions and dialog are critical for investor relations (Hoffmann, 2019; Hoffmann & Binder-Tietz, 2021; Kelly et al., 2010; Rao & Sivakumar, 1999).

A third element that sets investor relations apart from other communications functions is the level of regulation in the financial domain. Traditionally, listed corporations are obligated to publish regular financial reports, and to host an annual shareholders meeting. Over time, reporting requirements have expanded to include governance data and, most recently, sustainability or ESG (environment, social, governance) information (Laskin, 2022). Listed corporations may not distribute information preferentially. All material information must be disclosed to the entire capital market at once (ad-hoc publicity). Management transactions and corporate shareholdings have to be disclosed. Most IROs can tell tales of woe when it comes to the seemingly insurmountable complexity and density of financial communication regulations. On the other hand, the (regulatory) sensitivity of financial information ensures that IR is regularly involved in top management meetings to ensure that all applicable regulations are respected (Hoffmann & Binder-Tietz, 2021).

Influences on the Development of Investor Relations and Financial Communication

Three trends are likely to shape the future development of investor relations and financial communication: changes in the composition of capital market participants, an increasing focus on sustainability, and, of course, digitalization.

FIGURE 18.1 Stock trading on the floor of the New York stock exchange.

Source: Library of Congress. https://commons.wikimedia.org/wiki/File:No_Known_Restrictions-_New_York_Stock_Exchange_Floor_by_Thomas_J._O%27Halloran,_1963_(LOC).jpg.

For the longest time, the most common investment strategy among mutual funds can be described as active investing. Accordingly, a mutual fund conducted (buy-side) analyses of potential investment objects and employed a portfolio manager or investment committee that decided which assets to invest in, and which to avoid. Stock picking, traditionally, was the core value added of an actively managed investment fund. Increasingly, however, studies reveal that fund managers struggle to outperform the market over the long term (Shushko & Turner, 2018).

Yet, their services are quite expensive to investors. This has led to the rise of passive investing (Economist, 2006). Passively managed funds do not engage in stock picking, but rather replicate a stock market index in their portfolio – for example the Dow Jones Industrial Average (DJIA) or the Financial Times Stock Exchange 100 Index (FTSE 100). As a result, passively managed funds never underperform the market they replicate, and their management fees are very low. Today, among the four largest asset management firms globally, each managing assets in excess of 3 trillion USD, three specialize in passive investing: BlackRock, Vanguard, and State Street.

The rise of passive funds and the decline of active investing has disrupted and, to a degree, impeded the relationship management function of IR. After all, analysts and portfolio managers are the most important target audiences of IR. In the case of passive funds, however, portfolio managers play only a minor role as these funds' strategies are so simple that investment decisions can be largely automated. Simply put, in the case of passive funds, there is almost no one to talk to for IROs. Also, there is little use in fostering relationships with those administering passive funds, as these "fund managers" really have little to no decision latitude. Asset management firms specializing in passive funds do maintain so-called engagement or stewardship teams, however. These teams tend to focus on governance and sustainability issues, rather than details of financial performance. So passive funds are not just more difficult to engage from an IR perspective, they also imply a change in conversation focus.

The rise in passive investing and the concomitant decline in active investing opens a window of opportunity for shareholder activists. As there are fewer fund managers actively engaging corporations on questions of strategy and financial performance, this leaves ample opportunity for hedge funds that not only engage in stock picking, but actually very specifically identify and target underperforming corporations or those with strategic and/or tactic weaknesses to exert pressure on (Hoffmann & Fieseler, 2018). Shareholder activists tend to focus on governance concerns, questions of strategy and performance, and transactions (Brav et al., 2008; Del Guercio & Hawkins, 1999; Kahan & Rock, 2009). Their interventions are often quite disruptive to corporate leadership, so that IR takes on a critical role in preventing or managing activist attacks (Hoffmann & Fieseler, 2018).

Second, the past decades have witnessed a tremendous rise in societal and political concern over sustainability (Henn et al., 2022). These shifts in public sentiment have also resulted in a massive expansion of policy initiatives and regulatory efforts to strive for environmental, social and economic sustainability (Pizzi et al., 2020). As a result, sustainability topics have gained in prominence both in mandatory and voluntary corporate disclosures, they are also becoming ever more salient among financial audiences (Arvidsson, 2010). A majority of companies listed on Western markets today publish a sustainability report (Governance & Accounting Institute, 2021). In some markets, these reports are no longer voluntary. The European Union, in particular, has taken a leading role in mandatory sustainability reporting (see, for example, the Corporate Sustainability Reporting Directive (CSRD), and the European Sustainability Reporting Standards (ESRS)).

In 2020, Binder-Tietz and colleagues (2020) conducted a large-scale study among German listed corporations to explore how they approached the implementation of these novel sustainability reporting requirements. They found that all surveyed corporations published sustainability reports. Sustainability topics were also addressed in up to half of roadshow or capital market day presentations. Many corporations had not yet integrated sustainability into their equity story, but were planning to do so soon. Binder-Tietz et al.'s (2020) study also uncovered an interesting contradiction: When asked for the main addressees of sustainability reports, respondents named institutional investors and analysts – the key target audience of investor relations. However, when asked which corporate function was responsible for compiling and publishing the sustainability report, the same respondents pointed to the sustainability department, not the IR department.

Third, digitalization continues to change the face of financial communication. Already, the IR website is among the most important IR tools, reports and releases are usually published in a digital format, even meetings are increasingly conducted online, transcripts or recordings of these meetings are then posted on the IR website (Ettredge & Gerdes, 2005; Laskin & Hoffmann, 2023). Some analysts and investors take social media into consideration when analyzing a company (Alexander & Gentry, 2014), but social media are mostly popular among retail investors (cf., Zerfass & Köhler, 2017). As the now infamous GameStop short squeeze (Laskin, 2022) organized by disgruntled investors on Reddit shows, social media can be a platform for information sharing and even coordination within the financial community.

When looking toward the future, automatization is of particular interest for changes to the resources, processes and structures of IR departments. Given the small size of IR teams, automatization can be a chance to free up resources to be used in a more impactful way – for example in personal dialog with analysts, investors, and proxy advisors. That is why digital tools facilitating internal processes, such as customer relationship management (CRM) software or shareholder ID services, tend to be popular (Hoffmann et al., 2018; Laskin & Hoffmann, 2023). Both in the US and EU, XBRL (eXtensible Business Reporting Language) or iXBRL (inline XBRL) is increasingly employed to render corporate reports machine-readable. Automatization, thus, doesn't end at the corporation's boundaries. Capital markets today are digital spaces, where orders are input and processed, assets are transferred and stored digitally (Laskin & Hoffmann, 2023). As a result, they have reached unprecedented levels of speed and liquidity. High-frequency trading (HFT) is characterized by the processing of orders within milliseconds, allowing for tremendous trading volumes as well as the exploitation of miniscule asset price spreads (Chen et al., 2021).

A common critique of HFT is that it only benefits large investment firms that have specialized in this sort of trading, leaving less room for traditional traders (Chen et al., 2021). Retail investors can obviously not keep pace with traders employing HFT, which may systematically burden them with less favorable asset prices. At the same time, however, the emergence of digital technologies has rendered capital markets more accessible for retail investors and the average citizen. Particularly in the past years, and especially during the COVID-19 pandemic (Massa & Ponczek, 2020), the wide-spread popularity of trading apps, such as Robinhood, has revolutionized trading markets and made it very cheap and easy for retail investors to take part in stock market trading and to experiment with small investment amounts.

Investor Relations and Financial Communication in 2050

In 2050, investor relations and financial communication professionals will require significant expertise in the field of sustainability. Also, they will need high(er) levels of technological knowhow, as workflows are increasingly automated. They will continue to work in small, flexible teams, and their work will be characterized by even more cross-departmental cooperation and coordination. Their key value proposition to the organization will shift from preparing financial reports to engaging in finance-related conversations of strategic importance.

In terms of disclosures and reporting, expectations for dependably delivering timely, reliable, machine-readable information to the financial community will be higher than ever. AI-based tools employed within the organization will facilitate data access and aggregation, the composition and distribution of reports and announcements. Disclosures will apply an integrated perspective on financial and non-financial (but quantified) information. Sustainability departments will merge with the strategy and/or finance departments, as sustainability will be a core element of the corporate strategy, and thus, sustainability data will be collected and analyzed by the finance department alongside financial data. Integrated reports will become the norm – IROs will need to be able to explain sustainability data as fluently and clearly as financial data.

Integrated reports (Köhler & Hoffmann, 2018) – sometimes also called impact reporting (Adams et al., 2021) – requires close cross-departmental coordination, involving not just the finance department, corporate communications, and legal, but also HR, marketing, public/political affairs etc. Maintaining interfaces with these functions or departments, regular interactions and mutual updates will be a key element of the IR task.

IR teams are likely to remain small in size. However, (partial) automatization of disclosures and reporting will free up some resources to invest in focused relationship management. The diversity of audiences within the financial community is likely to increase. Aside from the well-established interactions with fund managers and analysts, IROs dedicate significant time to communicating with asset managers' engagement or stewardship teams. Proxy advisors also play a key role, as they shape the voting behavior of passive funds, in particular. Monitoring shareholder activists and ensuring early engagement in case of interventions is also crucial. Finally, on digital capital markets, reaching out to retail shareholders – directly or indirectly, through journalists and financial influencers – gains in importance. Retail shareholders are growing not just more numerous, but also more active and may play an important role in cases of activist interventions.

Automatization will be helpful in monitoring financial audiences – digital tools help IR keep up-to-speed on trading volumes, investor sentiment, retail shareholder conversations, trending topics etc. This will bolster the listening function, or the inbound function of financial communication (Vercic & Zerfass, 2016). As experts for the views and expectations of financial audiences, IROs will serve as valued advisors to corporate leaders in all matters related to strategy and finance (Zerfass & Volk, 2018).

Knowledge, Skills, and Abilities of IROs in 2050

Already, IROs tend to have expertise in multiple fields. In fact, the definition of the profession calls for expertise in "finance, communication, marketing and securities law" (NIRI, 2004). The future developments outlined above will demand expanding Knowledge, Skills, and Abilities of IROs even more. Sustainability is becoming a key issue investors are interested in. Thus, many IROs will also have to become sustainability officers, perhaps even taking over the responsibilities of managing corporate sustainability efforts to meet the demands of investors – and further stakeholders, such as employees, local communities, and even society at large. With pressure on corporations to find a balance between communicating about green efforts and being accused in greenwashing, it will be crucial to avoid de-coupling communicating sustainability from the actual practice of sustainability. And since IROs are already the ones communicating about sustainability and combining all corporate sustainability efforts into cumulative impact reports, IROs are likely to leaders of sustainability within the organization.

Second, the technological innovations affecting every single part of the corporate value creation chain will also require IROs to become experts in technology. For example, IROs will have to be able to explain not just what AI is but how AI can be utilized at every stage of the designing, producing, marketing, distributing, and servicing the corporation's products. Third, as explained above, listening to investors, financial analysts, proxy advisors, retail shareholders and other financial stakeholders is becoming more and more important. Thus, IROs will have to become expert listeners, capable not just of monitoring multiple conversations on a variety of channels simultaneously, but also being able to separate ideas from noise and generate actionable insights based on their analysis of the available data.

Conclusion

Investor relations and financial communication is a relatively recent strategic communications function. It has undergone significant and swift changes in the few decades of its establishment, professionalization, and institutionalization

(Köhler, 2018; Laskin, 2022; Laskin & Köhler, 2012). The next two decades promise a similar, if not increased pace of evolution, with IR gaining new responsibilities (esp. in the area of sustainability), facing a shifting stakeholder environment (e.g., the rise of passive investing, shareholder activism, retail investors, etc.), and employing new technologies to facilitate core responsibilities (i.e., disclosures and reporting) and strengthen contributions to corporate leadership (through listening capabilities and stakeholder engagement).

Pessimists warn that the investor relations department may entirely vanish in the future – if the finance and sustainability departments take responsibility for corporate reporting, and investor dialog is rendered obsolete due to passive investing or high-frequency trading. It is up to IROs to refute such pessimism. By taking charge of the sustainability challenge, by mastering new technologies, and by focusing on conversations of strategic importance with a wider set of audiences, investor relations and strategic communication can expand its portfolio and grow even more influential within the corporation's dominant coalition.

References

Adams, S., Tweedie, D., & Muir, K. (2021). Social impact reporting in the public interest: the case of accounting standardisation. *Qualitative Research in Accounting & Management, 18*(3), 390–416. https://doi.org/10.1108/QRAM-02-2019-0026

Alexander, R. M., & Gentry, J. K. (2014). Using social media to report financial results. *Business Horizons, 57*(2), 161–167. https://doi.org/10.1016/j.bushor.2013.10.009

Arvidsson, S. (2011). Disclosure of non-financial information in the annual report: A management-team perspective. *Journal of Intellectual Capital, 12*(2), 277–300. https://doi.org/10.1108/14691931111123421

Binder-Tietz, S., Hoffmann, C. P., Lamprecht, H., Van Poele, M., & Waskowiak, L. (2020). *Nachhaltigkeit in der Kapitalmarktkommunikation. Eine empirische Analyse der Nachhaltigkeitskommunikation deutscher börsennotierter Unternehmen an den Kapitalmarkt.* DIRK – Deutscher Investor Relations Verband.

Binder-Tietz, S., Hoffmann, C. P., & Reinholz, J. (2021). Integrated financial communication: Insights on the coordination and integration among investor relations and public relations departments of listed corporations in Germany, Austria and Switzerland. *Public Relations Review, 47*(4), 102075.

Brav, A., Jiang, W., Partnoy, F., & Thomas, R. (2008). Hedge fund activism, corporate governance, and firm performance. *Journal of Finance, 53*(4), 1729–1775. https://doi.org/10.1111/j.1540-6261.2008.01373.x

Chen, J., Boyle, M. J., & Munichiello, K. (2021). What is high-frequency trading (HFT)? How it works and example. *Investopedia.* Retrieved from https://www.investopedia.com/terms/h/high-frequency-trading.asp

Del Guercio, D., & Hawkins, J. (1999). The motivation and impact of pension fund activism. *Journal of Financial Economics, 52*(3), 293–340. https://doi.org/10.1016/S0304-405X(99)00011-2

Economist. (2006, January 26). *Passive aggression – America's shareholders settle for guaranteed mediocrity.* Retrieved from https://www.economist.com/finance-and-economics/2006/01/26/passive-aggression

Ettredge, M., & Gerdes, J. (2005). Timeliness of investor relations data at corporate web sites. *Communications of the ACM, 48*(1), 95–100.

Fama, E. F. (1980). Agency problems and the theory of the firm. *Journal of Political Economy, 88*(2), 288–307. https://doi.org/10.1086/260866

Governance & Accounting Institute. (2021). 92% of S&P 500® Companies and 70% of Russell 1000® Companies Published Sustainability Reports in 2020, G&A Institute Research Shows. *GlobeNewswire*. Retrieved from https://www.globenewswire.com/news-release/2021/11/16/2335435/0/en/92-of-S-P-500-Companies-and-70-of-Russell-1000-Companies-Published-Sustainability-Reports-in-2020-G-A-Institute-Research-Shows.html

Henn, M., Sloam, J., & Nunes, A. (2022). Young cosmopolitans and environmental politics: How postmaterialist values inform and shape youth engagement in environmental politics. *Journal of Youth Studies, 25*(6), 709–729. https://doi.org/10.1080/13676261.2021.1994131

Hoffmann, C. P. (2019). Investor relations communication. In R. L. Heath & W. Johansen (Eds.), *The international encyclopedia of strategic communication* (Vol. *2*, pp. 194–804). Wiley-Blackwell.

Hoffmann, C. P., & Binder-Tietz, S. (2021). Strategic investor relations management: insights on planning and evaluation practices among German Prime Standard corporations. *Journal of Communication Management, 25*(2), 142–159. https://doi.org/10.1108/JCOM-06-2020-0047

Hoffmann, C. P., & Fieseler, C. (2012). Investor relations beyond financials: Non-financial factors and capital market image building. *Corporate Communications: An International Journal, 17*(2), 138–155. https://doi.org/10.1108/13563281211220265

Jensen, M. C., & Meckling, W. H. (1976). Theory of the firm: Managerial behavior, agency costs and ownership structure. *Journal of Financial Economics, 3*(4), 305–360.

Kahan, M., & Rock, E. B. (2009). Hedge funds in corporate governance and corporate control. In L. E. Mitchell (Ed.), *Corporate governance* (pp. 389–461). Gower.

Kelly, K. S., Laskin, A. V., & Rosenstein, G. A. (2010). Investor relations: Two-way symmetrical practice. *Journal of Public Relations Research, 22*(2), 182–208. https://doi.org/10.1080/10627261003601630

Köhler, K. (2018). Investor relation in Germany – Institutionalization and professional roles. In A. V. Laskin (Ed.), *The handbook of financial communication and investor relations* (pp. 429–441). Wiley-Blackwell.

Köhler, K., & Hoffmann, C. P. (2018). Integrated reporting: Bridging investor relations and strategic management. In A. Laskin (Ed.), *Handbook of financial communication and investor relations* (pp. 209–220). Wiley-Blackwell.

Laskin, A. V. (2018). The third-person effects in the investment decision making: A case of corporate social responsibility. *Corporate Communications: An International Journal, 23*(3), 456–468.

Laskin, A. V. (2022). *Investor relations and financial communication: Creating value through trust and understanding*. John Wiley & Sons.

Laskin, A. V., & Hoffmann, C. P. (2023). Digital corporate communication and financial communication and investor relations. In V. Luoma-aho & M. Badham (Eds.), *Handbook on digital corporate communication* (pp. 91–102). Edward Elgar.

Laskin, A., & Köhler, K. (2012). Investor relations. The state of the profession. In D. Verčič, A. T. Verčič, K. Sriramesh, & A. Zerfass (Eds.), *19th international public relations symposium BledCom* (pp. 115–129). Pristop.

Laskin, A. V., & Laskin, A. A. (2018). Measurement and evaluation of investor relations and financial communication activities. In A. Laskin (Ed.), *Handbook of financial communication and investor relations* (pp. 275–281). Wiley-Blackwell.

Laskin, A. V., & Samoilenko, S. A. (2014). The investor communication strategies of newspaper corporations: A computerized content analysis. *International Journal of Strategic Communication*, *8*(3), 196–214.

Marston, C. L. (2004). *Survey of European investor relations*. The Institute of Chartered Accountants of Scotland.

Massa, A., & Ponczek, S. (2020). Robinhood's addictive app made trading a pandemic pastime. *Bloomberg*. Retrieved from https://www.bloomberg.com/news/features/2020-10-22/how-robinhood-s-addictive-app-made-trading-a-covid-pandemic-pastime

NIRI: The association for Investor Relations. (2023). *Definition of investor relations*. Retrieved from https://www.niri.org/about-niri

Pizzi, S., Caputo, A., Corvino, A., & Venturelli, A. (2020). Management research and the UN sustainable development goals (SDGs): A bibliometric investigation and systematic review. *Journal of Cleaner Production, 276*, 124033. https://doi.org/10.1016/j.jclepro.2020.124033

Rao, H., & Sivakumar, K. (1999). Institutional sources of boundary-spanning structures: The establishment of investor relations departments in the Fortune 500 industrials. *Organization Science, 10*(1), 27–42. https://doi.org/10.1287/orsc.10.1.27

Sushko, V., & Turner, G. (2018). The implications of passive investing for securities markets. *BIS Quarterly Review*, 113–131. Retrieved from https://ssrn.com/abstract=3139242

Vercic, D., & Zerfass, A. (2016). A comparative excellence framework for communication management. *Journal of Communication Management, 20*(4), 270–288. https://doi.org/10.1108/JCOM-11-2015-0087

Zerfass, A., & Köhler, K. (2017). Investor relations: Online-Kommunikation mit Analysten und Anlegern. In A. Zerfaß & T. Pleil (Eds.), *Handbuch online-PR: Strategische kommunikation in internet und social web* (2nd ed., pp. 181–196). Herbert von Halem.

Zerfass, A., & Volk, S. C. (2018). How communication departments contribute to corporate success: The communications contributions framework. *Journal of Communication Management, 22*(4), 397–415. https://doi.org/10.1108/JCOM-12-2017-0146

19

PROPAGANDA AND PSYCHOLOGICAL WARFARE ASPECTS IN THE STRATEGIC COMMUNICATION OF THE 21ST CENTURY

European Union's Place in the Global Order

Greg Simons

Introduction

Persuasive communications in the 21st century have become all pervasive, they are all around us as different organisations and groups are vying and competing for influence and power (Kamalipour & Snow, 2004; Macleod, 2019). This is not a new phenomenon in the history of organised human society, rather it has been a constant over time and space (Taylor, 2003). Communication technologies and the delivery of messages to improve the measure of effectiveness are continually fine-tuned over time and circumstances. This affects all aspects of our contemporary society – political, economic, social, military and diplomatic.

This chapter seeks to shed light on how propaganda and psychological warfare are integrated into the holy grail of higher order communications (at the strategic, rather than operational or tactical levels), strategic communication. The focus is very much upon the notion of how this is applied for political tasks. These are defined twofold, theoretically in an academic sense and in the sense of their operationalisation. A critical interpretation is taken, where the analogy of a crime is used in facilitating the use of this style of communication, it requires a combination of motive, means and opportunity.

There are a total of four sections in this chapter, the first of which engages in defining and mapping the concept and practice of organised persuasive communication, including the constituent elements and focus of this chapter – propaganda and psychological warfare. The next section moves to the issue and practice of strategic communication and the problems of reputation management in an increasingly turbulent 21st century. Following in the third section, the various academic definitions are illustrated through the case of the European Union's

DOI: 10.4324/9781003426653-22

FIGURE 19.1 Example of Propaganda from USSR.

Source: Wikimedia Commons. https://commons.wikimedia.org/wiki/File:The_Secret_Soviet_Bunker_(14360593542).jpg.

External Action Service, what, how and why they communicate to various audiences. In the final section before the conclusion, a brief analysis and estimate of the future of these forms of communication into the future as a profession and as a practice.

Organised Persuasive Communication (OPC): Propaganda and Psychological Warfare

It has been observed and noted that "Organized persuasive communication is essential to the exercise of power at national and global levels" and further, "manipulative, propagandistic organized persuasive communication within liberal democracies is a blind spot; it is rarely recognized let alone researched" (Bakir et al., 2019, p. 311). OPC embraces a broad range of approaches from coercive to non-coercive, manipulative to non-manipulative, dialogical, incentivisation, deceptive to non-deceptive, consensual to non-consensual. This entails using a wide range of promotional communication technologies as public relations or marketing to manipulative communication technologies as propaganda or psychological warfare.

Propaganda is a widely contested term that has many different definitions, it is also a highly controversial practice given the historical associations with Nazi Germany and the Soviet Union (Taylor, 2003). Often within the symbolic political environment of liberal democracy, propaganda is not something done by democracies, but rather a practice restricted to non-democratic settings. At its most neutral and simplistic level of definition, propaganda "means to disseminate or promote particular ideas" (Jowett & O'Donnell, 2012, p. 2). At a more sophisticated level of definition that also considers the communication process and purpose, "propaganda is the deliberate, systematic attempt to shape perceptions, manipulate cognitions, and direct behaviour to achieve a response that furthers the desired intent of the propagandist" (Jowett & O'Donnell, 2012, p. 7). It is a means of emotionally priming and mobilising audiences.

Propaganda has the function of being able to subjectively define and label the people, places, events and trends in the physical realm, which is a means to manufacturing the world view of those subjected to and accepting the propaganda communicated to them (Macdonald, 2009; Patrick, 2012, pp. 65–66). Engineering the world view of audiences is in turn a means for manufacturing their consent to realities, rules and the rulers by aligning perception and behaviour (MacLeod, 2019). Contrary to some constructed myths, propaganda can and often is used by democracies, both historically and contemporarily (Kamalipour & Snow, 2004; Sproule, 2005). In fact, in some respects democracies have been leading the way in terms of propaganda's operationalisation as a means of bringing about some form of societal change (Simons, 2022; Taylor, 2003). Linked to propaganda is the concept and practice of psychological warfare.

In its early stages (term first coined in 1920), psychological warfare focused upon propaganda, with connections to use by military forces and governments. It included a full range of persuasion activities, which includes the use of deception (Paul, 2008, pp. 11–12). Activities in the form of communications occur through the information realm, but are intended to create effects in the cognitive realm. "Psychological warfare seeks to win military gains without military force" (Linebarger, 2009, p. 37). The same can be said for politics too, political gains without the use of political coercion. In way of definition, "psychological warfare comprises the use of propaganda against an enemy, together with such other operational measures of a military, economic, or political nature as may be required to supplement propaganda" (Linebarger, 2009, p. 40). I would argue that it does not necessarily need to be directed against an enemy per se, but rather a target audience to be influenced and persuaded.

Strategic Communication Frames as a Means of Reputation Management

There are a very wide and varied selection of definitions of strategic communications, which means that its definition is simultaneously evolving and contested (Cornish et al., 2011, pp. 3–5; Nothhaft et al., 2018). The purpose and definition of strategic communications can be understood as the deliberate application of communication by an organisation (or other form of entity) to engage in conversations with audiences that are understood as being strategically important to achieving its organisational goals (Nothhaft et al., 2018). Paul (2011, p. 17) offers a slightly different definition as the "coordinated actions, messages, images, and other forms of signalling or engagement intended to inform, influence, or persuade selected audiences in support of national objectives." Furthermore, "strategic communication also includes examining how an organization presents itself in society as a social actor in the creation of public culture and in the discussion of public issues" (Hallahan et al., 2007, p. 27). Strategic communications not only requires definition and planning, but also its execution, which tends to be more of an art than science. "Effective strategic communication requires a grounding in theory, history, and techniques, as well as a specialised knowledge that on the ground practice provides" (Farwell, 2012, p. 227). One of the aims of an actor to communicate is to persuade and influence a selected audience.

At its comprehensive level of definition, persuasion is "a symbolic process in which communicators try to convince other people to change their attitudes or behaviours regarding an issue through the transmission of a message in an atmosphere of free choice" (Perloff, 2010, p. 12). It is a key component of issues management, which intends to create an organised response in identifying emerging trends, concerns and issues that are likely to affect an organisation in order to evolve and adapt to newly emerging environmental conditions (Heath, 1997, pp. 4–9). Information is power through its potential to harness influence through persuasion and is characterised as being the fifth dimension of strategy. The five dimensions of strategy include: (1) land, (2) water, (3) air, (4) space, (5) information and knowledge (Lonsdale, 1999). The fifth dimension is an intangible asset that can affect the functioning of the operational environment in the other four tangible environments. This is a means for an actor to project power.

In the context of this paper, power can be understood as the ability of an actor, through the successful use of influence and persuasion, to dominate the operational environment in terms of achieving their organisational goals and objectives. The context of power is that it is relative and interpersonal where those who possess power are empowered (Lasswell, 2009, p. 10). Accumulating influence and power through the fifth dimension of strategy has been made more problematic owing to the growth of digital communication and especially social media, which together with new communication technologies has the effect of flattening the communication hierarchies and empowering other groups and organisations. Not to mention the added effects of declining trust in mainstream media and politics (Eder, 2011). A more skilful and compelling approach to communication is required.

The construction and communication of one's own identity is a matter of creating a sense of inner group cohesion through creating common senses of belonging purpose and goals. But it is also a symbolic manifestation of intent in terms of relationships and interactions with external groups. As noted by Johnson-Cartee and Copeland (2004, p. 50), "social structures contribute greatly to an individual's behaviour," which plays a significant role in how the communicated message is approached. On the path to creating a compelling and resonating message to the outside world, it is a temptation to use pathos (emotions) to prime and mobilise audiences in the short-term – either the power of attraction (admiration) or repulsion (fear). For example, the construction of a narrative using experiential knowledge on either risks or rewards, something that is 'genuine' or illusionary (Gaffey, 2021) to reach and influence audiences. The result is a form of storytelling that exhibits an imperative for the audience to make a choice within a contextual setting of a conflict crisis or threat in which a subject or an object undergoes a securitisation process as it is both 'sacred' and at risk (Vultee, 2023). This can be seen in the EU's strategic communications in the context of attempting to secure an image of itself on the transforming and turbulent global stage as an important independent actor and force for good in the world.

The Example of the European Union's Communication Problem: Flawed Organised Persuasive Communication Campaign

The European Union seeks to communicate and project itself as an independent force for good in global affairs yet is afflicted by its relative decline and various crises. There is the motivation to try and project a constructed reality that fits with their ambitions, by using information as a tool to prime, mobilise and get selected international audiences to think and behave in a manner that is beneficial to the EU through engineering their perception and consent. In the current stage of international relations, the collective West (the Global North) is in a state of relative decline to several rising powers from the Non-Western world (the Global South) (Cooley & Nexon, 2020). A situation that prompts a context and motivation for powers to seek to minimise their weaknesses and try to project their strengths. Given the relative Western decline, including the European Union (EU) as their means of tangible power and strength (economy, military, industrial capacity, etc.) lack the capability and capacity they once had. This in turn limits the effectiveness of the first four dimensions of strategy but given the developments in technology and delivery of communication, the fifth dimension of strategy is the most viable being the least risky and least costly option for the goal of expanding or at the very least maintaining one's standing and influence in 21st century international relations.

This section seeks to understand and demonstrate how the European Union sees itself and projects this identity and purpose to the outside world through various official documents and through the words of the head of the EU External Action Service (https://www.eeas.europa.eu/_en), Josep Borrell. It is done within a global geopolitical context of Western relative decline. Hence, a story and a narrative are created and communicated through strategic communication to global audiences to influence the cognitive realm of the operational environment of international relations that could benefit the EU, if successful. In its internal documentation, the EU sees itself as an independent force for good in a chaotic system of international relations. This 'good' is derived from the slogans of the EU in terms of its adherence to 'liberal' values – namely democracy, rule of law and respect for human rights (EEAS, 2007). The interactions with 'good intentions' of the EU with other international actors is based upon the notion of conditionality, if the EU provides any form of assistance, then the recipient is obliged to make value and normative changes to the framework of governance. It is based upon the inherent assumption and presumption of the EU's inherent ideological superiority over other political systems.

Various key words as 'partnership' appear often in official documents, however, the underlying assumption is that the EU shall take the lead on defining the agenda, which is caged in terms of priorities such as promoting development and rehabilitation among countries of the Global South (EEAS, 2007, 2009). For example, the Brazil and the European Union comprehensive strategic partnership (as a form of strategic communication) proposed: Promoting peace and comprehensive security through an effective multilateral system; Enhancing the Economic, Social and Environmental Partnership to promote sustainable development; Promoting regional cooperation; Promoting science, technology and innovation; Promoting people-to-people exchanges (EEAS, 2008). Official EEAS documents as the ones mentioned above form the basis of laying out the narrative for the EU's strategic communications with the Global South, based upon EU identity and intent at the institutional level.

When EU communications and messaging comes down to the tactical and operational level, involving individuals rather than the institution, evidence of the use of propaganda and psychological warfare becomes apparent and the strategic messaging fragments. This is especially clear in Borrell's public statements and media interviews. For example, demanding that China take the EU seriously as an 'independent' international actor and not as a vassal of the United States, despite adhering to US trade and diplomatic demands on the EU in their relations with China. Hence, the onus of change is upon China and not the EU (Bermingham, 2023). This is an attempt to change the thinking and behaviour of China (psychological warfare), but in a rather clumsy and defensive manner.

In a speech to Latin American and Caribbean leaders, Borrell spoke of the need to urgently solidify a strategic partnership for the various usual reasons, such as having shared values and partnership, but also because of the geopolitical context (of a declining West) that was defined as a strategic imperative (EEAS, 2023). In a remarkably tone deaf manner that lack any awareness of cultural sensitivities and sociological context, Borrell went on to urge the audience to build a new world order together, "just like the Conquistadors" had in Latin America (decimating the native population) (Hands off Syria, 2022). Although, the intention of these communications is to persuade and influence through employing a blend of propaganda to prime and mobilise the audience and psychological warfare that was intended to persuade the audience to change their attitude and behaviour in a manner that benefits the EU foreign policy agenda, it is executed in a highly unprofessional manner that may well have the audience acting in a manner contra to the intention.

Perhaps the most colourful blunder made by Borrell in his attempts at communication with external audiences, which even dwarfs the above-mentioned blunders, in the sheer scale of insensitivity came in October 2022. The symbolic occasion was the inauguration of a pilot programme that created expression that Europe is a garden and most of the outside world is a jungle that could invade the garden. Borrell ended his address with "keep the garden, be good gardeners. But your duty will not be to take care of the garden itself but [of] the jungle outside" (Borrell, 2022). This implies a system of asymmetric relations between Europe and the Global South, which has echoes of the European colonial past. There is a great deal of attention paid to the quality of the global geopolitical transformation that disadvantages the West. However, it is highly risky for an actor to become an object of international relations rather than a subject of it. The Global South does not want to become an object of events to a declining power, it is not in their security or interests and no amount of strategic communication will change this point.

What Is the Future of the Influence Industry?

With increased and continually increasing competition and conflict in a transforming global order, persuasion has become pervasive in the everyday life of many people, and this is unlikely to change. Information and communication technologies are perceived as being a relatively low risk and low cost means of contesting influence and power, whether this is in the sphere of politics, military, business, foreign policy and so forth. Government communications have been steadily increasing in the number of staff and the amount of communicating (including strategic communications, propaganda and psychological warfare) as a means of influencing and engineering societal conformity on various contentious issues and policies and then asserting that this represents consensus (Urban, 2023). The size of the private and public communications sector that specialises in organised persuasive communication is likely to continue to increase.

There are likely to be other changes in terms of the approach to the communication of content, there are likely to be schisms appearing between the focus on ideological persuasion (subjective values, norms and politics) as opposed to pragmatic (objective interests and aims) persuasion by groups and organisations (Belabas, 2023). This is likely to become more intense with the increasing pressure and crisis of Western liberal politics and US-led geopolitics with the more culturally conservative and pragmatically oriented Non-Western world (the Global South). There is likely to be an increasingly proactive push by the Global South to define and implement strategic communications, propaganda and psychological warfare on their terms, for their interests and goals owing to the power that goes with the actor that is able to convincingly define the physical world around them.

In way of a series of predictions for the future of propaganda and psychological warfare in international politics and international relations, both as a practice and profession, several possibilities in terms of trends and processes emerge. 1) There needs to be a broader and deeper level of knowledge by workers beyond the current Western focus; 2) the development and enhancement of intercultural communication as Western messages to Non-Western audiences are becoming increasingly ineffective in their intended effects; 3) although a lot of focus is presently on operations in the digital environment as the place to complete, the analogue and physical environment should not be neglected or ignored as this will automatically concede a potential influence and persuasion advantage to those that do; 4) quantitatively speaking, in an (geo)politically sensitive global operational environment of international relations that is undergoing increased competition and conflict as actors vie for power and position, there is likely to be much more communication and especially of the manipulative and deceptive varieties; 5) the number of people in this sector of the industry are likely to increase, there is likely to be an increase in the size and number of government departments and more specialised private sector actors; 6) there may be a split in communication approaches to audience relationships with the Global North focused on a form of transactional ideology, while the Global South is more oriented towards a relational pragmatism.

Conclusion

Organised persuasive communications, such as strategic communication, propaganda and psychological warfare requires a clear and concise academic definition (even though they tend to be contested and evolving). The theoretical definition provides the foundational basis for how they are operationalised by practitioners and policymakers. As noted in the text of this chapter, there are numerous approaches to those communications, such as deceptive or non-deceptive, consensual or coercive, monological or dialogical, manipulative or non-manipulative. These forms of persuasive communication can be considered as a form of art, rather than a science. To prompt a communication campaign, which can use a mixture of difference concepts for an added cumulative effect upon an audience there firstly needs to be a source of motivation (competition or conflict for example). This is implemented through the opportunity to communicate and the human and technical means to deliver the message. Strategic communication by its very nature is a communication programme that must support the organisational aims and objectives where it is embedded.

The dos and don'ts of strategic communication, psychological warfare and propaganda are very well illustrated by the example of the EU, and the EEAS, in particular. The EU's abysmal state of strategic communications (and other communications) amply illustrate the need to not only be aware of the basic academic definitions of these components, but also how to effectively plan and implement them. There is a large disconnect between word and practice at one level, but also between the written word at the institutional level and the oral word at the individual level. In terms of the primary documents at the institutional level, there is a good consistency of word in terms of formulating the identity and intention of the EU to the outside world and what they expect from their partner. The documents are rather dry and reach a relatively small global audience. What is heard more and leaves an impression on the reputation and intent of the EU are the words of individuals as Borrell, whose communications violate many of the fundamental principles of organised persuasive communication. Based on the above, the greatest challenges likely to face the industry (academic and practitioner) is the decreasing trust and credibility of OPC and official institutions, combined with the requisite level of knowledge and skill of the professionals that are navigating an increasingly complex and crowded transforming global communication environment. There is, finally, the issue of needing to move increasingly away from a firmly Western-centric disposition and worldview, messengers and messages need to consider other interpretations of the physical world by broadening their exposure and understanding of other sociological, political and historical contexts. Otherwise, even though the theoretical and technical components may be sound, the human (focus on information-cognitive realm) elements will be faulty and render the influence and persuasive value to an ineffective level, perhaps even creating a backlash via audience outrage.

References

Bakir, V., Herring, E., Miller, D., & Robinson, P. (2019). Organized persuasive communication: A new conceptual framework for research on public relations, propaganda and promotional culture. *Critical Sociology*, *45*(3), 311–328. https://doi.org/10.1177/0896920518764586

Belabas, W. (2023). Moving toward more inclusive government communication in an era of superdiversity. *Administration & Society*, *55*(10), 1952–1973. https://doi.org/10.1177/00953997231190570

Bermingham, F. (2023, October 12). It is time China started taking Europe more seriously, says EU foreign policy Chief Josep Borrell. *South China Morning Post*. Retrieved from https://www.scmp.com/news/china/diplomacy/article/3237621/its-time-china-started-taking-europe-more-seriously-says-eu-foreign-policy-chief-josep-borrell

Borrell, J. (2022, October 13). European diplomatic academy: Opening remarks by high representative Josep Borrell at the inauguration of the pilot programme. *EEAS*. Retrieved from https://www.eeas.europa.eu/eeas/european-diplomatic-academy-opening-remarks-high-representative-josep-borrell-inauguration-pilot_en

Cooley, A., & Nexon, D. (2020). *Exit from hegemony: The unravelling of the American global order*. Oxford University Press.

Cornish, P., Lindley-French, J., & Yorke, C. (2011, September). *Strategic communications and national strategy*. A Chatham House Report. Chatham House.

Eder, M. K. (2011). *Leading the narrative: The case for strategic communication*. Naval Institute Press.

European Union External Action Service (EEAS). Appointing a European Union Special Representative to the African Union (2007). Acts adopted under Title V of the EU treaty council (Joint Action 2007/805/CFSP). Retrieved from https://www.eeas.europa.eu/sites/default/files/council_joint_action_2007-805-cfsp_en.pdf

European Union External Action Service (EEAS). Brazil-European Union Strategic Partnership Joint Action Plan. (2008). 2nd Brazil – European Union Summit. Retrieved from https://www.eeas.europa.eu/sites/default/files/2008_joint_action_plan_en.pdf

European Union External Action Service (EEAS). Strategic Partnership Between the Commission of the European Communities and the Food and Agriculture Organisation In the Field of Development and Humanitarian Affairs. (2009). Working document. Retrieved from https://www.eeas.europa.eu/sites/default/files/fao_ec_working_doc_final_en_0.pdf

EEAS. (2023, June 7). Latin America and the Caribbean: College read-out by high representative/vice-president Josep Borrell on a new agenda for relations between the EU and Latin America and the Caribbean. *EEAS*. Retrieved from https://www.eeas.europa.eu/eeas/latin-america-and-caribbean-college-read-out-high-representativevice-president-josep-borrell-new_en

Farwell, J. P. (2012). *Persuasion and power: The art of strategic communication*. Georgetown University Press.

Gaffey, J. (2021). *The construction of truth in contemporary media narratives about risk*. Routledge.

Hallahan, K., Holtzhausen, D., van Ruler, B., Verčič, D., & Sriramesh, K. (2007). Defining strategic communication. *International Journal of Strategic Communication*, *1*(1), 3–35. https://doi.org/10.1080/15531180701285244

Hands off Syria. (2022, December 2). E.U. official Josep Borrell to Latin America: "Like the conquistadors we must invent a new world." *Hands Off Syria*. Retrieved from https://www.youtube.com/watch?v=eSfTuedXusE

Heath, R. L. (1997). *Strategic issues management: Organizations and public policy challenges*. Sage.

Johnson-Cartee, K. S., & Copeland, G. A. (2004). *Strategic political communication: Rethinking social influence, persuasion, and propaganda*. Rowman & Littlefield.

Jowett, G. S., & O'Donnell, V. (2012). *Propaganda & persuasion* (5th ed.). Sage.

Kamalipour, Y. R., & Snow, N. (Eds.) (2004). *War, media, and propaganda: A global perspective*. Rowman & Littlefield.

Lasswell, H. D. (2009). *Power and personality*. Transaction Publishers.

Linebarger, P. M. A. (2009). *Psychological warfare*. Gateway Books and Tapes.

Lonsdale, D. J. (1999). Information power: Strategy, geopolitics, and the fifth dimension. *The Journal of Strategic Studies, 22*(2–3), 137–157.

Macdonald, S. (2009). *Propaganda and information warfare in the twenty-first century: Altered images and deception operations*. Routledge.

Macleod, A. (Ed.) (2019). *Propaganda in the information age: Still manufacturing consent*. Routledge.

Nothhaft, H., Werder, K. P., Verčič, D., & Zerfass, A. (2018). Strategic communication: Reflections on an elusive concept. *International Journal of Strategic Communication, 12*(4), 352–366. https://doi.org/10.1080/1553118X.2018.1492412

Patrick, B. A. (2012). *The ten commandments of propaganda*. Arktos.

Paul, C. (2008). *Information operations doctrine and practice: A reference handbook*. Praeger Security International.

Paul, C. (2011). *Strategic communication: Origins, concepts and current debates*. Praeger.

Perloff, R. M. (2010). *The dynamics of persuasion: Communication and attitudes in the 21st century* (4th ed.). Routledge.

Simons, G. (2022). The dark arts of political marketing: Use of propaganda in political campaigns. In B. I. Newman & T. P Newman (Eds.), *A research agenda for political marketing* (pp. 173–189). Edward Elgar Publishing.

Sproule, J. M. (2005). *Propaganda and democracy: The American experience of media and mass persuasion*. Cambridge University Press.

Taylor, P. M. (2003). *Munitions of the mind: A history of propaganda from the ancient world to the present day* (3rd ed.). Manchester University Press.

Urban, J. (2023, February). *Government communications in 2023 and beyond*. The Institute for Government.

Vultee, F. (2023). *A media framing approach to securitization: Storytelling in conflict, crisis and threat*. Routledge.

20

THE FUTURE OF MEDIA RELATIONS AND JOURNALISM

Exploring Law and Ethics

Jeremy Harris Lipschultz

Introduction

We may only imagine changes coming to media relations, law and ethics in the next quarter-century. A shift toward non-profit journalism models, social media relations and re-examination of US First Amendment law all suggest a rocky road ahead that continues to be fueled by personal branding and social influence.

About seven decades ago, Katz and Lazarsfeld (1955, 1964) explored *Personal Influence* and the connection between face-to-face and media communication. This groundbreaking research merged an interest in "the relative position of different community members" and "persons who were influential" (pp. 2–3). The "small intimate groups of family, friends, (and) co-workers" reinforced opinion stability, and functioned as "interpersonal communications networks" (p. 8). Mass media were studied as key "influences stemming from the outside" (p. 9). In response to campaign effects research that included advertising and political propaganda, Katz and Lazarsfeld (1955, 1964) identified four fundamental intervening variables:

1. Exposure, access or attention;
2. Medium type and character;
3. Content form, presentation and language; and
4. Psychological predisposition. (pp. 21–23)

While these researchers could not have predicted the characteristics of X/Twitter in 2024, they would have applied interpersonal and media communication theories to questions of exposure, content and predisposition. Katz and Lazarsfeld

DOI: 10.4324/9781003426653-23

(1955, 1964) understood the rise of political leaders within social network campaigns, but the context of US mid-20th-century social influence is challenging to apply now. Online impression management is one conceptual bridge that helps us understand social media self-presentation (Rosenberg & Egbert, 2011). Constantly connected individuals may use "wow" (emoji) content whether it portrays truth (Singer, 2023; Turkle, 1995). Individuals may use tactics that bring status within a social network. The larger social media become, the more likely it is that users will retreat to groups, including support group structures, that offer social value through meaningful engagement (Smith et al., 2014).

The Future of Media Relations and Journalism

More than eight billion people use an estimated 7.3 billion mobile devices, and *We Are Social* estimated that about 5.4 billion smartphones help explain 4.8 billion active social media users. Social media brand managers may share, optimize, manage and engage (SoMe) and use real-time listening and engagement in response to a crisis (Luttrell & Wallace, 2021). Weakened social and cultural fabric results in fertile ground for cynicism to grow. "A lack of faith in societal institutions triggered by economic anxiety, disinformation, mass-class divide and a failure of leadership has brought us to where we are today – deeply and dangerously polarized" (Edelman, 2023, para. 1). Effective social media storytelling by good and bad actors is relatively unfiltered compared to traditional news gatekeeping processes, and social influence power can motivate use (Smith & Place, 2013). It is fair to say that declines in original local newspaper reporting coupled with an interest in social media users exercising their voices has driven a sea of social noises – including misinformation and deliberate disinformation or we historically called propaganda. The lack of traditional news gatekeeping also de-values media relations because a wider swath of information may be shared to global audiences (Craig & Yetter, 2023).

The use of LinkedIn and other personal branding social media communication sites continue to be important seeds for spreading social influence within an integrated public relations campaign, but creativity is key to rising above the noise. It remains foundational to place a human face on organizational brands by leveraging media storytelling techniques. Beyond brand leaders, "social employees" and their online networks may continue to help market by spreading the word about new ideas, products and services (Brito, 2018, p. 46). Loyal fans and customers also may engage with a brand to raise awareness, discuss attributes, or review products, events and experiences. The more unique, the more likely it is that a branded campaign can temporarily raise awareness. While thought leadership may help shape a narrative, social crowds reflect sentiment. For example, user-generated content may respond to the tone of a post headline. Social media marketers measure metrics as key performance indicators

(KPIs) in strategic ways (Sterne, 2010; Vaynerchuk, 2013), and disruptive content can be used for good or bad. Social media accounts seek attention within noisy marketplaces (Webster, 2014), yet individuals have reasons to lurk without posting – especially when it comes to sharing news content about political controversies (Weeks & Holbert, 2013; Yun & Park, 2011).

PR and social media managers will continue to have opportunities to leverage their owned and shared social media crowds, even as they produce direct news releases, media kits and availabilities for working journalists. In practice, journalists of the future will be drawn to snackable news items that resonate with the TikTok (or whatever app comes next) generation. PR users already have been drawn to AI assistants that suggest content headlines and themes. Data that offer a summary of existing narratives will be valuable. Humans make judgments sometimes informed by personal interests, but the newest generative technologies appear to be learning from previously posted information and social media communication.

Hootsuite (2023) tested artificial intelligence (AI) that draft captions with a tone that is professional or friendly. Machine learning (ML) and natural language processing (NLP) and generation (NLG) emerged as virtual assistants that conversationally engage at all levels of the social marketing process (Quesenberry, 2025, pp. 308–309). "Marcom professionals should ensure AI is used responsibly and transparently as representatives of brands" (p. 311). Every popular tool has begun to integrate AI into user platform processes. While AI adoption speeds forward, European Union (EU) and US regulators trail in protection of user data privacy and effective legal guardrails (Satariano, 2023; Simonson, 2023).

Social Media Guardrails of Law and Ethics

US Federal Trade Commission (FTC) regulation emphasized social media commercial content transparency for products and services. Beyond law, the AMEC (2024) industry measurement association repeatedly has urged ethical use of data in its revised principles. There are no guarantees that platforms and practitioners will place users ahead of their own interests. In fact, most critical scholars conclude that "surveillance capitalism" is defined by a fight over power and money (Zuboff, 2019, p. 30). Neoliberal political economics is said to, "… reverse, subdue, impede, and even destroy the individual urge toward psychological self-determination and moral agency" (p. 31). There is a need to respond (Jones, 2023). AI assistants can be seen as cogs that work to diminish humanity of work and importance of ethical decision-making. The introduction of AI into integrated social PR marketing campaigns heightens a need for brands to exert content authority through trust and expert knowledge (Dietrich, 2023). Social media content frequently raise awareness through diffusion of new information, spark consideration of behavioral change, create fertile ground for advocacy and adoption, and leave a trail of tracking data (Hitz, 2018; Rogers, 2003). While data quality may be an issue, it has become apparent that regulation of personal data transfer and sale is needed.

The US First Amendment limits government regulation of political speech, but concerns have been raised about online content that is hateful, bullying or antisemitic (Conger & Hsu, 2023). Commercial advertising boycotts have shown to influence changes in platform terms of service (ToS) user agreements, but corporations are reluctant to limit free expression. Business practices tend to override long-term concerns about harmful speech (Freberg, 2019). Protection of "reputation and community for a brand on social media" may impact the bottom line (p. 277). A consistent brand voice is a component of reputation management (Luttrell & Capizzo, 2019). Companies tend to manage communication – especially during a crisis (O'Brien, 2023). A global pandemic, the rise of China-based TikTok, and proliferation of misinformation and disinformation have combined with AI adoption to disrupt social media communication (Matsa, 2023). EU regulators passed new laws, including the Digital Marketing Act, aimed at placing controls on unruly social media content (Mac, 2023). The 27 member nations sought to regulate large platforms. The EU "Right to Be Forgotten" was one earlier example of how human rights-based law diverges from US First Amendment precedent (Youm & Park, 20160, but federal law has gaps when it comes to data privacy.

In the US, the California Consumer Privacy Act of 2018 followed early EU regulation models. While federal privacy statutes have protected health and education data, state constitutions are broader in terms of fundamental privacy rights. California consumers may request disclosure of data collected and stored, but it remains difficult to stop the largest corporations from monetizing our private data for advertising purposes. For example, The Weather Channel was sued over lack of transparency in its sale of user location data to third parties. ToS user agreements tend to be written in legal jargon that few users read and understand. In general, these contracts fail to respect privacy and dignity as a human right (Mills, 2015). Protection of location history sometimes has devolved into a game between platforms, such as Google, and users (Nakashima, 2018). A user may click settings to protect data privacy, and then a software update erases the decision. Monitoring and vigilance are required to limit data collection, storage and sale in states without privacy laws.

The US Supreme Court in 2023 reviewed state laws in Florida and Texas that sought to regulate large social media sites. Republican (GOP) lawmakers had responded to the de-platforming of President Donald Trump during the January 6, 2021 election certification and US Capitol violence. The Court is faced with a broad re-examination of Internet law that protects sites as publishers (*Reno v. ACLU*, 1997). Lawmakers also have struggled to protect children from online obscenity and virtual pornography (*Ashcroft v. ACLU*, 2002; *Ashcroft v. Free Speech Coalition*, 2002).

In *Elonis v. United States* (2015) criminal true threats law was applied to a case that intersected with the First Amendment. The Court revisited the issues in a stalking case involving repeated use of Facebook Messenger (*Counterman v. Colorado*, 2023). A new mental state of recklessness was developed, but the Court split on whether objective or subjective understanding is required to prove the threatening nature of communication. The US Supreme Court justices balance First Amendment breathing space against the need to limit criminal threats. Location data may provide evidence of intent. Mobile phone data are particularly problematic in criminal cases that place a suspect at the scene of a crime. The Supreme Court voted 5 to 4 that cell site location information (CSLI) historical data may not be searched by police without a proper Fourth Amendment search warrant (*Carpenter v. United States*, 2018).

The EU General Data Protection Regulation (GDPR) appears to be a global standard for holding Meta Facebook and the other largest social media companies to be accountable for their actions. Still, the massive data that flow through popular sites gives power over people (Lerbinger, 2019). Given the struggle to find a workable legal solution to social media communication regulation, we need to explore how ethics may help modulate potentially dangerous online communication.

The US Supreme Court recent began a variety of inquiries about how defamation, copyright, student expression, data privacy, stalking and threats are impacted by social media communication. It is likely that by 2050 there will be a re-categorization of private figures, public figures and public officials that may, for example, retreat from the *New York Times v. Sullivan* model that has broadly protected free expression in the age of the Internet and social media communication (Barbas, 2023). History teaches us that press freedom protected progressive political movements that strengthened racial equality and civil rights in the 1960s.

If present and future laws fail to save us from reputational and other atrocious harms then individual and organizational policies and ethics will need to be strengthened.

A Need to Revisit Ethics

Individual beliefs and values are important when it comes to limits on human behavior that may be difficult to monitor and regulate (Ward, 2019). AI may be similar to previous waves of technology adoption in that it has the potential to either make matters better or worse. Core values, such as personal integrity, are the best hope for creating a more honest and authentic social media. Truth, accuracy and disclosure are found within codes of ethics (PRSA, 2023), but it is up to people and their virtual assistants to practice the best behaviors. People, though, often act in self-interests over the greater public good. At the corporate level, we need continued critical thinking about corporate social responsibility (CSR) practices (Pompper, 2018, 2015).

We may consider electronic word-of-mouth (eWOM) as a useful framework for understanding social media communication ethics (Bi & Zhang, 2022). The historic definition of social network sites is a commonly used foundation for exploring online behavior (boyd & Ellison, 2008). Social media communication are a form of virtual competition because algorithms tap individual psychological motivation to return and remain at a site (EZrachi & Stucke, 2016). Network analyses suggest that, at least on X/Twitter, users cluster around like-minded others (Himelboim, McCreery & Smith, 2013). Leaders emerge at the center of online communities of influence, and these groups may amplify misinformation and disinformation (Huffaker, 2010; Johnson et al., 2022). Social media ethics may be seen as a response to the negative effects from surveillance capitalism that can destroy media and democracy (Jones, 2023). Individual care-based ethics and corporate social responsibility (CSR) could be social mechanisms that contribute to inoculation from propaganda and vaccination against viral content (McWilliams & Siegel, 2001). A polarized political example, such as about the function of diversity and inclusion programs within higher education and corporate life, could involve a PR campaign to raise the inclusive climate by promoting cultural intelligence (Men et al., 2023). Group support for progressive ideas should weaken social fear to remain silent in the face of a vocal minority pushing regressive ideas (Noelle-Neumann, 1984).

A broader freedom to express popular and unpopular ideas since Twitter became X, though, opened users to manipulation by suspicious content. Bad state actors, such as Russia, used US social media platforms to spread propaganda that potentially weakens democracy. The use of political disinformation is clearly not ethical, but user ignorance of truths spreads falsehoods across social networks (Myers et al., 2023). It is simple for propagandists to utilize social marketing brand storytelling principles in the interest of creating political division (Quesenberry & Coolsen, 2023).

Productive media relations and journalism must happen within a transparent and trusting relationship that is driven by personal and professional ethics. In fact, the work of journalism, media and communication higher education is to produce graduates that distinguish themselves from the din of unfiltered social media communication. These industries and our free society depend upon verified and trusted news and information sharing.

Freedom and Guardrails

Communication freedom is a treasured value, and it should be protected, as online interaction blurs human and rapidly spreading AI technologies. Individuals must use new tools with care. The rights of free expression have never insulated people from the civil harms of defamation and invasion of privacy. In these cases, the legal remedies for reputation damage or intrusion on private spaces are lawsuits that seek large monetary damages. Entrepreneurial technology development demands scrutiny by the public and our public officials. The US Supreme Court's precedent of First Amendment protection tips the scales against EU-style privacy protection guardrails. Authentic and mature public debate is needed about the direction of policies designed to balance free expression and privacy. Individuals, employees, students and communication practitioners need clear social media policies within organizations and external laws that find a balance between freedom and protection.

The future of social media communication returns us to fundamental interpersonal and mediated communication. Psychological motivation, sociological realities, political constraints, and economics inform us that change will continue. PR and journalism practitioners will need stronger media literacy skills to navigate an AI landscape. The blending of human cognition and emotion with human-like technologies is likely to point us toward new waves of chaotic change. In real-time, we must learn to deconstruct social media content to identify sources and motivation for advocacy. Source and message credibility is not always easy to determine within memes, short video and other online content that is freely shared across platforms by somewhat anonymous accounts Shifman, 2013). Our desire to be entertained, too often, is more important than consuming truthful and authentic content. AI content mimics reality, and it now may be used to convert text to video and audio (Robledo, 2023).

Conclusions

Katz and Lazarsfeld's (1955, 1964) prediction about interpersonal and media communication may be appropriately extended in the current milieu of social media communication:

> Primary groups… may serve as channels for mass media transmission; this might be called the *relay function* for interpersonal relations … person-to-person influences may coincide with mass media messages and thus either counteract or reinforce the message.
>
> *(p. 43)*

Opinion sharing within communication networks may be visualized on X/ Twiiter, and political polarization helps explain the virality of misinformation, mal-information and disinformation within the modern context. Network users respond to psychological and social expectations that drive them to return to connect with friends and others (Raacke & Bonds-Raacke, 2008). This suggests that decades from now group norms about social reality, shared values within political or other contexts, and influence transmission will continue to function as both change agents and structural support for the status quo. These can be seen as drivers of political and social conflict, as society seeks to reorient around real economic and environmental changes brought by growing population and scarce resources. From these conditions, we may continue to find emergence of communication leaders leveraging a position of "*strategic social location*" (Katz & Lazarsfeld, 1955, 1964, p. 113). "Within these networks, key communications roles – initiators, transmitters and influentials – can be identified and these, in turn, can be related to *nomination*, social *location* and cultural *certification*" (p. 115). Katz and Lazarsfeld (1955, 1964) understood, for example, that a news an information "gatekeeper" offers content "in the sense that he introduces an idea to a group, but he may or may not serve as a transmitter within the group and may or may not be influential at all" (p. 119). In the current era of social network analysis, we may confuse network centrality with influence through X retweets, Reddit upvotes, and other empirical measures. A decline in traditional group membership, though, may signal the relative importance of online temporary groups that rise within a particular moment. While the #BlackLivesMatter and #NotOkay social movements, for example, leveraged social and media communication attention and activated some to respond, we know that most social media communication lacks significant engagement.

It is likely, then, that PR and journalism practitioners will share value in the need for their businesses and organization to rise above a cacophony of opinions, real-time viral memes and other content that debases humanity. Symbiotic relationships between journalists and their reliable sources will continue to be cultivated only when shared values and mutual understanding of needs realigns within a social media communication context (Lipschultz, 1991, 2024). In other words, media relations will continue to add value for the smaller numbers of traditional working journalists when they trust the source, content and interest for audiences.

References

AMEC. (2024). https://amecorg.com

Ashcroft v. ACLU, 535 U.S. 564 (2002).

Ashcroft v. Free Speech Coalition, 535 U.S. 234 (2002).

Barbas, S. (2023). *Actual Malice: Civil rights and freedom of the press in New York Times v. Sullivan*. University of California Press.

Bi, N. C., & Zhang, R. (2022). Electronic word-of-mouth and social media. In J. H. Lipschultz, K. Freberg, & R. Luttrell (Eds.), *The Emerald handbook of computer-mediated communication and social media* (pp. 37–50). Emerald.

boyd, d. m., & Ellison, N. B. (2008). Social network sites: Definition, history and scholarship. *Journal of Computer-Mediated Communication, 13*(*1*), 210–230. https://doi.org/10.1111/j.1083-6101.2007.00393.x

Brito, M. (2018). *Participation marketing*. Kogan Page.
California Consumer Privacy Act of 2018, AB-375. https://leginfo.legislature.ca.gov/faces/billTextClient.xhtml?bill_id=201720180AB375
Carpenter v. United States, 585 U.S. 296, 138 S Ct 2206 (2018).
Conger, K., & Hsu, T. (2023, November 30). Advertisers say they do not plan to return to X after Musk's comments. *The New York Times*. https://www.nytimes.com/2023/11/30/technology/elon-musk-dealbook-advertisers.html
Counterman v. Colorado, 600 U.S. 66, 143 S.Ct. 2106 (2023).
Craig, D. A., & Yetter, C. (2023). Virtual virtue? Opportunities and challenges explicating intellectual virtues through journalistic exemplars in the digital network. *Journal of Media Ethics*, *38*(4), 224–240. https://doi.org/10.1080/23736992.2023.2265337
Dietrich, G. (2023, November 30). What's next? What you need to know for marketing success in 2024. *BuzzSumo Webinars*. https://youtu.be/KJH4yqSN4Bk?si=yBYlWMW-zBy0bst4
Edelman. (2023, January). 2023 Edelman Trust Barometer. https://www.edelman.com/trust/2023/trust-barometer
Elonis v. United States, 575 U.S. 723 (2015).
Ezrachi, A., & Stucke, M. E. (2016). *Virtual competition: The promise and perils of the algorithm driven economy*. Harvard University Press.
Freberg, K. (2019). *Social media for strategic communication: Creative strategies and research-based applications*. Sage.
Himelboim, I., McCreery, S., & Smith, M. (2013). Birds of a feather tweet together: Integrating network and content analyses to examine cross-ideology exposure on twitter. *Journal of Computer-Mediated Communication, 18*, 154–174. http://dx.doi.org/10.1111/jcc4.12001
Hitz, L. (2018, July 26). *How to build an audience-aligned social marketing strategy*. Sprout Social. https://sproutsocial.com/insights/build-audience-aligned-strategy/
Hootsuite Education. (2023). Hootsuite social trends 2023 in higher education. *Hootsuite*. https://www.hootsuite.com/research/social-trends
Huffaker, D. (2010, October). Dimensions of leadership and social influence in online communities. Human Communication Research, 36(4), 593–617. http://dx.doi.org/10.1111/j.1468-2958.2010.01390.x
Johnson, T. J., Wallace, R., & Lee, T. (2022). How social media serves as a super-spreader of misinformation, disinformation, and conspiracy theories regarding crises. In J. H. Lipschultz, K. Freberg, & R. Luttrell (Eds.), *The Emerald handbook of computer-mediated communication and social media* (pp. 67–84). Emerald.
Jones, J. (2023). Reclaiming media: Answering surveillance capitalists with care-based democracy. *Journal of Media Ethics, 38*(4), 241–254. https://doi.org/10.1080/23736992.2023.2265343
Katz, E., & Lazarsfeld, P. F. (1955, 1964). *Personal influence, The part played by people in the flow of mass communications*. The Free Press.
Lerbinger, O. (2019). *Corporate communication: An international and management perspective*. Wiley Blackwell.
Lipschultz, J. H. (1991). A comparison of trial lawyer and news reporter attitudes about courthouse communication. *Journalism & Mass Communication Quarterly, 64*(4), 750–763. https://doi.org/10.1177/107769909106800416
Lipschultz, J. H. (2024). *Social media communication: Concepts, practices, data, law and ethics* (4th ed.). Routledge.

Luttrell, R., & Wallace, A. (2021). *Social media and society: An introduction to the mass media landscape*. Rowman & Littlefield.

Luttrell, R. M., & Capizzo, L. W. (2019). Public relations campaigns: An integrated approach. Sage.

Mac, R. (2023, November 16). X races to contain damage after Elon Musk endorses antisemitic post. *The New York Times*. https://www.nytimes.com/2023/11/16/technology/elon-musk-endorses-antisemitic-post-ibm.html

Matsa, K. E. (2023, November 15). More Americans are getting news on TikTok, bucking the trend seen on most other social media sites. *Pew Research Center*. https://www.pewresearch.org/short-reads/2023/11/15/more-americans-are-getting-news-on-tiktok-bucking-the-trend-seen-on-most-other-social-media-sites/

McWilliams, A., & Siegel, D. (2001). Corporate social responsibility: A theory of the firm perspective. *Academy of Management Review, 26*, 117–127. https://doi.org/10.2307/259398

Men, L. R., Qin, Y. S., Mitson, R., & Thelen, P. (2023). Engaging employees via an inclusive climate: The role of organizational diversity communication and cultural intelligence. *Journal of Public Relations Research, 35*(5–6), 450–471. https://doi.org/10.1080/1062726X.2023.2222859

Mills, J. L. (2015). *Privacy in the new media age*. University Press of Florida.

Myers, S. L., Thompson, S. A., & Hsu, T. (2023, October 26). The consequences of Elon Musk's ownership of X. *The New York Times*. https://www.nytimes.com/interactive/2023/10/27/technology/twitter-x-elon-musk-anniversary.html

Nakashima, R. (2018, August 13). AP exclusive: Google tracks your movements like it or not. *Associated Press*. https://www.apnews.com/828aefab64d4411bac257a07c1af0ecb/AP-Exclusive:-Google-tracks-your-movements-like-it-or-not

Noelle-Neumann, E. (1984). *The spiral of silence: Public opinion—Our social skin*. University of Chicago Press.

O'Brien, M. (2023, November 22). OpenAI brings back Sam Altman as CEO just days after his firing unleashed chaos. *Associated Press*. https://apnews.com/article/altman-openai-chatgpt-31187f7f6eca8ff9d0eef7585aac6ace

Pompper, D. (2015). *Corporate social responsibility, Sustainability and public relations negotiating multiple complex challenges*. Routledge.

Pompper, D. (Ed.). (2018). *Corporate social responsibility, sustainability, and ethical public relations: Strengthening synergies with human resources*. Emerald Publishing.

PRSA. (2023). The ethical use of AI: For public relations practitioners, guidance from the PRSA board of ethics and professional standards. *Public Relations Society of America*. https://www.prsa.org/professional-development/ai-insights

Quesenberry, K. A. (2025). *Social media strategy: Marketing, advertising and public relations in the consumer revolution* (4th ed.). Rowman & Littlefield.

Quesenberry, K. A., & Coolsen, M. K. (2023). *Brand storytelling: Integrated marketing communications for the digital media landscape*. Rowman & Littlefield.

Raacke, J., & Bonds-Raacke, J. (2008). Myspace and Facebook: Applying the uses and gratifications theory to exploring friend-networking sites. *CyberPsychology & Behavior, 11*(2), 169–174. http://dx.doi.org/10.1089/cpb.2007.0056

Reno v. ACLU, 521 U.S. 844 (1997).

Robledo, A. (2023, December 14). None of these anchors are real: Channel 1 plans for AI to generate news, broadcasters. *USA Today*. https://www.usatoday.com/story/tech/news/2023/12/14/channel-1-ai-news/71925360007/

Rogers, E. M. (2003). *Diffusion of Innovations* (5th ed.). Free Press.
Rosenberg, J., & Egbert, N. (2011). Online impression management: Personality traits and concerns for secondary goals as predictors of self-presentation tactics on facebook. *Journal of Computer-Mediated Communication 17*(1), 1–18. https://doi.org/10.1111/j.1083-6101.2011.01560.x
Satariano, A. (2023, December 8). E. U. agrees on landmark artificial intelligence rules. *The New York Times*. https://www.nytimes.com/2023/12/08/technology/eu-ai-act-regulation.html
Shifman, L. (2013). Memes in a digital world: Reconciling with a conceptual trouble-maker. *Journal of Computer-Mediated Communication, 18*(3), 362–377. http://dx.doi.org/10.1111/jcc4.12013
Simonson, J. (2023, October 6). 5 best social media management tools. *Forbes*. https://www.forbes.com/advisor/business/best-social-media-management-software/
Singer, J. B. (2023, Summer). Closing the Barn door? Fact-checkers as retroactive gate-keepers of the Covid-19 "Infodemic." *Journalism & Mass Communication Quarterly, 100*(2), 332–353. https://doi.org/10.1177/10776990231168599
Smith, B. G., & Place, K. R. (2013). Integrating power? Evaluating public relations influence in an integrated communication structure. *Public Relations Research, 25*(2), 168–187. http://dx.doi.org/10.1080/1062726X.2013.758585
Smith, M. A., Ranie, L., Sneiderman, B., & Himelboim, I. (2014). Mapping Twitter topic networks: From polarized crowds to community clusters. *Pew Research Center*. http://www.pewinternet.org/2014/02/20/mapping-twitter-topic-networks-from-polarized-crowds-to-community-clusters/
Sterne, J. (2010). *Social media metrics*. Wiley.
Turkle, S. (1995). *Life on the screen: Identity in the age of the internet*. Simon & Schuster.
Vaynerchuk, G. (2013). *Jab, Jab, Jab, Right Hook: How to tell your story in a noisy social world*. HarperCollins.
Ward, S. J. A. (2019). *Disrupting journalism ethics: Radical change on the frontier of digital media*. Routledge.
Webster, J. G. (2014). *The marketplace of attention: How audiences take shape in a digital age*. The MIT Press.
Weeks, B. E., & Holbert, R. L. (2013, Summer). Predicting dissemination of news content in social media: A focus on reception, Friending, and partisanship. *Journalism & Mass Communication Quarterly, 90*(2), 212–232. https://doi.org/10.1177/1077699013482906
Youm, K. H., & Park, A. (2016, Summer). The "Right to Be Forgotten" in European Union Law: Data protection balanced with free speech? *Journalism & Mass Communication Quarterly, 93*(2), 273–295. https://doi.org/10.1177/1077699016628824
Yun, G. W., & Park, S.-Y. (2011). Selective posting: Willingness to post a message online. *Journal of Computer-Mediated Communication, 16*(2), 201–227. https://doi.org/10.1111/j.1083-6101.2010.01533.x
Zuboff, S. (2019). *The age of surveillance capitalism: The fight for a human future at the new frontier of power*. PublicAffairs.

21

MEASUREMENT AND ANALYTICS IN 2050

Quantifying Digital and Analog Behaviors

Nathan J. Carpenter

Introduction and Definitions

As described by the international Association for Measurement and Evaluation of Communication (AMEC), *measurement* is fundamentally concerned with "ascertaining the size, amount, or degree of something by using an instrument or device; assessing the importance, effect, or value of something" (AMEC, 2023a). For public relations, this has historically involved using surveys, interviews, and focus groups to measure public opinion, and quantifying the volume and tone of discussions in print, radio, television, and digital networks. Measurement typically relies on the use of frameworks and benchmarks as standards by which assessments can be made. Related to measurement is *analytics*, which Macnamara (2018) describes as "the process of discovery and interpretation of meaningful patterns in data. It involves the application of statistics and computer programming to process large volumes of data to identify means (averages), significant trends, clusters, and relationships" (p. 144). Analytics provide the information that make measurement and assessment possible by describing what happened, prescribing a course of action, or predicting future activity (Sponder and Khan, 2018, p. 175).

For public relations, measurement and analytics are essential for developing strategy and crafting tactical responses in a variety of situations. As explained by Freberg (2019), they are "the key to determining whether or not we were successful in our efforts to engage our audiences, accomplish our set objectives for the short and long term, and provide value for the intended parties" (p. 208). At issue for measurement and analytics are a series of interconnected questions: what exactly can be measured, by which analytical methods, and to what ends?

DOI: 10.4324/9781003426653-24

Hollifield and Coffey (2023) describe our present moment as one in which analytics have been "mainstreamed" into many sectors of society. Social media platforms, for example, provide users access to built-in analytics dashboards that summarize basic information about the reach and number of engagements of each of their posts, and web hosting services and indexing companies provide performance metrics and rankings for individual websites. If measurement and analytics are mainstream now, what will they look like in 2050? This chapter examines the potential future of measurement and analytics by examining patterns from the not-too-distant past and calling to attention contemporary factors that seem to be driving change. What follows is an educated guess about what we might expect to see in the not-too-distant future.

A Brief History

Scholarship of the history of public relations suggests that measurement practices have gone through several transformations, typically in response to changes in social practices or the emergence of new communication technologies. Watson (2012), traces timeline that begins with rudimentary practices of newspaper monitoring in the 18th and 19th centuries, followed by the development of publicity agencies in the early 20th century that created systematic processes for clipping, quantifying, and categorizing newspaper coverage about their clients. These typically measured the volume of columns published and the number of inches of text that expressed favorable or unfavorable opinions about clients, and eventually developed into larger-scale media monitoring services to also cover radio and television (p. 391).

Agencies during the mid-20th century also created novel measures such as *advertising value equivalency* (AVE) to estimate the monetary value of publicity by comparing media coverage to the cost of similar advertising space. Running parallel to media monitoring and measurement of the 20th century were social scientific methods such as opinion surveys, interviews, and focus groups that were deployed with varying degrees of rigor and validity (pp. 391–393). Watson (2012) also suggests that professional standards and guidelines for measurement did not fully emerge until 1960s, and academic attention to measurement in the 1970s and 1980s promoted the emergence of organizations and campaigns that promoted best practices for measurement and evaluation in the 1990s (pp. 394–395). Today, organizations such as the international Association for Measurement and Evaluation of Communication (AMEC), "the world's largest media intelligence and insights professional body" (AMEC, 2023b) influence the trajectory of media measurement and evaluation in public relations and other professional organizations by setting standards and offering evaluation frameworks. For example, beginning in 2010, AMEC has used the "Barcelona Declaration of Research Principles" to establish an industry-wide consensus about the importance of setting goals, using measurement and evaluation to clearly identify outcomes and impact for stakeholders, the necessity of using both qualitative and quantitative methods of analysis, measurement both online and offline communication, and fostering transparency in the research process (AMEC, 2023c).

Our present moment is differentiated from the previous ones by the "digital turn" of the late 20th and early 21st centuries, which have seen an explosion in the amount of data available for measurement and analysis. Web traffic and social media provide seemingly non-stop sources of user-generated data that present major opportunities for understanding changing consumer interests, public opinion, unfolding crisis situations, and campaign effectiveness (Fan & Gordon, 2014). In response to the continuous flow of information produced by digital and social media, organizations and agencies have essentially become their own publishing houses and media intelligence firms (Rees, 2020). In a nod to the news clippings agencies of the 20th century, the 21st century has seen the rise of an entire industry devoted to collecting and analyzing social media data. Despite the influence of AMEC and other professional organizations dedicated to improving measurement and evaluation, these analytics industries face several challenges. As Lipschultz (2022) explains, many metrics such as "engagement" and "influence" are not governed by standards, many social media accounts may artificially inflate their follower counts and may not reflect accurate audience sizes, engagement metrics may have different meanings across different platforms, comments and replies are not always understood within the full context of a conversation, and the data may not always fully explain users' motivations to post (p. 366)

Main Influences on Measurement and Analytics Between Now and 2050

The last 25 years have witnessed widespread technological and social changes, perhaps most noticeably experienced in the widespread adoption of mobile communications, ubiquitous internet connectivity, exponential growth of computing power, and the dominance of user-generated and on-demand media. Social media platforms have been particularly transformative and disruptive, growing from simple text-based forums and networking sites to billion-user juggernauts that capture attention with continuous streams of multimedia content curated by algorithms and spawning an entire industry devoted to processing, analyzing, and analyzing the data produced by their users. Over the next 25 years, growth and disruption in digital media will likely continue to be primary drivers of change. As we head toward the year 2050, the primary influences on the development of measurement and analytics will be likely related to the availability of data, the technologies used to analyze data, consumers' and audiences' responses to being measured and analyzed, and new standards and frameworks that will be introduced by professional organizations.

First, consider the major influences on the availability of data, particularly the influences on the digital media that are most frequently used to measure audience engagement and public opinion. At present, organizations expend significant resources on social media monitoring and listening, practices that require complex and often unseen economic and political relationships between organizations, analytics providers, social media platforms, and regulatory agencies. Social media platforms are increasingly restricting access to data or charging more for it. Twitter (now X) infamously its free public API and replaced it with professional and enterprise accounts that cost hundreds, if not thousands of dollars per month (Porter, 2023). Apart from its advertising platforms, Meta has restricted commercial researchers from directly studying audiences through its API, and academic researchers must now undergo a lengthy application process to examine datasets related to specific, predetermined projects. Governing bodies are also likely to continue to influence the availability of consumer data. The European Union's General Data Protection Regulation (GDPR) restricts how personal user data can be processed and shared, and proposed privacy regulations in the United States are likely to enact similar constraints. Even as existing platforms become more restrictive and governments enact restrictive regulation, we should also expect additional sources of data to become available as new digital media platforms and experiences emerge. New social media platforms such as Mastodon, Threads, and BlueSky are implementing decentralized technical protocols and community models that could radically expand access to user-generated data (Knight, 2022). The use of virtual reality (VR) and augmented reality (AR) are growing, and wearable devices will likely add to the body of consumer and user data that can be used to measure engagement and public opinion (Lipschultz, 2020, p. 242). If these new platforms and experiences maintain independence and avoid being bought out by existing media moguls, they will challenge the status quo. As Hollifield & Coffey explain, "when a single company is considered the currency for the industry (such as Nielsen with television), the lack of competition can be a deterrent to developing new metrics quickly" (2023, p. 24). Competition could mean new metrics for measurement and evaluation.

Second, the methods used to analyze data are becoming increasingly complex and efficient, thanks to increases in computing power. Machine learning (ML) and artificial intelligence (AI) are already helping to improve trend identification and predictive analytics. At present, text and numerical analysis has been the primary drivers for most types of analytics, but advances in image detection and speech-to-text processing are making it easier to collect, measure, and analyze multimedia content. Existing monitoring and scoring practices such as sentiment analysis will become much more accurate and nuanced through ML and AI applications making it easier for analysts to determine public opinion and audience reception of campaigns. Additionally, advances in AI are likely to increase analysts' power to predict future trends, identify brewing crises before they become firestorms, and assist in crafting successful campaigns by modeling probable reactions to variations on campaign messaging (Zavo, 2023). In a somewhat paradoxical fashion, ML and AI are also complicating the media landscape as AI-generated content and "deepfakes" can quickly spread and distort the information ecosystem. ML and AI tools may be able to detect and counter the attempts of bad actors, but the digital environment is likely to become a much busier place in the near future and the work of identifying the signal in the noise will remain a challenge. Increasing attention to the use of ML and AI is attracting more data scientists to the public relations profession, which may have a profound effect on the culture, values, and the fundamentals that are taught in future public relations programs.

Third, audience perception of data collection and analytics has an understated influence on measurement and analytics. In the current system of surveillance capitalism, consumers are ambivalent about data collection practices and seem willing to exchange a fair amount of user-generated data in exchange for the convenience of using digital services (Zuboff, 2015). That ambivalence could easily turn into more active cooperation or outright hostility, depending on the extent to which platforms and analytics platforms create ethical value that respects users' rights and enable the equitable allocation of risks and rewards (Allen et al., 2021). People who believe that they are being disproportionately targeted, are providing excessive surplus labor to companies, or that their privacy is being violated may decrease their engagement with digital media, move to more privacy-minded platforms, or support legislation that regulates how user-generated data may be collected and analyzed. Vincent et al. (2021) have suggested a framework that a discontented public might use to leverage their data production to force technology and analytics firms to improve relationships with those who create data. These include "data strikes" in which people delete or withhold data, and "data poisoning" in which people intentionally produce inaccurate or corrupted data to disrupt processing and analysis. Agencies and tech companies that rely on consumer data for measurement, analytics, and research will need to maintain trust by providing transparency and choice for the consumers who produce data.

Finally, as history has demonstrated, scholarly and professional scrutiny has led to the development of standards and frameworks that validate and legitimize certain practices of measurement and analytics while rejecting others. The Institute for Public Relations helped codify research practices for planning and evaluation, insisting that measurement should include outputs, outtakes, and outcomes (Lindenmann, 2006). AMEC's 2010 Barcelona Principles rejected AVEs as a useful measure for public relations and encouraged professionals to consider instead a range of qualitative measures in place of quantitative ones (Magee & O'Reilly, 2010). Analysis from professionals and scholars such as Michaelson et al. (2023) and Laskin (2016) recommends that agencies perform stronger measurement of audience behaviors as part of the evaluation process. Organizational leadership will continue to shape the profession by defining the practices that matter and rejecting those that are found to be invalid, misleading, or no longer valuable.

Measurement and Analytics in 2050

If measurement and analytics practices were considered mainstream in the 2020s, then it should come as no surprise that they are omnipresent in 2050. In 2050 it is easy to think of the insights and analytics pages from past social media platforms like Facebook and Twitter as quaint. The previous generation of platform metrics – clicks, likes, impressions – only quantified very rudimentary types of digital behaviors.

We have a slate of new metrics and analytics that were inconceivable in the first part of the 21st century. For example, we used to estimate engagement with video content online by measuring how long a video played in a user's web browser. We used to set a baseline – "3-second views" as we used to call them – to determine whether there was basic engagement with video content. Now, thanks to the fact that facial recognition and eye-tracking hardware and software are built into virtually every new device, we can measure not only the exact duration of a video view but *how* the user viewed the video. We can measure how long they looked directly at the video as well as the specific sections of the screen they were scanning. This allows us to determine if they were following particular elements of the message, including the extent to which they followed the main subject of the video and read any of the text. Facial recognition software also scans users' faces as they view content, helping us determine their exact emotional reactions and level of comprehension of the message.

Since the late 2020s, wearable technologies have been providing continuous streams of information about their wearers' movements and patterns of engagement with the world around them. Pioneering headset products like the Apple Vision Pro were at first a bit obtrusive, but gradually became smaller, more convenient and comfortable, and as ubiquitous as smart phones, watches, and eyeglasses. Competition among big tech companies led to a proliferation of these devices, making them affordable for nearly everyone and gradually replacing most smart phones. A large segment of the population uses these wearables in everyday life to provide augmented reality overlays to assist with wayfinding, environmental annotation, and interpersonal communication. Data from these wearables give us the capacity to track certain elements of what users see in the real world, where they see them, how long they see them, and measure them in correlation with other biometric information to determine their reactions. We have further incentivized the collection and analysis of behavioral information by allowing users to earn credits by providing additional biometric information that we can map alongside their media consumption.

Quantum computing makes it possible to process all this information in real time, and we use it to adjust our campaigns and messaging as quickly as we collect audience reactions. The old axiom that measurement and evaluation should take place at every stage of a campaign has been replaced by the notion that measurement and evaluation are *always* ongoing. For example, the videos we create for campaigns involve multiple variations that can be altered in real time according to viewer's response. If our facial recognition system determines that a viewer is not responding well to a particular argument, it can present alternative arguments or subjects until the viewer responds in a more favorable way.

Similarly, we have adapted the social media monitoring and listening tools from the 2010s into real-time response systems that can read and evaluate user-generated content from across a variety of platforms and respond with messages that automatically adapt according to the perceived emotions and reactions from the audiences being analyzed. We replaced the simplistic sentiment analysis systems that scored social media posts and news stories according to positive and negative keywords with AI systems capable of precisely determining emotions, intentions, and other forms of expression such as sarcasm. Previous systems of sentiment detection and analysis were deemed so inaccurate that one of AMEC's 2035 Barcelona Principles encouraged analysts to reject keyword-based sentiment analysis in favor of more nuanced AI models of language detection.

While the technology has come a long way since the 2020s, we are still dealing with many of the same economic and social issues in the 2050s. Our largest challenge stems from the political economy of data. Even though we produce, consume, and analyze more data than ever before, the digital media ecosystem is deeply fragmented. The most dominant social media networking and microblogging platforms like Facebook and Twitter collapsed in the late 2020s, and the void was filled by thousands of decentralized and interoperable social media platforms managed by volunteers and hobbyists who could set their own rules for content moderation and data collection policies. Collectively, these platforms created a federated universe of social media sites that were independent of mainstream social media which became known as the "Fediverse." At first, data from the Fediverse was plentiful, but in the mid-2030s managers and operators of these platforms searched for creative ways to support their platforms and found that licensing or selling data from their sites was the most lucrative means of doing so. Similarly, the big tech platforms that produce wearable devices and headsets have realized that they also need to subsidize the costs of their products by selling user data. The result is that there is now a constant competition for data among platforms and agencies that conduct digital analytics. Contracts and fees for data services are inconsistent, and the quality of data depend on the types of communities using each platform. Analysts are constantly having to evaluate the landscape for the best platforms to examine and are perpetually negotiating and renegotiating terms of access. This has been an expensive proposition, and only the best-funded agencies can acquire data streams at volume. Even though computing power has grown exponentially since the 2020s, quantum computing turned out to be much more expensive and power-intensive than initially projected. In the same way that data have become harder to obtain, the computing required to process data in real time is available only to the wealthiest agencies.

We are now realizing, with a good degree of irony, that most professionals involved in measurement and analytics are not actually doing measurement and analytics, but rather spend most of their time negotiating access to data streams. We have seen a recent downsizing of actual analysts in major agencies as automated systems are taking over the day-to-day work of data collection, measurement, and analysis. Most of the work of collecting user inputs and modulating messaging is performed by AI agents programmed by public relations strategists who only occasionally need to step in to make minor corrections to the algorithm. Unsurprisingly, small to medium scale public relations agencies have largely vanished since the mid-2030s, as they were unable to afford access to the most important data streams and computational techniques in order to remain competitive with large agencies.

Perhaps the most interesting development in measurement and analytics in 2050 is the acknowledgement of the need to research audiences that aren't a significant part of the digital ecosystem. In light of ubiquitous wearable devices, automated data analysis, and adaptive messaging, we are beginning to acknowledge that there is a large contingency of the general public that is absent from these systems of measurement and analysis, either by poverty or by choice. They are nearly impossible to measure, as they do not use wearable devices or create content in social media platforms, thereby producing little to no data within the existing digital infrastructure. This also makes them unreachable through most messaging systems as they are not continuously connected to data and information streams. In response, a growing body of public relations scholars and practitioners has been rediscovering 20th century social scientific methods of measurement and assessment, namely qualitative surveys, focus groups, and interviews, and are discussing ways to integrate them alongside dominant practices of digital analytics.

Conclusion: Anticipating the Knowledge, Skills, and Abilities Necessary for Measurement and Analytics in 2050

This chapter has considered the past, present, and future of measurement and analytics in public relations. It presents a future world in which data collection and analysis is ubiquitous and messaging can be programmed to automatically adapt to audience reactions. While it isn't intended to provide a perfect prediction of the future, it is intended to be something of a warning for the future of public relations. At present, the profession seems to demand technical measurement and analytics skills that more closely resembles data science than public relations. Therefore, it is important to ascertain that we differentiate the knowledge, skills, and abilities that distinguish public relations from other disciplines.

First, public relations professionals are well-situated to be able to understand the context and audiences they are examining. They excel at communicating what the data *mean* from within the context of specific campaigns, organizational goals, and audience attributes (Hollifield & Coffey, 2023). This requires knowledge of not only how to appropriately process and analyze data, but also to select appropriate sources of data, assess the validity of those data, and provide a rationale for making these decisions, each of which are unlikely to be accomplished by AI systems. Second, public relations professionals are trained to be excellent storytellers. They can effectively leverage multimodal communication – written, oral, and visual forms – which enables them to effectively convey the process of measurement and analytics and explain the return on investment (ROI) of a campaign. Finally, public relations professionals are adaptable. While we may not yet be able to predict the scope and scale that technological disruption may exert over public relations by the year 2050, it is reasonable to expect significant changes to our models and methods of measurement and analysis. History tells us that public relations professionals have been able to effectively implement a variety of tools and frameworks to analyze audiences and assess campaigns, and that they will be able to continue to do so in the future.

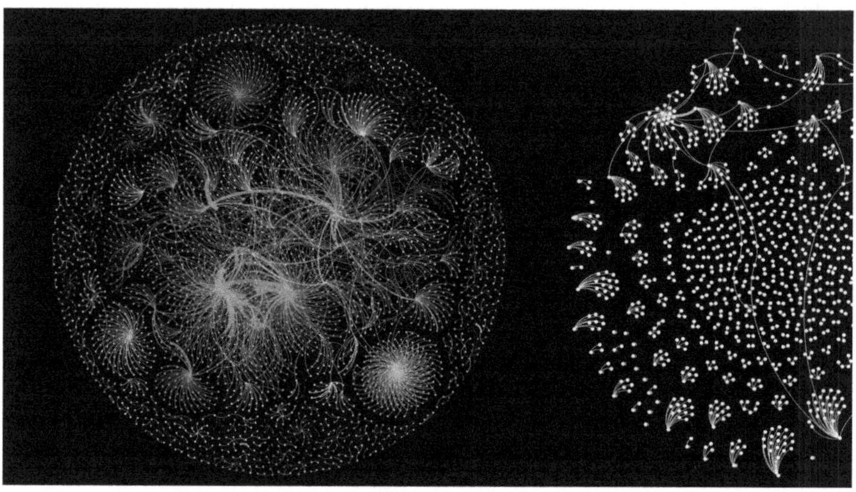

FIGURE 21.1 Social network analysis graph mapping relationships and interactions among social media users.

Source: Author.

References

Allen, J., Bella, K., Hewett, N., & Mulligan, C. (2021). *Data-driven economies: foundations for our common future*. [White paper]. World Economic Forum. Retrieved November21,2023,fromhttps://www.weforum.org/publications/data-driven-economies-foundations-for-our-common-future/

AMEC. (2023a). "Glossary." Retrieved November 20, 2023, from https://amecorg.com/glossary/#measurement

AMEC. (2023b). "Who We Are." Retrieved November 20, 2023, from https://amecorg.com/about/.

AMEC. (2023c). "Barcelona Principles 3.0." Retrieved November 20, 2023, from https://amecorg.com/barcelona-principles-3-0-translations/

Fan, W., & Gordon, M. (2014). The power of social media analytics. In *Communications of the ACM* (Vol. *57*, Issue 6, pp. 74–81). ACM. https://doi.org/10.1145/2602574

Freberg, K. (2019). *Social media for strategic communication: Creative strategies and research-based applications*. Sage Publications.

Hollifield, C. A., & Coffey, A. J. (2023). The industry and profession of media analytics. In *Media analytics* (1st ed., pp. 13–34). Routledge. https://doi.org/10.4324/9780429506956-3

Knight, W. (2022, November 14). The man behind Mastodon built it for this moment. *Wired*. Retrieved from https://www.wired.com/story/the-man-behind-mastodon-eugen-rochko-built-it-for-this-moment/

Laskin, A. V. (2016). Levels of evaluation: An agency's perspective on measurement and evaluation. *Public Relations Journal*, *10*(2), 1–31.

Lindenmann, W. K. (2006). *Public relations research for planning and evaluation*. Institute for Public Relations. Retrieved from http://www.instituteforpr.org/topics/pr-research-for-planning-and-evaluation

Lipschultz, J. H. (2020). The future of social media measurement and management. In *Social media measurement and management* (1st ed., pp. 241–270). Routledge. https://doi.org/10.4324/9781351108072

Lipschultz, J. H. (2022). "Big data" analytics. In *The Routledge companion to public relations*. Routledge. https://doi.org/10.4324/9781003131700-33

Macnamara, J. (2018). Metrics, analytics and beyond: The evolving evaluation landscape. In *Evaluating public communication* (1st ed., pp. 143–175). Routledge. https://doi.org/10.4324/9781315391984-4

Magee, K., & O'Reilly, G. (2010). A new dawn for measurement? *PR Week*, 3. Retrieved from https://login.lp.hscl.ufl.edu/login?url=https://www.proquest.com/trade-journals/new-dawn-measurement/docview/664964874/se-2

Michaelson, D., Stacks, D., & Wright, D. (2023). Assessing "Cause and Effect": Objective based measurement for public relations. *Organicom : Revista Brasileira de Comunicação Organizacional e Relações Públicas*, *20*(42), 17–32. https://doi.org/10.11606/issn.2238-2593.organicom.2023.206972

Porter, J. (2023). Twitter announces new API pricing, posing a challenge for small developers. *The Verge*. Retrieved from https://www.theverge.com/2023/3/30/23662832/twitter-api-tiers-free-bot-novelty-accounts-basic-enterprice-monthly-price

Rees, S. (2020). The digital public relations turn: Understanding how digital media is changing public relations practice. In *Public relations, branding and authenticity* (1st ed., pp. 35–45). Routledge. https://doi.org/10.4324/9780429022685-3

Sponder, M., & Khan, G. F. (2018). *Digital analytics for marketing*. Routledge. https://doi.org/10.4324/9781315640914

Vincent, N., Li, H., Tilly, N., Chancellor, S., & Hecht, B. (2021). Data leverage: A framework for empowering the public in its relationship with technology companies. Association for Computing Machinery. In *Proceedings of the 2021 ACM conference on fairness, accountability, and transparency* (pp. 215–227). https://dl.acm.org/doi/10.1145/3442188.3445885

Watson, T. (2012). The evolution of public relations measurement and evaluation. *Public Relations Review*, *38*(3), 390–398. https://doi.org/10.1016/j.pubrev.2011.12.018

Zavo, L. (2023, September 13). Implementing AI in the public relations industry. *Forbes*. Retrieved from https://www.forbes.com/sites/forbesbusinesscouncil/2023/09/13/implementing-ai-in-the-public-relations-industry/?sh=641835344ba8

Zuboff, S. (2015). Big other: Surveillance capitalism and the prospects of an information civilization. *Journal of Information Technology*, *30*(1), 75–89. https://doi.org/10.1057/jit.2015.5

INDEX

Note: **Bold** page numbers refer to tables; *italic* page numbers refer to figures and page numbers followed by "n" denote endnotes.

For Product Safety Concerns and Information please contact our EU
representative GPSR@taylorandfrancis.com
Taylor & Francis Verlag GmbH, Kaufingerstraße 24, 80331 München, Germany

www.ingramcontent.com/pod-product-compliance
Ingram Content Group UK Ltd.
Pitfield, Milton Keynes, MK11 3LW, UK
UKHW022350190926
475702UK00015B/2215
9781032730936